Downton: monument on S wall chancel by P. Scheemakers, to Margaret, Lady Feversham (+ 1755).

Royal Commission on the Historical Monuments of England

Churches of South-East Wiltshire

London · Her Majesty's Stationery Office

Printed in the United Kingdom for Her Majesty's Stationery Office.   Dd 738902   C 200   CCN 485739   4/87

CONTENTS

LIST OF BUILDINGS DESCRIBED WITH THEIR CIVIL PARISHES

		Civil Parish
ALDERBURY	St Mary	*Alderbury*
ALLINGTON	St John Baptist	*Allington*
AMESBURY	St Mary and St Melor	*Amesbury*
BERWICK ST JAMES	St James	*Berwick St James*
BOSCOMBE	St Andrew	*Allington*
BRITFORD	St Peter	*Britford*
BULFORD	St Leonard	*Bulford*
CHARLTON	All Saints	*Downton*
CHITTERNE	All Saints	*Chitterne*
CHITTERNE	St Mary	*Chitterne*
CHOLDERTON	St Nicholas	*Cholderton*
COOMBE BISSETT	St Michael	*Coombe Bissett*
DOWNTON	St Lawrence	*Downton*
DURNFORD	St Andrew	*Durnford*
DURRINGTON	All Saints	*Durrington*
EAST GRIMSTEAD	Holy Trinity	*Grimstead*
FARLEY	All Saints	*Pitton and Farley*
FUGGLESTONE	St Peter	*Wilton*
HOMINGTON	St Mary	*Coombe Bissett*
IDMISTON	All Saints	*Idmiston*
IVYCHURCH	Former Priory	*Alderbury*
LANDFORD	St Andrew	*Landford*
LAVERSTOCK	St Andrew	*Laverstock*
MADDINGTON	St Mary	*Shrewton*
NETHERHAMPTON	St Catherine	*Netherhampton*
NEWTON TONEY	St Andrew	*Newton Toney*
NUNTON	St Andrew	*Odstock*
ODSTOCK	St Mary	*Odstock*
ORCHESTON	St George	*Orcheston*
ORCHESTON	St Mary	*Orcheston*
PITTON	St Peter	*Pitton and Farley*
PORTON	St Nicholas	*Idmiston*
REDLYNCH	St Birinus	*Redlynch*
REDLYNCH	St Mary	*Redlynch*
ROLLESTONE	St Andrew	*Shrewton*
SHREWTON	St Mary	*Shrewton*

LIST OF ILLUSTRATIONS

GENERAL

TABLES

CHAIRMAN'S FOREWORD

Churches of South-East Wiltshire is the result of a change of approach by the Royal Commission in its programme of investigation. Originally, Wiltshire had been divided into a number of areas for recording purposes, where the intention was to publish the information comprehensively, parish by parish, in the traditional manner.

By the late 1970s it had become apparent that this treatment would be inappropriate. It would take too long to complete, in view of the richness of the material which had to be recorded, the limited resources of the Commission and other pressing cases requiring attention by the Royal Commission elsewhere.

It was decided, therefore, to complete the work which was already in progress on the first area – that of the south-east of the county around Salisbury – and to produce other publications, which would be based upon certain selected parts of the record. The remainder of the recordings would be placed in the archives of the National Monuments Record.

This book covers some fifty-five places of worship. The introduction deals with the historical development of the buildings and this is followed by descriptive accounts of each church. There is a series of lists in which the detailed evidence, for example, on faculties or patronage, is given in tabulated form.

The full inventory of each church, which includes all the fittings and the furnishings except for the bells and plate, as well as numerous additional photographs, is not published here. It is deposited as an archive in the National Monuments Record at the Royal Commission's offices at 23 Savile Row, London W1, where it is available to the public.

FERRERS

ACKNOWLEDGEMENTS

The Commissioners wish to acknowledge the work accomplished by their executive staff in the preparation of this work; in particular, the late Mr John Bassham (photography), Mr Desmond Bonney (Principal Investigator, Salisbury Office), Dr Thomas Cocke (field investigation and drafting of text), Miss Lizbeth Gale (editorial), Dr Bridgett Jones (documentary research), Mr Nicholas Moore (investigation), Ms Kate Owen (editorial), Mrs Glenys Popper (editorial), Mr John Reeves (investigation), Mr Tony Rumsey (photography), Miss Veronica Smith (typing), Mr Peter Spencer (draughtsmanship) and Mr Humphrey Welfare (archaeology).

The following persons kindly gave their assistance with various aspects of the text: Miss Sarah Brown and Miss Jill Kerr, formerly of the Corpus Vitrearum Medii Aevi; Mr Victor Chinney; Mr Howard Colvin; Mrs Elizabeth Eames; Mr Clive Wainwright of the Victoria and Albert Museum.

We are grateful to the Marquess of Bath, the Earl of Pembroke and the Earl of Radnor for permission to use their family archives. Our thanks are also due to the staff of the following bodies: the Diocesan and County Record Offices, County Hall, Trowbridge; the former Diocesan Record Office in Salisbury, particularly Miss P. Stewart; the Wiltshire Archaeological Society, Devizes Museum; the Salisbury and South Wiltshire Museum, particularly Miss T. Hunt. We are grateful to all these institutions and to the individuals who permitted us to photograph buildings or topographical material in their care. Of our major sources, the faculty plans and drawings were photographed at the Diocesan Record Offices at Salisbury and Trowbridge and the watercolours by Buckler and Kemm at the Devizes and Salisbury Museums; we again thank these bodies for allowing this.

The maps opposite page 1 and on page 10 are reproduced from the 1983 Ordnance Survey 1 to 50,000 2nd Series Sheet 184: Salisbury and the Plain and the map on page 233 is reproduced from the Ordnance Survey 1 to 2500 Sheet SU1441/1541 with the permission of the Controller of Her Majesty's Stationery Office, Crown copyright reserved.

Successive Bishops of Salisbury, Archdeacons of Sarum and the staff of the Diocesan Office have given every assistance to the project. Finally we owe an especial debt to the incumbents, churchwardens and parochial church councils of the churches of the area, without whose ready co-operation this survey would have been impossible.

EDITORIAL NOTE

Full ground plans of each building are presented at a uniform scale of 24 feet to the inch and unless otherwise indicated are taken from RCHM surveys made between April 1979 and November 1981.

Plans are not date-hatched, allowing use of the plans as primary documents, but diagrammatic plans, at a smaller scale, are included to explain the development, sometimes conjectural, of the more complex churches.

Faculty plans are included for a number of buildings. Where a faculty plan is shown with an RCHM scale, this represents an existing building; where no such scale is included, the faculty plan depicts a demolished church. No RCHM plans exist for those buildings illustrated by a faculty plan with an RCHM scale.

KEY TO LINE DRAWINGS

GENERAL

P	Pulpit	+	Altar
F	Font	p	Piscina
S	Sedilia	a	Aumbry
G	Gallery	s	Stoup
L	Organ loft	rs	Rood stair

 Change in plan level

········ Feature no longer extant

DEVELOPMENT DIAGRAMS

▨▨▨ Existing work

▬▬ New work

░░░ Conjectural

In Tables 5–11 the numbers which occur at the end of each entry refer to illustrations. A complete list of illustrations can be found on pages ix–xv.

CONVERSION TABLE
1 inch = 25.4 mm
1 foot (12 inches) = 304.8 mm
1 yard (3 feet) = 914.4 mm
1 mile (1760 yards) = 1.6 km

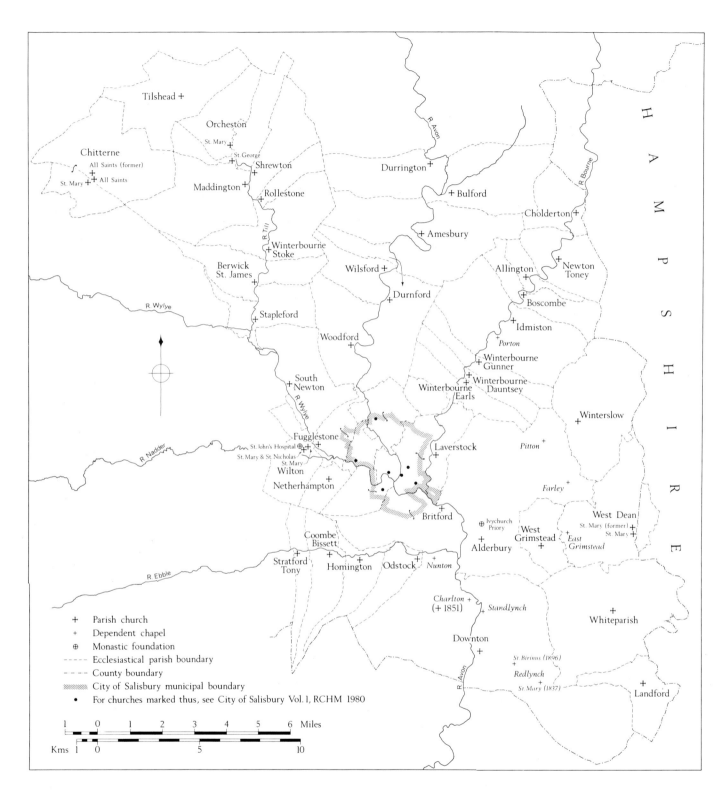

Tilshead +

Orcheston
St. Mary +
St. George +

Chitterne
All Saints (former)
+
St. Mary + + All Saints

Shrewton

Maddington +
+ Rollestone

R Avon

Durrington +

+ Bulford

Cholderton +

+ Amesbury

Winterbourne
Stoke +

Berwick
St. James +

Wilsford +

R Wylye

Stapleford +

+ Durnford

Allington
+
+ Boscombe

+ Newton
Toney

R Bourne

Woodford
+

+ Idmiston

Porton

South
Newton +

R Wylye

Winterbourne
Gunner
+
+ Winterbourne
Dauntsey

Winterbourne
Earls

+ Winterslow

Fugglestone
St. John's Hospital ⊕ +
St. Mary & St. Nicholas +
St. Mary
+
Wilton

Netherhampton +

+ Laverstock

Pitton

Farley

R Nadder

West Dean
St. Mary (former) +
+ St. Mary

Britford

⊕ Ivychurch
Priory

West
Grimstead
+

East
Grimstead

Coombe
Bissett +

Stratford
Tony +

+
Homington

+ Odstock
Odstock + Nunton

+ Alderbury

R Ebble

Charlton +
(+ 1851)

+ Standlynch

Whiteparish
+

Downton
+

St Birinus (1896)
+

Redlynch

St Mary (1837)
+

+
Landford

R Avon

H
A
M
P
S
H
I
R
E

+   Parish church
+   Dependent chapel
⊕   Monastic foundation
- - -   Ecclesiastical parish boundary
– –   County boundary
▨▨   City of Salisbury municipal boundary
●   For churches marked thus, see City of Salisbury Vol.1, RCHM 1980

Miles
1   0   1   2   3   4   5   6

Kms 1   0   5   10

1.   Outline map of south-east Wiltshire showing the positions of the churches discussed. (Ecclesiastical boundaries accord with those of the tithe maps of *c*. 1840.) *Crown copyright reserved.*

CHURCHES OF SOUTH-EAST WILTSHIRE

DISCUSSION

The aim of this survey has been to continue the usual practice of this Commission of investigating each church in depth, but to examine the results in a more analytical way than hitherto. No archaeological excavation has been possible.[1] The discussion that precedes the accounts of the individual buildings studies them together as an example of the development of parish churches. The conclusions are tentative rather than definitive, but they are founded upon detailed evidence; so although they relate only to this particular area and to buildings of unexceptional quality, they may encourage similar studies elsewhere which, cumulatively, could form a basis for wider generalisations.

The evidence upon which the book is based consists, for each church, of full photographic coverage, plans and drawings based upon new surveys (except for some of those churches entirely rebuilt in the 19th century, in which cases contemporary plans are used) and a detailed written account of the development of the building, all its elements being recorded and discussed. Since the bulk of this material cannot be published in full, it is deposited in the archives of the Commission where it is available for consultation. This published account is, therefore, not a complete inventory of every feature and fitting.

Precise dating of the various parts of pre-Victorian church buildings and fittings is generally not possible in south-east Wiltshire as, in the absence of documentation, stylistic evidence must be used. In order to create a consistent framework for the whole period from Saxon times to the present day, particular features of a church are dated, where feasible, to an approximate year, rather than by the traditional stylistic labels of Romanesque, Early English, Decorated, Perpendicular, Jacobean etc. Such labels are used extensively, however, in the introductory discussion, where the architectural development of the churches is treated in a wider chronological context. However, for certain features such as fonts, the forms and mouldings of which changed very gradually, the evidence for their development in the Romanesque and Early English periods on the one hand and in the Decorated and Perpendicular on the other, is gathered and discussed in two parts; early medieval and late medieval.

The plans of the churches are not date-hatched in the manner traditional in RCHM volumes. This change of practice allows the reader to use the plans as primary documents independently of the interpretation in the accompanying text. It also avoids the need for arbitrary decisions, for instance whether a feature, such as the west wall of Stapleford church, which was taken down and faithfully rebuilt in the 19th century, should be described as medieval or Victorian. For the more complex churches there are diagrammatic plans to illustrate the known or likely stages of development.

The survey covers Anglican churches and chapels (Nonconformist chapels have been recorded for separate treatment by the RCHM; among them is the only Roman Catholic church of architectural significance, St Edith's in Wilton, which was built as a Primitive Methodist meeting-house).[2] The two monastic foundations of the area which preserve medieval fabric, the Augustinian priory of Ivychurch and the hospital of St John, Wilton, are also discussed in this volume.

TOPOGRAPHICAL AND HISTORICAL INTRODUCTION

The churches covered by this survey lie within thirty-six modern civil parishes in south-east Wiltshire[3], one of six areas into which the county was originally divided by the Royal Commission for recording purposes. The churches now within the municipal area of Salisbury – Bemerton, Fisherton, Harnham and Stratford-sub-Castle – have already been described in the Commission's *Inventory of Monuments in the City of Salisbury* Vol I (1980) and are, therefore, excluded.

Despite its relatively small size the area exhibits considerable variety. The landscape includes the bare chalk downland of Salisbury Plain in the north west, the rich sheltered valleys of the rivers converging on and near Salisbury and, in the south east, the more wooded countryside on the margin of the New Forest. The pattern of settlement varies from the nucleated villages concentrated along the main valleys of the chalklands – some of which, like the Orchestons and the Chitternes, are notably isolated – to the dispersed hamlets and farmsteads in the extreme south of the area; it includes, also, the small, ancient centres of Wilton and Downton, both of borough status. Some of the communities, like the Winterbournes, have lived relatively independent of great landowners, but others have for long felt the influence of powerful institutions or families: Wilton, for example, was dominated first by its great Benedictine abbey/nunnery and then by the earls of Pembroke who succeeded it. Such variations in physical geography and social conditions are clearly to be seen in the churches of the area, as in the building materials used, and in the degree of sophistication to be found in fittings or funerary monuments.

The survey comprises fifty-five places of worship, past and present, varying in size from aisled cruciform churches, as at Amesbury or Downton, to simple two-cell buildings such as Standlynch chapel. Size and status are, however, not necessarily related. A dependent chapel like Nunton could be relatively ambitious whereas a parish church, especially one associated with a small downland community such as Rollestone, might be small and simple.

The majority of the buildings are now parish churches although several, especially in the east part of the county, were traditionally chapels within larger parochial jurisdictions, for instance East Grimstead under West Dean, or Pitton and Farley under Alderbury. Some of the churches enjoyed special status. Amesbury, though not the church of the priory, must have been related to it. Wilsford and Woodford, Durnford and Coombe Bissett were attached to prebends, while Alderbury, Britford and Homington were peculiars of the Dean and Chapter of Salisbury.[4] Standlynch, although possessing the rights of baptism and burial, never acquired independence from the lords of the manor or from the parish priests of Downton.

Nearly all the churches in the area are medieval in origin and most incorporate some medieval fabric. Three churches were built on virgin sites in the 19th century, two in Redlynch and one in Charlton; in the 20th century one was built, for the Army camp at Bulford.[5] Almost half of the medieval churches, however, were destroyed or drastically altered in the mid 19th century. Eight were demolished completely. In three a part was allowed to survive as a mortuary chapel, as at West Dean and Chitterne St Mary. Others were dismantled and some of their medieval features incorporated in larger buildings. Fortunately, contemporary topographical drawings and plans combined with written accounts allow the original buildings to be reconstructed and their surviving fittings and architectural features to be assigned their proper places.[6] This survey can thus include these totally or partly demolished buildings in its catalogue. It does not, however, provide entries for those churches and chapels which had vanished by or during the 16th century, the most notable of these being the monastic churches of Amesbury and Wilton and the twelve parish churches of Wilton and its suburbs.[7] There were also a number of free chapels (*see* Table 2), particularly in the forest areas in the south east of the county. One of these survives: the single-cell 12th-century chapel of St Leonard at Whelpley, near Whiteparish, but it does not appear to have been used for worship since the 16th century and the fabric has been much rebuilt (Jackson 1867b, 317–18; Taylor 1968, 41–2). Former chapels in private houses, whether medieval or later, have also been omitted. The only one extant, though disused, that in Wilton House, was constructed by James Wyatt *c.* 1810 and altered by T.H. Wyatt in the mid 19th century.

The area is not renowned for ecclesiological rarities; fittings and furnishings in general being of standard types. The only unusual dedication is that to St Melor at Amesbury. Amesbury Abbey possessed relics of this princely Breton martyr from an early date (VCH 1956, 242–3; Chandler 1979, 17). The commonest dedication, as elsewhere in England, is to St Mary; All Saints and St Andrew follow, each with half as many dedications.

SOURCES

The principal printed source is *The History of Modern Wiltshire* by Sir Richard Colt Hoare and his collaborators, published in parts from 1822 to 1844: although the quality of the descriptions varies considerably from church to church, the sketch plans of the churches indicate their shape and the siting of their fittings before Victorian rebuilding. This source is supplemented by the drawings made by John Buckler in the first decade of the 19th century, which record each church in one or two external views and sometimes include details of internal features such as fonts or arcades.[8] Their standard of reliability appears to be remarkably high.[9]

Another important topographical source is the series of watercolours of a number of the churches painted by Robert Kemm of Amesbury in the 1860s.[10] Although his exterior views add little to what can be learnt from Buckler, his general interiors are unique records of pre-Tractarian arrangements of furnishings, and his details of piscinae, stained glass, bosses and similar objects often record features that have since vanished or suffered restoration.

The Faculties granted for the alteration or rebuilding of churches and now deposited in the Diocesan Record Office at Trowbridge supply important evidence for changes to the fabric, especially those which retain original plans submitted with the applications. In the 18th century Faculties rarely included plans since they dealt largely with the allocation of pews and the provision of galleries, but in the 19th century they comprised not only plans and elevations of proposed new buildings in detail but also, on occasion, records of the original buildings before alteration or demolition. Similar documentation is contained in the records of the Incorporated Church Building Society, which gave grants towards the provision of increased seating.[11] Other parish records, now mostly on deposit at the Wiltshire County Record Office at Trowbridge, are disappointing in their references to church building however informative they may be about other aspects of church life. Even the Churchwardens' Presentments, designed to secure a regular report on the fabric, rarely went beyond generalities. References to church work may also be found in the archives of the great families of the area who financed it, notably in the Pembroke papers at Wilton and the Radnor papers at Longford.

Some parishes have historical notes compiled by their Victorian incumbents, for example Cholderton (*see* Barrow 1889) and West Dean (*see* Master 1885) both of which include accounts of church restoration. The album assembled for Landford incorporates contemporary photographs. Newspaper articles, usually written when churches were re-opened after restoration, may give useful details. Recent guide books prepared for several of the churches vary considerably in quality. There are also some autobiographical accounts of church life which illuminate the history of the buildings: the Reverend Thomas Mozley described his rebuilding of Cholderton Church in the 1840s; and Edith Olivier portrayed the church of St Mary and St Nicholas, Wilton, in its prime under her father, Canon Dacres Olivier, rector from 1867 to 1912.

The *Wiltshire Archaeological Magazine*, the journal of the Wiltshire Archaeological Society, is an important source. At the beginning of this century, C.E. Ponting, the Marlborough architect, who had almost a monopoly of the ecclesiastical commissions in the county, regularly contributed descriptions of the churches visited on the Society's annual outing as well as more detailed articles on those he was restoring. Some decades earlier the *Magazine* had contained lengthy and sometimes acrimonious discussions of major churches such as Amesbury, Downton and Britford. The Society has also published the mid 17th-century parliamentary surveys of the churches and the 19th-century notes on them by the antiquary Sir Stephen Glynne. Associated with the work of the Society are the scrapbooks compiled, parish by parish, by its successive editors Canon Jackson and Canon Goddard and now in the library of the Society of Antiquaries in London and the library of the Wiltshire Archaeological Society at Devizes respectively. The *Magazine* continues to attract articles on Wiltshire churches, whether on general topics such as fonts or Royal Arms, or on individual buildings.

The local volumes of the Victoria History of the Counties of England and the Buildings of England series are also essential to the study of the area. The VCH, while so far covering only a few of the parishes in south-east Wiltshire, includes in its third volume summaries of the ecclesiastical history of the county and of its religious houses. The Wiltshire volume in the Buildings of England series is generous in ideas about buildings and about the development of architectural themes although its accounts are essentially selective. There are authoritative books on the church plate of the county (Nightingale 1891a) and on its bells (Walters 1929); these render any detailed account of these objects unnecessary.

BUILDING MATERIALS

The predominant material used for walls in the area has always been the local flint. At Britford the Saxon nave was constructed of uncoursed, roughly-knapped flint mixed with some stone rubble, but the present pointing makes it difficult to be precise about the technique of laying. The later Saxon church of Breamore, just across the Hampshire border to the south, was built in the same manner; there, unlike Britford, the original quoins largely survive. The few examples of flints set herringbone fashion seem random and should not be interpreted as evidence of early medieval work, late examples often appearing near the top of a wall in rebuilt sections. Although intermixing flints with dressed stone became common practice, walls entirely of flint continued to be built in every century. The chancel of Tilshead church is an example of 13th-century work in flint rubble, but whether it and other similar masonry was intended to be rendered is not known. Certainly the walls at Durnford and West Grimstead show traces of rendering, but neither its application nor its removal can be dated. The fine treatment of the flint in the external faces of the walls of the early 14th-century chancel of Downton church suggests that flint was not always considered a cheap material best hidden away. Here the flints were cut into small 'bricks', 2 in. by 2½ in. (51 mm by 64 mm), and carefully coursed. The method of its construction is indicated by the survival of putlock holes lined on top and sides with stone slabs. Putlock holes are also evident in the roughly contemporary flint and stone rubble walls of the Borbach/Evelyn Chapel at West Dean. They were even considered necessary in the construction of the low and rustic north aisle wall of the church of West Grimstead.

2.   Britford: exterior from NW.

3.   Downton: exterior from NE.

4. Standlynch: exterior from NW.

The earliest datable examples of flint and stone chequering in the area are apparently those in the chancel at Chitterne St Mary of *c*. 1400, and the towers of Durrington and Stratford Tony, of a century later. As in secular buildings, the technique appears to have reached its fullest development in the 17th century, for example in the rebuilt west front of Standlynch Chapel, dated 1677. But it is often difficult to distinguish 17th-century from 15th-century work, as, for instance, in Odstock tower. The relative size of the stone chequers varies from the massive blocks of the tower at Stratford Tony to the more modest blocks at Rollestone; this difference seems not so much a matter of date as of the greater or lesser degree of sophistication practised by the builders. Consistent chequering came about only in the 19th century. In the work of the 1830s at Orcheston St Mary it was executed in the traditional manner, but in later 19th-century buildings such as the chancel and north wall of Homington church, the stone is cut with mechanical regularity.

It is important to note that walling of flint or flint and stone chequering can often be rebuilt without leaving any trace of the operation once the masonry has been uniformly repointed. At Amesbury the lower part of the east end of the nave north wall is of chequered flint, recognisable as a late medieval or 17th-century repair to the 12th-century rubble flint of the rest of the wall. At Maddington, however, the insertion of a window in the chequered flint north wall of the nave just west of the porch, perhaps in the 17th century, and its removal in the late 19th century, would never be suspected were it not for 19th-century topographical drawings.

The stone used in the medieval churches of the area came from three sources all within or close to its boundaries: the Chilmark or Tisbury limestone, familiar from Salisbury Cathedral; the Greensand from beds near Chilmark and at Hurdcott, west of Wilton; and the brown heathstone of the New Forest region. Bath stone was not introduced until the 19th century. Purbeck was rarely used and then only for fittings such as fonts.

Greensand seems to have been more commonly used in the 12th century than later, both for external features such as the buttresses at Durnford and for internal work such as the piers and arches of arcades. It ceased to be used, perhaps because it was found not to weather well. The New Forest heathstone appears to have been employed in a similar way during the 12th century in the churches of Whiteparish, West Grimstead and Landford, near where it is found, and to have suffered a comparable decline, but because of its greater durability its use was revived in such later works as the largely 17th-century tower of Downton. The 12th-century mixture of heathstone or greensand with buff-coloured stone, either in alternate courses (as in the arcades of Stapleford, West Grimstead, and the chancel arch of Whiteparish) or set as contrasting chequers (as in the tympana of the doorways of Durnford and Berwick St James), suggests that the builders consciously planned this polychromy. It must not be forgotten, however, that the internal masonry now visible was stripped of plaster only in the 19th century and that this concealing plaster may have been intended from the first.

Finely jointed ashlar was always a mark of quality in a building, so that its use in the 13th-century chancel of Amesbury church, which was paid for by the priory, is not unexpected.[12] In general, however, the use of ashlar in church building seems particularly characteristic of important additions made during the 14th and 15th centuries. At Stapleford the south faces of the Decorated south chapel and of the Perpendicular clearstorey and porch are of ashlar; so, too, is the clearstorey of Berwick St James and the west tower of Orcheston St George. All these works were enriched with mouldings.

5. Amesbury: exterior from NW.

Although chalk cob was a common walling material in secular buildings it does not appear to have been used in churches, unless some examples lie concealed beneath plaster, nor are there any records of its discovery and destruction in the 19th century. Similarly, thatch does not seem to have been used to roof churches: it is not shown even in early 19th-century views of unrestored church buildings. The usual roof coverings are lead (as, for instance, at Stapleford where late 18th-century work survives intact over the south chapel), stone tiles (as over the chancel of Amesbury) or, much the most common, clay tiles. Clay tiles were particularly suited to the catslide roofs covering nave and aisle, as at West Grimstead, Downton and, formerly, at Homington.

The earliest use of brick in a church of the area is at Amesbury, c. 1500, where random brick tiles are to be seen amongst the flintwork of the south aisle.[13] Generally, however, brickwork mixed with masonry is a sign of 18th-century or early 19th-century repair. It can occur either on a small scale, as in the chancel and north 'transept' gables of Coombe Bissett, or in more extensive works, as in the nave of Stratford Tony where brick and flint are set in regular alternate bands extending along the walls.

The church at Farley is a complete example of fine, late 17th-century brickwork. Here the bricks are of two sizes, 9 in. by 4½ in. by 2⅝ in. (229 mm by 114 mm by 67 mm) and 9½ in. by 4⅝ in. by 2¼ in. (241 mm by 117 mm by 57 mm), laid in English bond. The same bond was used in the nave of Stratford Tony and in the 18th-century towers of Netherhampton and West Grimstead. The latter is so plain that it can hardly date from before 1770. Vitrified brick appears only in the parapet of the south aisle at Downton. In the 19th century stock brick was used for the chancel at Winterbourne Stoke and for the north aisle at Bulford and probably for other cheap rebuildings since removed. Some restrained polychrome brickwork of the mid 19th century occurs at Landford and Alderbury.

6. West Grimstead: exterior from W.

7. Winterslow: exterior from SW showing former timber belfry on masonry S tower/porch, removed in 1849–50, *Buckler c.* 1805.

Traditional timber framing survives in only a few porches such as the 16th-century south porch of Durnford; there are, however, many examples of timber porches erected in the 19th century. More distinctive of the area until the rebuildings of the mid 19th century were timber belfries which were to be found in twelve of the churches. As depicted in the Buckler drawings they appear to be post-medieval, but this impression may be due to their undoubtedly late weather-boarding. Usually they were erected on the masonry stump of a tower or tower/porch, but at West Dean the east wall of the belfry was carried on wooden posts which rose from the floor of the nave (Master 1885, 285). Perhaps in medieval times some parishes were content to house their bell or bells in a cage just off the ground—still the arrangement at the church of Quarley, just to the east in Hampshire. Some of the churches may also have had timber and lead spires such as that of the priory church at Amesbury, the account of which at its destruction after the Dissolution suggests a structure of some size.[14] The west tower of Durnford was crowned by a lantern; a piece of its leadwork survives inscribed with early 17th-century graffiti perhaps contemporary with its construction.[15]

HISTORICAL DEVELOPMENT

THE ANGLO-SAXON PERIOD

Although the history of most parish churches in south-east Wiltshire, as in England generally, cannot be traced before the Conquest, the area was important in Anglo-Saxon times. Except in the disastrous years of the 870s and in the early 11th century, the county remained relatively unscathed by Danish attacks and its religious institutions could maintain continuity if not prosperity. From the 9th century onwards Wiltshire had its own bishop, whether seated at Wilton or Ramsbury. The convent at Wilton was by the Norman Conquest regarded as one of the most distinguished monastic houses in England (VCH 1956, 231). The nunnery at Amesbury, though less well documented, had traditionally, and probably, a foundation date in the late 10th century (VCH 1956, 242). Both houses enjoyed royal

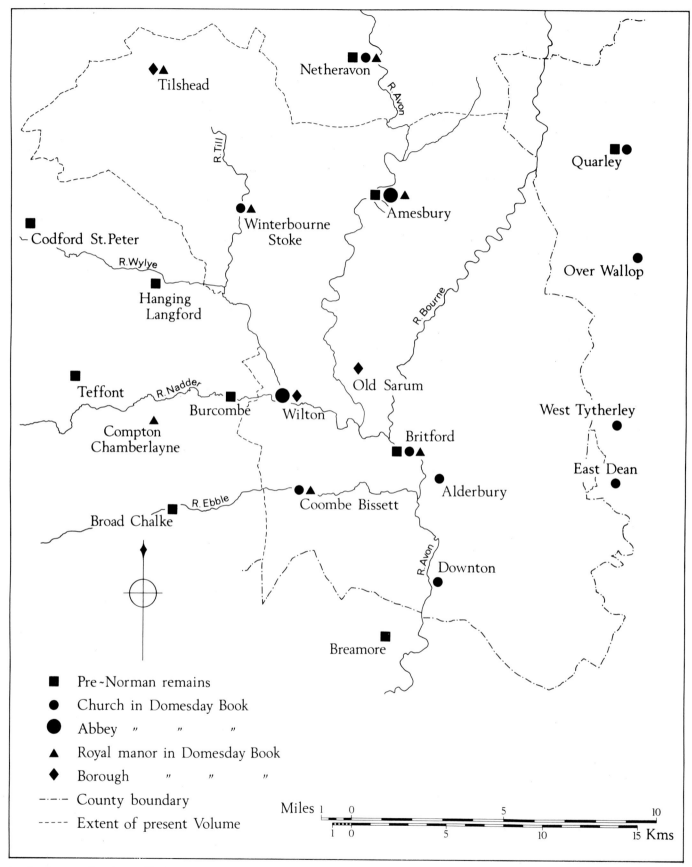

8.   Outline map of south-east Wiltshire and surrounding area showing sites of particular significance in Saxon and early Norman periods. *Crown copyright reserved*.

patronage. The bishops of Winchester possessed a large estate in the south east of the county, given to them probably at the institution of the See in the later 7th century and perhaps originally more extensive. The principal secular lord was the king, who retained very considerable lands in the county.

Little is known of the local churches. Five were recorded in Domesday: at Alderbury, Britford, Coombe Bissett, Downton and Winterbourne Stoke (VCH 1955, 33–4). There must also have been churches for lay worship at Old Sarum; also at Wilton and Amesbury unless at these two the laity used part of the nuns' churches. Of the Domesday churches all but Coombe Bissett have been claimed as minster churches (OS 1973, 56–7). Downton and Alderbury might be classified as belonging to the 'old minster' type in which a mother church served by a group of priests was the focus of the religious life of a relatively wide area, rather than to the later system in which the smaller unit of a parish was served by one priest. Both Downton and Alderbury gave their names to Hundreds and both retained large sprawling parishes with dependent chapels until the 19th century. At Downton the provision of a substantial estate for a rector between 1066 and 1087 may have been part of the process whereby a college of priests serving a minster was replaced by a parish priest (VCH 1956, 7). It is possible that Amesbury and Wilton also had minster churches of this type. Amesbury was the centre of a large royal estate and, like Alderbury and Downton, gave its name to a Hundred. The later rural deanery of Wilton, the unusually restricted size of which suggests an earlier and smaller local grouping, may preserve the boundaries of a minster district (VCH 1980, 46). The minster status of the churches of Britford and Winterbourne Stoke is, however, less certain. Neither is distinctive in the size of its parish or in its relation to its Hundred. Both would appear to owe their early importance to their presence on royal estates. Britford was sufficiently distinguished to be an occasional royal residence. The church of Winterbourne Stoke was rich enough to be a suitable gift from William I to the great Norman abbey of Jumièges.

Only two churches in the area contain visible remains of the Anglo-Saxon period: the 8th to 9th-century nave of Britford, with decorated arches leading formerly to flanking porticūs,[16] and the two cross-heads preserved at Amesbury. This paucity of material evidence is compensated for by other monuments just beyond the boundaries of this survey (*see* Illus. 8): the almost complete, late Saxon church of Breamore to the south; the tower/nave of Netheravon to the north; to the west, the famous figurative relief at Codford St Peter and cross fragments in Broad Chalke and in Hanging Langford (the fragment from the last is now preserved in the church of Steeple Langford). The churches of Burcombe, just west of Wilton, and Quarley, just east of

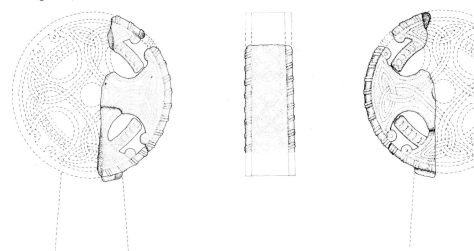

9. Amesbury: reconstruction of larger Saxon cross-head, found 1907.

Cholderton, have Saxon features which could date from before or after the Conquest.[17]

Even from this enlarged area no clear picture of architectural development or artistic style emerges. Britford is relatively early in the Saxon period, Breamore and Netheravon late; their plans differ markedly. The style of interlace around the circumference of the larger Amesbury cross-head is comparable with that of the cross-heads at Ramsbury but quite unlike that of the cross shafts of Codford St Peter or Hanging Langford, yet the last three have all been assigned dates within the 9th century. The key to the developoment of Saxon art in the area ought to be found in Wilton, at times almost a second capital of Wessex, but little record survives of the pre-Conquest buildings or sculpture of Wilton, nor can any surviving late Anglo-Saxon manuscripts be associated with the abbey.[18] None of the medieval parish churches of the borough can be proved to have existed before the Conquest although excavation might reveal evidence of earlier origins.

The further possibility remains that some churches with fabric entirely of later date might yet retain the ghost of an Anglo-Saxon predecessor in their plan. The inconsistencies in plan of both Downton and Winterbourne Stoke church may best be explained as the result of following the outline of earlier, possibly Saxon, work. The cruciform plan adopted in both is not on its own an indication of Saxon origin since it is common in churches of the Romanesque and early Gothic periods. No church in the area has the distinctive salient angles to the crossing, a feature which has been identified as marking Anglo-Saxon work in the Dorset churches of Sherborne, Wimborne and elsewhere (RCHM 1952, xlviii). The church at Breamore is not truly cruciform but has a longitudinal plan of nave, tower/chancel and sanctuary, with porticūs flanking the tower but not forming transepts.[19] The church of Tilshead has a similar plan (except that the nave is aisled) and might be of late Saxon origin. The village seems to have reached the peak of its development in the 11th century when it was recorded in Domesday Book as a borough. There is no apparent sign of pre-Conquest work in the fabric of the church but any traces of the specifically Saxon feature of porticūs against the tower would be unlikely to have survived the later erection of tombs against the external walls and their subsequent removal, not to mention a lowering of the ground level in the restoration of 1845.[20]

The Romanesque Period

The Norman Conquest can have had little immediate impact on the architecture of south-east Wiltshire. The principal landholders remained the same: the king, the bishops of Sherborne/Salisbury and Winchester, the abbesses of Wilton and Amesbury. The boroughs of Wilton and Tilshead did not suffer any disastrous drop in population, unlike their counterparts in Dorset (VCH 1955, 22). In addition to the two nunneries mentioned above, Domesday Book records only five churches in the area (see p.11), although this does not mean that others did not exist. The earliest identifiable fabric in the great majority of churches in the area is of the 12th century (VCH 1955, 33).[21] Most churches were probably not founded until then.

Documentary evidence confirms that the present parochial system became fully developed in the 12th and the early 13th century (VCH 1956, 3). Although the bishop of Salisbury's registers do not begin until 1297, references in charters together with the evidence of architectural remains indicate that at least three-quarters of the medieval churches of the area were in existence by 1200. Their appropriation by outside bodies began early. Jumièges already owned Winterbourne Stoke by the time of Domesday although it was not until c. 1250 that a vicarage was formally instituted. The great majority of the churches appropriated in the 12th and 13th centuries,

10. Durnford: interior looking W showing Romanesque nave and blocked window.

11. Amesbury: interior looking W showing Romanesque nave and blocked clearstorey windows.

however, went to support the cathedral establishment at Salisbury, either directly to the Dean and Chapter as a prebend or to a particular officer such as the treasurer. Of the religious houses of the area, Wilton was in the main content with the patronage rather than the rectories of the churches in its care, but Amesbury acted very differently. Apparently as part of the refoundation grant, the priory received the rectories of the four local parishes of Amesbury, Bulford, Durrington and Maddington which it retained in its own hands until the Dissolution, serving the churches by chaplains rather than by formally instituted vicars.

The links of patronage do not seem to have affected the architectural character of the churches: the four belonging to Amesbury share no distinctive features, and those belonging to the Salisbury Chapter, such as Durnford or Alderbury, are not noticeably larger or more splendid than the others in the area. Since it was on the whole the richer rectories that were appropriated it is hard to know whether any feature of quality in a prebendal church was due to interest on the part of the prebendary or to the general wealth of the village. There are direct links between the ornament used at the prebendal church of Durnford and some of the sculptured fragments from the cathedral at Old Sarum (*see* pp.16,17) but these can as well be attributed to the proximity of Durnford to Old Sarum as to common patronage.

While much 12th-century work can still be seen in the churches, not enough remains to·present a comprehensive picture of a Romanesque church of the area. Relatively complete Romanesque naves survive at Amesbury, Durnford, Winterbourne Stoke, Berwick St James, Stapleford, Coombe Bissett and Bulford, together with over a dozen fonts and fifteen doorways. The few surviving windows are either *ex situ* as at Odstock, or blocked as at Amesbury or Durnford. No Romanesque chancel can be identified unless the short chancel of a later medieval building, as for example Orcheston St George, is sometimes evidence of 12th-century origin.

Most of the 12th-century churches of the area probably originated as two or even one-cell buildings such as the chapel of St Leonard at Whelpley, but few unaltered examples survive. Standlynch, founded traditionally in 1147, has a plan of Romanesque type in which the line of the inner wall of the nave is continued to form the line of the outer wall of the chancel (see also RCHM 1984, lxxx); all the identifiable fabric is, however, later. The most frequent elaboration of the plan is the occurrence of a south aisle, as at Stapleford or Winterslow. Such aisles are probably additions to existing naves, but there is no evidence in the masonry of the arcades to show that the arches were cut through existing walls.

An arcaded nave was not always found in the more ambitious Romanesque churches of the area. Bulford, Durnford, Winterbourne Stoke and Berwick St James have airy unaisled naves, broad in proportion to their length. That these proportions are deliberate is suggested by the dimensions of the nave at Berwick St James which is exactly twice as long as it is wide.

Three groups of Romanesque arcades may be distinguished on the basis of the form of their piers: square piers, with very simple impost mouldings; large round piers, with square, scalloped capitals; and more slender round piers, with round moulded capitals. The first form occurs at Winterslow (south arcade), at Nunton (arch to chancel chapel) and at Tilshead (north and south arcades) where each impost block has a continuously chamfered lower edge defined by a groove above. The imposts of the chancel arches at Bulford and Nunton are similarly moulded but those at Nunton have rich carving.[22]

The four arcades belonging to the second group, at Coombe Bissett, Downton, Shrewton and Stapleford, are probably some fifty years later than the 'impost' type. They are all similar in form, although the decoration of the scalloped capitals differs in detail. The arcades at Shrewton may once have shown a development from the early, impost type of the W respond of the N arcade to the more developed scalloped type of the S arcade, but because of the rearrangement of the piers during the 19th-century restoration of the church this hypothesis cannot be confirmed.

The third group of arcades has the round piers of the second type but instead of square scalloped capitals has round moulded ones, prefiguring the classic Early English form though with very different mouldings. The capitals of the north arcades at Winterslow and Whiteparish both show the same treatment of rolls, which vary in number from capital to capital and which are set sparingly down a bulky drum. The two easternmost piers of the Whiteparish south arcade and the surviving pier and responds of the Ivychurch arcade have similar capitals cut into a form of scalloping, so emphasising the essentially Romanesque character of the design. The same combination of the moulded and a scalloped type occurs in the south arcade at Durrington.

The form of the arches of the arcades does not help to date them more precisely. The round, chevron-encrusted arches at Stapleford are as clearly Romanesque as the plain, round chancel arches of Durnford or Bulford, but the use of dogtooth in their outermost orders suggests that they were not built until late in the 12th century. In the one original arch of the south chapel at Nunton (which has responds of the elementary first type), the arches of the Downton north arcade (which have piers of the second, scalloped type) and the arches of the Whiteparish north and south arcades (which have piers of the third, moulded type) the orders are unchamfered and thus, seemingly, early even though the heads of the arches are pointed.

Substantial remains of Romanesque towers exist only in two churches, at Idmiston and Wilsford. A third tower, complete although over-restored in the 19th century, lies just outside the area to the north, at Figheldean.[23] Each stands at the west end of its respective church whereas the more numerous 13th-century towers in the area are sited mostly on the south side.

12

13

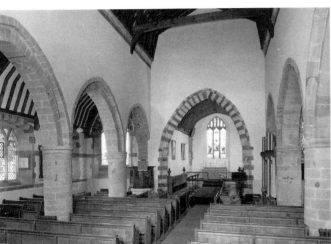

14

15

12. Nunton: interior looking SE showing S respond of chancel arch, and S chancel arcade.

13. Tilshead: interior looking E.

14. Whiteparish: interior looking E.

15. Stapleford: nave arcade.

16. Wilsford: exterior from SW in 1857 showing tower before restoration.

17. Stratford Tony: exterior from N showing re-used Romanesque arch in later porch.

The Romanesque feature which survives most frequently is the doorway. Most doorways are *in situ* and remain in use; those at Woodford and at Orcheston St George were still sufficiently valued in the 15th century to be retained in Perpendicular rebuildings. At Stratford Tony a late Romanesque arch survives, much altered, incorporated in a post-Reformation porch. The doorways of the area were decorated with ornamental rather than figurative carvings, apart from a few animals on capitals.[24]

The doorways, with the single exception of that at South Newton, are of one order rising from shafts. In some the arch of the order is that of the door opening, in others the arch acts as a frame to a narrower doorway. Two sets of typological differences occur, and in about equal numbers: between doorways with tympana and those without and between roll-moulded and chevron-enriched arches.

A distinct group emerges among the churches in the Avon and Till valleys (at Durnford, Woodford, Stapleford, Berwick St James and Winterbourne Stoke): opposed doorways set about a third of the way up the nave from the west end having tympana and shafts with scalloped capitals carrying single orders of rich sawtooth chevron projecting at a right angle from the wall face.[25] The most important church in this group is Durnford, not only because of the elaboration of its two doorways but also because their decoration is clearly connected with the major contemporary sculpture found at Old Sarum, such as the 'ravioli' motif lining the inner jamb of the south doorway (Stalley 1971, 76) and the intersecting arcading round the bowl of the font (Henry, Zarnecki 1957, 21–2). The north doorway at Berwick St James seems a less skilful version of that at Durnford: the lion's mask at the apex is omitted and the pattern of contrasting greensand and buff stone lozenges at Durnford is here reduced to alternating courses of greensand and buff stone in the tympanum and lozenge hatchings scratched on the lintel;[26] the south doorway (now blocked) lacks any decoration. At Winterbourne Stoke ideas from Durnford were perhaps considered after the erection of the south doorway and before the erection of the north doorway, since the simpler roll-moulded arch of the former, typical of the area, gives way in the latter to a more ornate chevron similar to that of Durnford. This difference may, however, merely reflect the greater importance of the N door; moreover, a close dating sequence could be misleading since the dogtooth border to the arch of the south doorway at Stapleford shows that the Durnford influence could linger on late in the 12th century.

Shaft bases do not assist in establishing a dating sequence for the doorways because in most cases they have been defaced, obscured or doubtfully restored. The 'elephant's foot' type of double roll occurs at Wilsford, Landford, Amesbury (for the base of the respond) and, reversed, at Durrington, but it merely confirms an already probable date for these buildings in the first part of the 12th century.

18. Netherhampton: tub font (destroyed), *Buckler c.* 1805.

Any classification of fonts must be yet more tentative, not only because the sample is limited to a dozen or so of probably 12th and early 13th-century date, but also because they have been subject to successive repairs and resettings, especially in the 19th century.[27] With the exception of Rollestone, few of the stems and bases of the fonts appear to be original. Conversely, the shallowness of the font bowl and the absence of any evidence for a lock on the rim to secure the cover does not prove a post-medieval date, since the rim can be easily abraded or cut away.

The most primitive and so, in theory at least, typologically the earliest form is the plain tub font, of which an example survives unaltered at Winterslow. Drawings, of 1804, 1864 and 1867 respectively, suggest that the fonts at Netherhampton, West Dean and West Grimstead were originally of this form (*see* Table 6).[28] The fonts at Winterbourne Gunner and Boscombe seem to mark a further stage in the development of the type, comprising a tub bowl (i.e. one with only slightly rounded sides) supported on a proper stem rather than on a crude plinth and decorated with a roll-moulding either on the stem or, as at Boscombe, at the junction of bowl and stem. The fonts at Winterbourne Stoke and (formerly) Shrewton belong to the same type, although they were executed with a degree of skill which suggests a date in the latter part of the 12th century. Probably of the same date, though different in type, is a third group of fonts which share the bowl and stem form but which have a wider and shallower bowl with sides springing abruptly from the base (e.g. Stratford Tony, Rollestone and Pitton). Again the mouldings are simple. Of the same type, though almost certainly 13th-century in date, are the fonts at Berwick St James and Odstock, the latter grievously retooled.

Firmly datable to the late 11th or the 12th century because of their bold Romanesque ornament are fonts of this third type with decoration covering all or most of the sides of the bowls: at Tilshead, decorated with broad grooves between opposed herringbone, probably of *c.* 1100, and at Stapleford with a band of feather fluting.[29] The most elaborate is the font at Durnford, of *c.* 1150, with its rich band of intersecting arcading probably derived, like the doorways, from work at Old Sarum (Henry, Zarnecki 1957, 21–2). Less ornate but equally striking is the decoration round the bowl of the font at Chitterne All Saints (originally in St Mary's). The Cholderton font has a more Early English type of decoration, with stiff-leaf capitals linked to form horse-shoes round the base of the bowl; presumably the lost base incorporated shafts to these capitals.

Shafts are, however, a more typical adjunct of the rectangular table form of font, the last of the early medieval font types. That at Bulford, a good plain example, is probably 12th century but its presence is undocumented before the church's restoration in 1905. The more complex, richly moulded design of the Coombe Bissett font, which, though circular, incorporates shafts to carry the bowl, must be 13th

19. Wilsford: base of S respond shaft, W doorway.

20. Orcheston St George: Romanesque male head reset in N wall, nave.

21. Standlynch: Romanesque male head reset in S porch.

century. The table fonts at Amesbury and Downton are of the design, common in southern England in the 12th and 13th centuries, in which the bowl is decorated with shallow arcading along the sides (Pevsner 1967, 18). Both have lost their supporting shafts; at Amesbury, the bowl had already been given a square solid base by the later Middle Ages.

A general examination of ornament suggests that few regional characteristics are detectable. Table 4 illustrates clearly the preference in the area for sawtooth chevron (i.e. chevron projecting at a right angle to the wall surface rather than parallel to it) and for scalloped rather than cushion or any other form of capital. The widespread use of stars, saltires or lozenges, especially in borders, is too common in Romanesque ornament for any local significance to be attached to it.

Only one major piece of Romanesque figurative sculpture, apart from the fragments from the Augustinian priory of Ivychurch, survives: the relief depicting two figures on either side of a cross now set above the inside face of the north door at Landford. The subject has been identified as the Invention of the Cross by St Helena and dated to c. 1130.[30] The original setting and function of the panel are uncertain. It was found buried in the foundations of the south-east corner of the former chancel of Landford church when it was demolished in 1857. The association with the sanctuary together with the relatively modest size of the panel (2 ft 4 in. by 1 ft 8 in: 0.71 m by 0.51 m) and the presence of six slots neatly cut into the stone, suggest that the relief may have contained relics of the Cross or of St Helena and stood over an altar. Two Romanesque carved male heads survive ex situ, one in the north wall of the nave at Orcheston St George and the other above the inner face of the doorway to the porch at Standlynch. Though roughly the same size they bear little similarity to each other, even allowing for the thick paint covering the Orcheston sculpture. The Standlynch head is roughly square and has a beard and moustache marked by grooving; that at Orcheston is long and thin with protruding eyes and cheekbones and a clean-shaven chin.

There also survive a few ex situ carved capitals, as at Pitton, or grotesque beast heads, as at West Grimstead. Such examples give a slight indication of the vast amount of Romanesque sculpture that has disappeared. The original corbel table of the nave at Amesbury is well preserved (so far as it is visible) on the south side, though it has been much restored on the north. A small monster head built into the north wall of the south aisle at West Grimstead may have served as a label stop to a doorway or arch moulding. Lastly, there are two relatively large but much worn carvings of monstrous animals at Odstock, found during the 1871 restoration of the church and incorporated as corner-stones to the new porch.

22

23

22. West Grimstead: grotesque head reset in N wall, S aisle.
23. Odstock: grotesque beast reused in N porch.

24   25   26

24, 25. Ivychurch: reliefs of St Peter (24) and St Paul (25), formerly on W front of present house.
26. Landford: relief depicting the Invention of the True Cross, reset above rear-arch, N doorway.

27. Ivychurch: double capital from former cloister.

The Romanesque sculpture from Ivychurch Priory needs to be considered separately in view of its quantity and the lack of stylistic links between it and work in the parish churches of the area. About thirty capitals survive from the double arcade of the cloister, of which half are intact. One, now in Salisbury museum, is decorated with seated figures under an arcade. The others, of a type found widely across England, are decorated with ten different decorative motifs, based on the scallop but adapted with beading or foliage motifs. Of the relatively few single capitals, one example has volutes and another scallops. The most important pieces of sculpture to survive are two standing male figures rather under three feet (0.91 m) high and carved in high relief. The figures are impressive works of the 1160s. One depicts St Peter, in a frontal pose and holding two large keys while blessing; the other figure, shown in profile, represents St Paul (Arts Council 1984, 190–1).[31] Their original siting, however, is hard to reconstruct. The St Paul was recorded in the early 19th century in an engraving in *Modern Wiltshire*; a drawing had been made of the St Peter a century before, in the margin of a plan of Ivychurch of *c.* 1730 (BL Kings Libr. Topog. gen. XLIII, 42–4; *see* also Arts Council 1984, 372).

28. Stratford Tony: 13th-century piscina in S wall, chancel (*see also* 461).

29. Orcheston St George: 15th-century piscina in sill of SE window, chancel.

THE EARLY ENGLISH PERIOD

Noteworthy in this area is the apparent lack of influence upon the numerous new churches erected in the 13th century of what might be assumed to be the key building, Salisbury Cathedral. This is the more unexpected in view of the number of local churches appropriated to the cathedral dignitaries. There is no use of Purbeck shafts in arcades or single arches, unless the 19th-century marble shafts in the chancel (now tower) arch at South Newton replace originals of Purbeck.[32] Use of window shafts is rare; exceptions are the east windows of Fugglestone and, if the original design has been accurately restored, also at Durrington. The general proportions of windows even in the large churches of Amesbury and Downton differ from those of the cathedral, being relatively taller and narrower. Some of the moulded capitals (for instance in the nave arcade at Nunton) resemble those of the cathedral, especially the chapter house, but not so closely as to establish the cathedral as the model.

The local churches appropriated to monastic houses rather than to Salisbury Chapter received no more lavish treatment. Amesbury Priory must have paid for the Early English chancel and transepts added to Amesbury church, but the contemporary chancels of two of their other churches, Durrington and Maddington, were simple buildings. Although the members of Salisbury Chapter were unambitious patrons, the Winchester Chapter, the priory of St Swithun, and the bishop of Winchester were more generous. The chancel at Downton, rebuilt at the end of the 13th century, is relatively large and elaborately detailed and resembles that at Bishopstone, the other neighbouring church belonging to the bishop of Winchester. There is also a link between Downton and Enford (a church some three miles north of Durrington), which belonged to the Winchester Chapter and whose chancel was rebuilt in the 13th century; in both churches a substantial vestry was built contemporary with the chancel and connected with it through a passage.

The distinctive contribution made in the 13th century to the churches of south-east Wiltshire was the provision of new chancels. With few exceptions they are unambitious and lack the quality of those of other Early English parish churches in the county such as, for example, Potterne. Amesbury is the only one of major design to survive, although that at Berwick St James is of some distinction.[33] The extent to which Romanesque work was incorporated is hard to estimate, but the discovery of 12th-century sculptural fragments buried in the chancel foundations underneath 13th-century walling at Maddington, Odstock and Landford suggests that earlier chancels were completely dismantled.

The favoured design for a chancel of the period appears to have been a relatively long and low building with an east window of three stepped lancets and single lancets along the side walls. Towards the west end there was often a doorway or low-side window. Low-side windows survive at Tilshead and Downton, closed as originally by shutters. Possibly they were only opened during times of service to provide additional light and ventilation (Cook 1954, 176–7).

These Early English chancels were provided from the first with aumbries and piscinae although seats in the form of sedilia were not installed until the end of the century. At Durnford there are twin aumbries set in the east wall and flanking the altar; in the position usually occupied by image brackets in a later medieval chancel. Piscinae are generally of simple design except for the late 13th-century example at Stratford Tony which is of Purbeck marble and has richly moulded jambs and trefoiled head, and a bowl carved with two fish. Elsewhere the most elaborate form is that in which the tall recess of the piscina is divided by a shelf, the upper part serving as the credence and the lower as the piscina proper.[34] The piscina at West Dean (now split and with the roles of the two sections reversed) is finely but not elaborately moulded. Other types of piscina are few; drains were set directly into the sills of the late 15th-century windows to the south of the altar at Orcheston St George, and at Pitton. There is a pillar piscina at Allington and an angle piscina built into the pastiche Gothic west front of the old church at Wilton.

The character of Early English naves in south-east Wiltshire is less well defined, perhaps because they either incorporate Romanesque work or have been much altered in later times. The nave at Idmiston clearly replaces earlier work since the plinths of the arcade piers incorporate re-used fragments of Romanesque carved stonework. One almost unaltered example is the nave at Odstock where both the north and the south walls have an exactly corresponding arrangement of a moulded two-centred doorway towards the west end and lancet windows to the east.

Otherwise the most obvious evidence of Early English work in naves is the addition of arcades. Thirteenth-century arcade piers were always round, but they varied in form between a stubby column on a high plinth, as in the nave arcades of Orcheston St Mary and West Grimstead, and tall slim shafts as in the south arcade at Downton. This latter type was particularly favoured for responds, not only of arcades but also of single arches opening to chancels, towers or chapels.[35] The sole more complex type of pier found in the area is the quatrefoil cluster at Idmiston.

While the development between the Romanesque and the Early English types seems well established in general, individual examples display inconsistencies. In the nave at Whiteparish the piers are tall and relatively slender but their moulded capitals are still crudely composed; whereas at West Grimstead the north arcade pier, which is stubby and of more primitive appearance typologically, carries a capital with well co-ordinated mouldings. As a type, the stubby pier continued in use throughout the 13th century in remote or unambitious buildings such as the churches at Nunton and Orcheston St Mary.

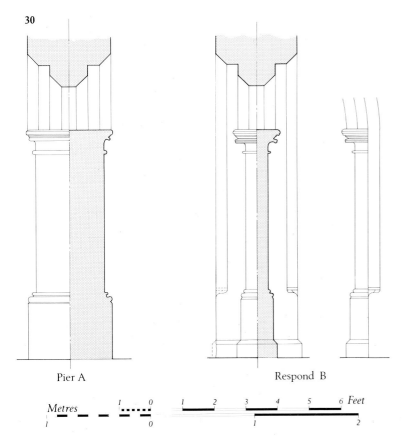

30

Pier A   Respond B

Metres

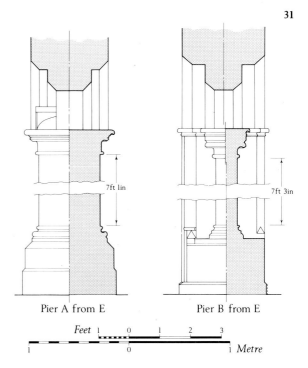

31

30. West Grimstead: elevations and sections of nave arcade pier (L) and W respond of archway to S chapel (R).
31. Downton: elevations and sections of easternmost pier N arcade (L) and second pier from E, S arcade (R).

7ft 1in

7ft 3in

Pier A from E   Pier B from E

Feet

Metre

32. Stapleford: capital and corbel, W respond of archway to N chapel.

33. Stapleford: capital and corbel, S respond of chancel arch.

Early English arch mouldings were in general uncomplicated. By far the commonest is the double chamfer. More elaborate examples are the east arch of the crossing at Downton and, dating from the end of the century, the arch of the east doorway in the north wall of Amesbury chancel.

In a few churches, perhaps of the later rather than the earlier part of the 13th century, the inner orders of an arch are borne not by full shafts but by dwarf shafts resting on sculpted corbels. Stapleford has two such examples. The earlier is the arch to the north chapel; here the male and female corbel heads, though they have been defaced and partly restored, are of some quality. The same elements are crudely reproduced in the late medieval chancel arch, perhaps because it replaced a 13th-century arch. In the late 13th-century tower arch at Stapleford the innermost order is continuous except for two responds carved with heads. At Idmiston some of the responds to the tower and arcade arches are carried not on dwarf shafts but directly on corbels.

One local characteristic was a preference for south towers sited so that their lowest chambers might be used as porches. The examples cannot be dated precisely because the tower openings tend to be simple, but a date in the second half of the 13th century is indicated by the curious shouldered and hollow-chamfered arch of the Pitton doorway. A very similar door existed in the same position in the old church at Winterbourne Earls. There is no obvious reason for the unusual positioning of these towers; it was not due to practical difficulties such as restricted churchyards or abrupt changes in ground level around the buildings since in all examples the sites allow for a conventional west tower. Most of the churches of this type (e.g. Pitton, Allington, Winterslow) are in the north-east part of the area, in and around the Bourne valley, and are somewhat similar in appearance, suggesting, perhaps, that each parish imitated its neighbour. These towers may have been intended primarily as *clochers-porches*, to house a bell or bells which had previously, as at Quarley (Hants), hung in a cage at ground level. None of the towers was of any great height originally. Until the 19th century those of the Bourne valley group were constructed of masonry in their lower stages only, the belfries being of wood. Others, such as at Chitterne St Mary, were heightened in the 15th or 16th century.[36]

The decorated capitals in the area exhibit a certain variety but no consistent pattern. At Shrewton the responds of the chancel arch have scalloped capitals adorned with large flat leaves. At Downton a similar combination of scalloped and foliage elements is also found in the north respond of the arch from the nave to the south transept but the leaf forms are in a band above the scallops. Both these Transitional forms could be dated to *c.* 1200 but for the fact that in the south respond of the same arch at Downton, scallops have been completely discarded in favour of the later form of stiff-leaf in which the leaves are comparatively naturalistic. By contrast, the stiff-leaf of the north transept chapel of Amesbury, which is no later than *c.* 1250, has leaves more conventionally cut in crocket-like fronds resembling those in Salisbury chapter house. The two elegant waterleaf capitals now incorporated in the lectern of West Dean church probably derive from those at the east end of the church of the Augustinian priory of Mottisfont (Hants), only a few miles to the east of West Dean. Finally, the east respond of a portal of four recessed orders attached to the west end of the nave of Amesbury has capitals delicately carved with a kind of crocket applied so as to produce the effect of Corinthian acanthus and volutes.[37] Their quality as well as their type place them apart from the general developments in the area.

The Early English treatment of the moulded capital follows the same form as in the rest of the country. It is more coherent than the crudely spaced rolls typical of the Romanesque moulded capital. Above the neck ring there is a plain bell and then

34

35

36

37

38. Pitton: S doorway, S tower.

34. Shrewton: capitals, S respond of chancel arch.
35. Downton: capitals, S respond of arch between S transept and aisle (*see* also 299).
36. Downton: capitals, N respond of arch between S transept and aisle (*see* also 299).
37. Amesbury: capital carrying vault rib, SE angle of N transept chapel.

39. West Dean: waterleaf capitals re-used in lectern.

40. Winterbourne Stoke: capitals, E respond of arch to N transept.

41. Winterbourne Stoke: arch to S transept.

mouldings grouped in two or three bands or rolls, with grooves between, the upper roll projecting but with an oversailing abacus. The capitals of the eastern parts of Amesbury church may be considered as a model since they are the most uniform work of the period. The mouldings consist not of two rolls and a hollow, but of two flat bands divided by a groove, with projecting members enriched by a narrow fillet. The other work of comparable quality, the east crossing arch at Downton, has capitals of a very similar type but with two grooves around the bell, thus creating three bands. Although this latter arrangement of mouldings can be found at Salisbury Cathedral, the Downton mouldings have the flatness of the Amesbury capitals rather than the swelling profile of those at Salisbury. The mouldings of the capitals of the nave arcade of Nunton and of the south chapel arch at West Grimstead are more deeply cut and come near to achieving the hour-glass profile typical of Salisbury work of the later 13th century, e.g. the cathedral cloister. The north and south arches of the crossing at Winterbourne Stoke illustrate the difficulty of charting the development of moulded capitals. The south arch has capitals with one groove creating two bands and with a deeply undercut bell, the capitals being supported on shafts grouped round a virtually free-standing central pier. On the north side the capitals are more coarsely treated, with almost no undercutting but with mouldings of two grooves and three bands. The south arch can be regarded as the more refined and therefore the later of the two, or the north arch can be considered as a debased version of that on the south.[38]

A few remains of painted decoration survive from the Early English period. On the east wall of the chancel at Durnford there is a restored but apparently authentic scheme of masonry outlining, enlivened with hook-like flourishes. A fragment of similar outlining survives at West Dean, and according to 19th-century sources other examples formerly existed both at West Dean and at Winterslow. Painted tendril patterns have been revealed on the nave walls at Durnford and in the soffits of the Stapleford nave arcade. The most important example of wall painting recorded in the area was the cycle of the Life of Christ, probably of *c.* 1300, in the church of Winterbourne Dauntsey, which was described and photographed in some detail before its demolition. As Borenius observed, 'we are not here face to face with the work of some provincial rustics' (1932, 45). The artist was clearly familiar with work of high quality, whether at Clarendon Place or in Salisbury. The Last Supper on the east wall of the former refectory at Ivychurch, also apparently of *c.* 1300 and also destroyed in the 19th century, is even more likely to have been influenced by the wall paintings commissioned by Henry III for Clarendon Palace,[39] since the canons of Ivychurch served the palace chapel.

42. Winterbourne Dauntsey: wall painting of the Adoration of the Magi, photographed before destruction in 1867 (*see* also 214).

In the words of Sir Nikolaus Pevsner (1975, 25), 'Wiltshire is not a Decorated county', and its south-east corner is no exception. The few important examples of Decorated work appear to be set pieces, commissioned by individual patrons. A close association with the patron is typical of the period: the chancel at Downton, the outstanding work of the early 14th century in the area, was under the patronage of the bishops of Winchester; the south aisle of West Dean church was added c. 1333 by Robert de Borbach to serve as his chantry chapel; the south chapel of Stapleford, which is small but unified in design, is equally the result of a personal commission although the name of the founder of the chapel has not been established.

Individual patronage appears to have been responsible not only for the addition of complete chapels but also for the insertion of single windows and tombs. The donation of a new window was often prompted by the desire to light an altar. At Bulford a window was made at the south-east corner of the nave where it could light an altar which was set to the south of the chancel arch and to which was added in this same period a cinquefoiled niche as a form of reredos behind and above it. The sheer size of these Decorated windows marked a change from earlier forms. In the chancel at Amesbury the two four-light traceried windows, each of which replaced a single lancet, took up so much of the wall that they came to endanger the stability of the fabric. The relatively modest chancel of Stratford Tony, only 22 ft by 15 ft (6.71 m by 4.57 m), was lit by two two-light windows in each side wall and a three-light window which fills most of the east wall.

There were no extensive rebuilding schemes in the period, except for Britford where the upper part of the Saxon nave was refashioned and a new crossing, transepts and chancel added. Chancels were replaced only at Downton and Stratford Tony. Naves were untouched except for the addition of an aisle, as at Maddington and West Dean, or the alteration of an earlier aisle, as at South Newton and Whiteparish. Arcade piers and capitals were now polygonal, not round. The west towers at Berwick St James and Durnford seem to have been added at this period but their date is indicated only by the width of the tower arch and its continuous moulding.

Much more common were additions designed to enhance the appearance and usefulness of existing buildings. Sedilia were inserted in several churches of the area, as in many parts of England.[40] At West Dean the 13th-century chancel was adapted to accommodate seats by cutting two recesses into the south wall and supporting the wall above with a re-used shaft and capital. The sedilia of Stapleford and Downton are of the usual design of an arcade of four openings of which a piscina occupies the easternmost and stepped seats the other three, although in both churches the arrangement of the openings and the ornament of the upper parts were extensively altered in the 19th century. The sedilia at Britford are much less elaborate, with the three stepped seats arranged in the sill of the window to the south of the altar, and the piscina cut into the east jamb of the window.

Chancels were further decorated by the addition of tiled floors, almost certainly for the first time. The surviving tiles in the churches of the area nearly all date from the late 13th and early 14th century.[41] Those at Britford, Stapleford, West Dean and Winterbourne Stoke belong to a group of the Wessex school deriving its decorative designs from those used at Clarendon Palace and Salisbury Cathedral during the period 1250–60. The same influence has also been identified at the site of Amesbury Priory (Stevens 1937, 364–5).[42] The body fabric of the tiles is light red to pinkish buff in colour and includes lumps of haematite; over it the glaze appears orange-brown with purple-brown spots. Although no kiln associated with these tiles has yet been securely identified, the discovery in 1939, during the excavations on the site of

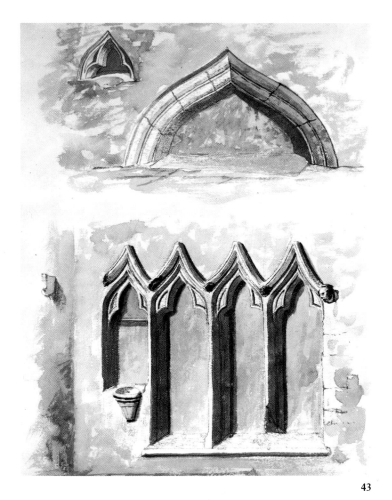

44

45

43

Clarendon Palace, of a heap of wasters of this type suggests Clarendon as a possible source (Eames 1980, 189–90, 194–5). The type has therefore been called 'Clarendon 2' to distinguish it from the tiles produced at Clarendon in the early 1240s. Manufacture of Clarendon 2 tiles probably began about 1260 or soon afterwards and may have continued into the early years of the 14th century. Some tiles of a different type, similar to those manufactured at Nash Hill, Lacock, and possibly made there, were also used at Amesbury Priory and probably date from *c.* 1300–25 (Eames 1974, 134–8).

The major characteristic of Decorated work in south-east Wiltshire is simplicity, whether expressed in the balanced proportions of the Downton and Stratford Tony chancels or in the plain mouldings of arches and windows. The use of continuously-moulded chamfered arches is most striking in the crossing at Britford, but it is also found in the east and west crossing-arches of Winterbourne Stoke, the chancel arch of Stratford Tony and the tower and chancel arches of Berwick St James. The jambs of the doorway and the windows of the relatively ambitious south aisle of West Dean are merely chamfered and not moulded.[43] The priest's doorway in the chancel of Stratford Tony is so plainly treated, with chamfered jambs and a two-centred head, that it could easily be claimed as a survival from the mid 13th century if it were not integrated with the moulded plinth of the 14th-century building.

More ornate are the various types of Decorated window.[44] The two-light side windows in the chancel at Downton have the most interesting design. Their tracery consists of a six-foil star with the foils alternately round and pointed, of a kind paralleled at Malmesbury Abbey. The design recurs only in the west window of the

43. Stapleford: details of fittings, prior to restoration; tomb recess and piscina, S chapel; piscina and sedilia, chancel S wall (*see* also 457); *Kemm* 1864.
44. Britford: tiles, now missing, recorded at 1872 restoration.
45. West Dean: 14th-century tiles reset in former piscina now aumbry.

46. Odstock: rubbing of incised slab in tomb recess, S side of nave.

chapel at Standlynch, in a less complex version. Otherwise, nearly all the Decorated windows in the churches of the area have tracery of the reticulated quatrefoil type, varying from the complexity of the Amesbury north chancel window to the more restrained form of the east window at Stratford Tony where the three principal lights are crowned by three quatrefoils arranged in a triangle, the space remaining between the quatrefoils and the outer rim of the window being occupied by two mouchettes. In the window of the south chapel at Stapleford a more ambitious attempt to insert quatrefoils in a similar position and blind mouchettes on either side of the upper quatrefoil resulted in some confusion in the lay-out of the tracery. In churches with reticulated tracery in the east window, the side windows of the chancel might have, as at West Dean, tracery of two ogee trefoil-headed lights enclosing a quatrefoil above, flanked by blind mouchettes. Alternatively, as at Stratford Tony, they might have straight-headed side windows with the top half of the tracery omitted and the mouchettes pierced. The two-light window with a single quatrefoil in the head became very common in isolation, particularly as the principal window of a chapel (e.g. the south window of the Winterbourne Stoke south transept), of an aisle (e.g. the west window of the Winterslow north aisle), or as a belfry opening (Maddington).[45]

The only other type of Decorated tracery found in the area is the dagger form, possibly introduced at a rather later period than the reticulated. It is used on a large scale in the south chancel window at Amesbury. The heads of the four lights are drawn up into elongated cinquefoils; over each pair of lights is a cusped dagger and between and over the two daggers is another, much larger, dagger filling the head of the window. The west (and, until the restoration of 1880, also the east) window at Pitton is a simpler version of the same design with only three cinquefoiled lights and two quatrefoils. Whiteparish has a further variant, with the daggers omitted and the head filled with three steeply-stepped cinquefoils.

Although grave-slabs carved with a cross-fleury survive from the 13th century, it is in the 14th century that tombs in this area become substantial and acquire a more architectural expression. The most common type is a waist-high recess open to the church under an ogee arch which, at West Dean, Odstock and Downton, is cusped into a cinquefoil. Similar tombs at Durnford and Stapleford have arches of simpler form but with richer mouldings of sunken rolls. Only the Odstock tomb retains what is apparently the original effigy: an incised slab of a gowned figure holding a (?)heart to his breast, under a spikily-cusped and crocketed gable (*see* Blair 1979 *passim*). Two other more conventional effigies of rather earlier date survive at Britford and at Fugglestone, both now *ex situ* and somewhat damaged; neither is large. Both figures wear the same type of simple tunic and have their arms crossed over their breasts; the Britford figure holds the foot of a cup or chalice in his left hand. At Winterbourne Earls and brought from the former church of Winterbourne Dauntsey there is a small, worn slab showing a half-length angel holding a heart, presumably from over a heart burial.

47. Britford: late 13th-century effigy, now in chancel found in 1873.

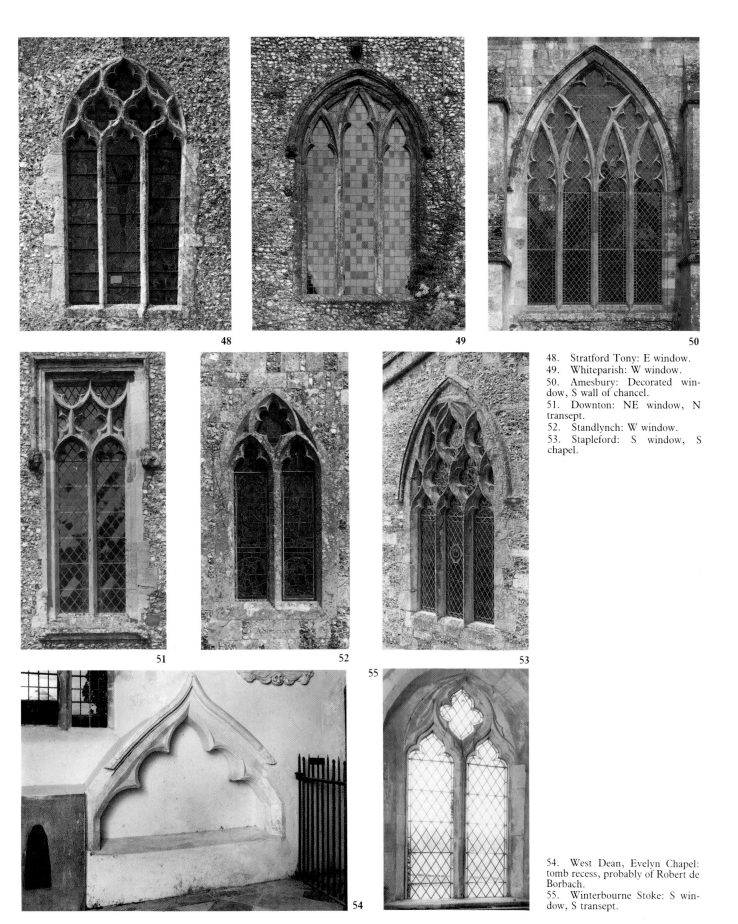

48

49

50

48. Stratford Tony: E window.
49. Whiteparish: W window.
50. Amesbury: Decorated window, S wall of chancel.
51. Downton: NE window, N transept.
52. Standlynch: W window.
53. Stapleford: S window, S chapel.

51

52

53

55

54

54. West Dean, Evelyn Chapel: tomb recess, probably of Robert de Borbach.
55. Winterbourne Stoke: S window, S transept.

29

THE PERPENDICULAR PERIOD

The Perpendicular style left a decisive imprint on the church architecture of the area, as elsewhere in Britain, even though the buildings were not as completely transformed as in East Anglia or Somerset. The basic forms of Perpendicular continued in use, in church towers at least, until well into the reign of Queen Anne.

Perpendicular design in the churches of south-east Wiltshire follows the forms typical of the West Country. It is characterised by relatively low-pitched, arch-braced or ceiled wagon roofs, tracery-panelled responds to arches, embattled and pinnacled aisles and two-storied porches. The masonry of important works is of ashlar with robust mouldings. Influence from the towns in the west of the county, particularly Bradford on Avon, is suggested by the similarity between the treatment of the west window, doorway and the label stops of the church at Orcheston St George, and that of the same elements of the church at Westwood, close to Bradford and with a Bradford patron.

The religious houses of the area were still prepared to contribute to considerable rebuilding schemes in the churches which they controlled. Amongst the churches belonging to Amesbury Priory, Amesbury itself was completely remodelled, including the chancel, and at Bulford a new east window and a new roof were provided for the chancel. The chancel of Chitterne St Mary, which belonged to the Dean and Chapter of Salisbury, was rebuilt to a modest size but to a high standard. The refacing and remodelling of the south side of the nave at St Mary's, Stapleford and its appropriation by Easton Priory in 1444 may well be connected.

Unfortunately, what must have been the principal Perpendicular monuments in the area are the least well preserved. During the 15th century the early medieval church at Amesbury was enlarged by the building of a new south aisle and comprehensively refitted with great east and west windows and elaborate roofs and furnishings, all of high quality, but in 1852–3 a large part of this work was removed in an attempt to recover the Early English appearance of the building (pp.72–3, 103). The former

56. Orcheston St George: exterior from SE before alteration of nave (*see* also 394), *Buckler c.* 1805.

church of St Mary at Wilton, which was a substantial building of the 15th and 16th centuries, with decorative carving on the capitals of the north arcade and on the font, was mostly demolished in the 1840s after its replacement by the 'Lombardic' St Mary and St Nicholas (pp.70, 213, 215). Ivychurch Priory, extensively refurbished in the early 16th century, was taken down even more recently; in 1889 (*see* p.150).

Nearly all the Perpendicular work was a remodelling of earlier buildings rather than a new design. Orcheston St George appeared, until the nave was altered in 1833, as a neat embattled building of the late 15th century, but a Romanesque doorway in the north wall of the nave and a lancet window in the south wall revealed that earlier fabric survived. Remodelling was in general confined not to chancels, as in the 13th and 14th centuries, but to naves and towers. At both Idmiston and Woodford, the Early English chancels were completely omitted from the thorough reconstructions of the nave, aisles, tower and porch. In a similar building programme at Coombe Bissett the chancel was at least partly refenestrated to match the new work.

The principal aims in the rebuilding of naves appears to have been greater height and better lighting. Roofs were reduced in pitch and the upper nave walls made into clearstoreys. In the nave at Amesbury the windows of the Romanesque clearstorey were either blocked or replaced by straight-headed Perpendicular windows. In churches such as St Mary's, Stapleford, the Perpendicular clearstorey windows were probably new insertions. In general, clearstoreys were only provided for aisled churches though one was added over the wide, unaisled nave of Berwick St James church. The clearstorey of Berwick St James church also demonstrates the rich and careful design which could be employed on such an operation even in a parish of modest wealth: the Perpendicular ashlar walling is clearly distinguishable externally from the Romanesque work below by bands of heavy roll-moulding which extend right round the nave and above and below the clearstorey windows.[46] The Stapleford clearstorey has gargoyles and fleurons carved in the string-course over the windows and here the care for detail was such that each window was built successively higher towards the east, to correspond with the slope of the hill on which the church is set. The treatment of the windows themselves was more standardised: they are straight-headed with trefoil or cinquefoil cusping of each light.

Arcade forms in the area developed gradually over the 14th and 15th centuries. The arcades at Wilton, Coombe Bissett and Amesbury are of conventional 15th-century form, each pier having four attached shafts with hollows between; in other churches piers are single shafted as in earlier centuries, although polygonal in section rather than round or square (except for the curious pier at South Newton, which consists of four conjoined half-octagons). The hollowing of the octagonal sides of the pier and responds of the south arcade at Woodford to produce a fluted effect can be dated by the other features of the arcade to the 15th rather than to the 14th century.

The differences in form between the north and south arcades of the nave at Homington indicate how the arcades of a relatively modest church could change between the 14th and the 15th century. The north arcade is still of the Early English type described above, i.e. with stubby piers on high plinths (*see* p.21), but piers are now polygonal (possibly the squat proportions and the crude bases with angle spurs remain from an earlier arcade). The south arcade is much taller and requires only three bays, instead of four as in the north arcade, to cover the length of the nave. The arches in both arcades are double-chamfered but the chamfers of those on the south are hollowed. In the south arcade curves are more pronounced in the capitals (the necks have an ogee profile rather than the slight swelling found in those of the north arcade) and also in the abaci, which are rounded on both upper and lower faces.

A common alteration of the period was the insertion of deeply moulded west doorways (even where there were already substantial side-portals to the nave as at

58. Stapleford: clearstorey windows, S side of nave, stepped to accord with sloping site.

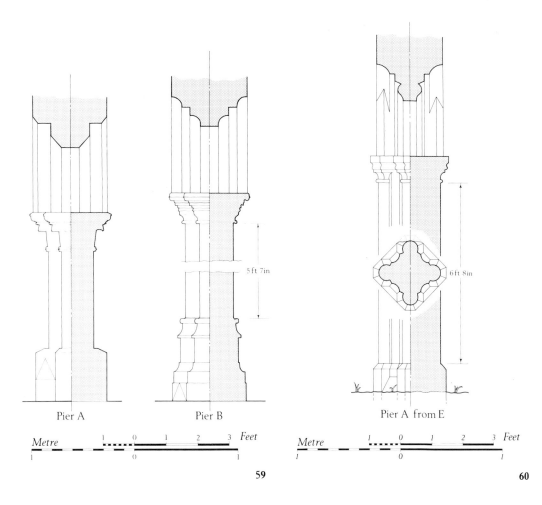

Pier A   Pier B   Pier A from E

5ft 7in

6ft 8in

Metre   1   0   1   2   3 *Feet*

Metre   1   0   1   2   3 *Feet*

59

60

59. Homington: elevations and sections of central pier N arcade (L) and W pier S arcade (R) (*see* plan p. 144).

60. Wilton, St Mary: elevation and sections, E pier, S arcade (*see* plan p. 213).

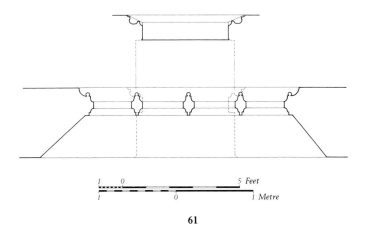

1   0   5 *Feet*

1   0   1 *Metre*

61

61. Winterbourne Stoke: section, W window and W doorway (*see* also 539).

Downton and Winterbourne Stoke) and, above them, large panel-traceried windows. Whether such doorways and windows were inserted in a west tower or in the west end of a nave, they were conceived as a single composition: at the west end of the nave at Downton the head of the doorway almost protrudes into the sill of the window; in the tower of Orcheston St George the reveals of the west window repeat the hollow mouldings of the doorway jambs below. Nor was this unity of effect lost internally.

62. Stratford Tony: angle gargoyle, W tower.

63. Odstock: rubble filling, stair-tower.

The tower arches at Orcheston, Woodford and, especially, Durrington were made very tall in order to reveal the full height of the west window.

Church towers were frequently rebuilt in the Perpendicular period and nearly always sited at the west end. Where the taste for south towers still survived, as at Coombe Bissett and Homington, the lowest stage of these towers was no longer used as a porch, since no doorway to the outside was provided.[47] Openings in the upper stages tend to be relatively simple, the most elaborate being of two lights with a quatrefoil over, although the simplicity of the openings may sometimes be the result of later rebuilding. Buttresses are diagonal and are usually applied to the west angles alone; an exception is the stepped and angled south-east buttress at Woodford.[48] Towers were usually crowned by battlements with a pinnacle rising from each angle, though in many places this design has been destroyed or altered during the last century. Sculpture of any kind is confined to the angle gargoyles of Winterbourne Stoke and Stratford Tony.

Inconsistencies within the west tower and west end of Odstock church suggest that the development of towers may have been more complex than it would seem from their present, comparatively uniform, appearance. Here the presence of diagonal buttresses at the eastern angles of the tower, within the church, suggests that the tower was built free-standing and then joined to the body of the church, the west wall of the nave being canted to accommodate the buttresses. The stair-tower, though in the usual position at the north-east corner abutting the nave, is disproportionately large and has had its eastern third filled with rubble since at least the early 17th century, which, together with the modest size of the belfry stage, indicates that an ambitious design had been curtailed.

The detailing of doorways, windows, arcades and roofs in general conforms to established Perpendicular types. All major doorways and windows have four-centred heads and heavy hood-moulds. Mouldings are thick and unrefined except for the relatively delicate north doorway of the nave of Stratford Tony. It may be significant that for the decoration of features more monumental than doorways, such as tower

64

65

64. Odstock: interior looking W showing canted W wall.

65. Durrington: interior looking W to tower arch.

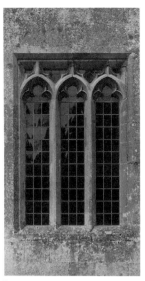

69. Durrington: W window.

66. Coombe Bissett: S window, S tower.

67. Woodford: S aisle window.

68. Coombe Bissett: N aisle window.

arches or large window splays, tracery panelling was preferred to shafts and complex mouldings; at Amesbury a start was even made on the casing of the great responds of the crossing with small-scale panelling.[49] Beneath the panelling of the Durrington tower arch the jambs are merely chamfered and the responds of the arch have simple capitals. At Orcheston St George the opening of the tower arch lacks any articulation and the tracery panelling is applied directly to the soffit.

Three-light windows, as for instance the south window of the tower at Coombe Bissett, sometimes have the common Perpendicular type of panel tracery with continuous mullions running from sill to head, but more often the mullions of the upper, traceried, lights rise from the heads of the lower lights not from their mullions. The large west window at Winterbourne Stoke and the even larger (former) east window at Amesbury were both designed with continuous mullions but each with distinctive tracery: in the former, a window of four lights, a transom runs across the centre lights; in the latter, of five lights, the three central lower lights rose into the arched head of the window. In another form, tracery was omitted and the cusped lights were stepped directly under the arched head of the window; in the Durrington west window this form was adapted to a large scale by the addition, below a transom, of a lower tier of simple trefoil-headed lights. Even if a window were straight-headed, an element of tracery could be created either by the insertion of mouchettes between the heads of the lights, as in the north aisle windows at Coombe Bissett, or by the addition of half-quatrefoils set above and between the heads of the main lights, such as had been used in the 14th century in the side windows of the chancel at Stratford Tony and was still acceptable a century later for the windows of the Woodford south aisle. This latter form might be elaborated by the addition of a row of whole quatrefoils as in the windows in the east walls of the transepts at Downton, or it might be reduced to pierced spandrels as in the less ambitious window on the north side of the nave at Orcheston St George.

Some types of Decorated tracery persisted well into the Perpendicular period. The type with a two-light window and quatrefoil above occurs in the Perpendicular upper stages of the towers at Winterbourne Stoke and Coombe Bissett. The small nave of Rollestone has two large, completely dissimilar, 15th-century windows. One is two-centred with sexfoils set in a Decorated, reticulated pattern; the other is

70. Coombe Bissett: N window, N chapel.

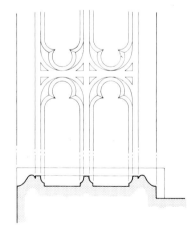

71. Orcheston St George: section of tracery panelling, tower arch.

35

72. Rollestone: N window, nave.
73. Rollestone: S window, nave.

72

73

four-centred, with stepped, cusped lights and continuous mullions. These windows were presumably inserted at different times, but in the chancel of Chitterne St Mary, which is all of one mid 15th-century build, the east window has continuously mullioned panel tracery with continuous mullions of a Perpendicular type and the side windows a more complex Decorated form of tracery with twin mouchettes.

There are no major roofs surviving from before the 15th century with the exception of those at West Grimstead, where nave and chancel have double-framed roofs of the 14th century with principals scalloped back above and below the purlins. The arch-braced tie beams are apparently additions of the 15th or 16th century. In the 15th century flat-pitched roofs were inserted in most of the more important churches in the area although frequently removed in the course of Victorian restorations. They consist of moulded tie beams and arch braces carried on sculpted corbels, with purlins and a ridge. Carved bosses mark the intersections of the principals. The most imposing example of this type is the nave roof of Amesbury church where tracery is introduced into the spandrels of the arch braces and above the tie beam; the roofs of the nave and aisles at Idmiston are similar although less ambitious in scale. Another type of roof construction is to be found in the east truss of the chancel roof at Bulford, which is constructed as a hammer-beam. This form may have been adopted merely to prevent the east window being blocked by a tie beam of the type used in the other trusses of the same roof.[50] The only true example of a hammer-beam roof occurs at Cholderton. The principals rise up carrying two pairs of purlins – the upper pair linked by an arch-braced collar – to the ridge, with no decoration except for the moulding of the principals and the carved spandrels of the hammers. The explanation for this unexpected appearance of an East Anglian roof-type in Wiltshire is that the roof was bought at auction in Ipswich in 1840, transported to Wiltshire and re-erected over a new church at Cholderton (*see* Appendix 2).

The other medieval form of roof common in the area was the ceiled wagon vault. The finest surviving examples are at Amesbury over the north and south transepts and over the south aisle. The ribs are arranged to form a continuous arc, and their

74

75

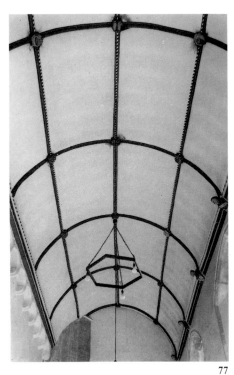

76

77

74. Bulford: interior of chancel looking E.
75. Amesbury: interior looking E.
76. West Grimstead: nave roof.
77. Amesbury: S aisle roof.

springings and intersections are marked by decorative bosses. The only other intact example is over the south chapel at Nunton. Elsewhere are a number of roofs originally of this type which have been altered either by the insertion of tie beams in the 17th century or by the stripping of the plaster ceiling in the 19th century, as over

78. Britford: chancel roof.
79. Amesbury: boss, S transept roof.
80. Idmiston: boss, nave roof.
81. Amesbury: corbel, S transept roof.
82. Amesbury: boss, S aisle roof.

78

the chancels at Britford, Winterbourne Gunner and Whiteparish and over the nave and chancel of St Andrew's, Durnford.[51] The timbers exposed by the removal of plaster ceilings can never have been intended to be seen since they are of meagre proportions and lack any moulding. Perhaps for the same reason these roofs have the primitive single-framed construction typical of the 13th century although they are most unlikely to be of such an early date. In several churches, as at Durnford, the steep creases of the former roofs can be seen above the present roofs.

It is possible that several local workshops were responsible for the carving of the corbels and the bosses. At Amesbury the style of corbels and bosses in the nave roof is very different from that displayed in the approximately contemporary roofs of the south aisle and transepts. In the nave roof human heads or faces are the commonest motifs, but in the other roofs half-length figures, beasts and foliage patterns are more numerous. The well characterised depictions of men and women in contemporary dress in the nave corbels of Amesbury are also found in the nave corbels of Berwick St James and Idmiston and may come from the same workshop. Some individual motifs amongst the bosses in the Amesbury south aisle roof, for instance the foliate knot, are repeated in the roof of St George's church, Harnham and in four bosses (now in Salisbury Museum) which survive from the roof of Ivychurch refectory; this again may indicate a common authorship.

79

80

81

82

83

84

85

86

87

83. Berwick St James: man with noose around neck, corbel, nave roof.
84. Amesbury: male head, corbel, nave roof.
85. Idmiston: man with twisted face, corbel, N aisle roof.
86. Idmiston: nun with beads, corbel, N aisle roof.
87. Idmiston: male bust, corbel, nave roof.

The churches of south-east Wiltshire are no exception to the general rule that the Perpendicular period is one of rich and varied fittings. Although examples of a wide range are recorded, not many of any one category survive. Rood screens, for example, are known to have existed in at least fourteen churches in the area but only that at Amesbury remains reasonably intact, and it was banished from the church for fifty years after the restoration of 1851–2. It is of wood with double doors in the centre and flanking bays of panel tracery over a simple panelled dado. Only fragments of the

89

88

90

stone screen at Chitterne St Mary are preserved in the Victorian church; the original had a four-centred archway with pierced spandrels and, on either side, two bays each with two tiers of trefoil-headed lights with pierced quatrefoils above.[52] More typical, perhaps, was the wooden screen of Winterbourne Dauntsey, destroyed in 1867, of which a photograph and a measured drawing survive.[53] It consisted of a more or less continuous series of lights with crude tracery but with fine running ornament on the rail below and the beam above. The only parallel to this work now to be found in the area is the screen at Laverstock, made up in the 1930s to incorporate authentic medieval panels of complex tracery patterns. The panels are perhaps of Welsh origin.

The provision of rood screens does not usually appear to have involved the construction of elaborate stairs and turrets to gain access to the roof lofts. Only at Durnford is there evidence of a rood stair turret (now dismantled) projecting from the body of the nave. Otherwise the surviving stairs are, like those at Idmiston, scrambling affairs cut through the thickness of the nave walls and accessible from the ground only by ladders except where, as at Coombe Bissett, the tower stair could double for belfry and roof loft. The only parclose screen recorded in the area, that across the south transept of Amesbury church, was destroyed in the 19th century.

The form and decoration of other liturgical fittings of this period, such as fonts and piscinae, also tend towards simplicity rather than complexity. The most elaborate piscina of the later medieval period is that in the south aisle at Amesbury, but the hood-mould and carved spandrels are crudely worked. It is, at least, clearly

Perpendicular in style and certainly a piscina, unlike other possible examples such as the triangular-headed recesses by the south-west door of Amesbury and at the foot of the Idmiston rood stair, which lack both drains and architectural features. The Amesbury recess may be a stoup, on account of its position by a doorway. Other stoups survive by the north doorway at Durnford and the south doorway at Bulford.

The development of late medieval fonts does not fall readily into a neat sequence. A distinguishing feature is the polygonal bowl and, usually, a polygonal stem. Idmiston font has a polygonal Purbeck bowl probably of 13th-century date and a sparsely moulded stem. The former font at Maddington had a comparable bowl but was probably much later since its stem was ribbed in a style also found in the Perpendicular font at Woodford. The sides of the bowl of the Woodford font are carved with bold quatrefoils alone, but the similar and contemporary font at Wilton (discarded in 1845) had a more elaborate decoration of trefoils on the bowl and figures under tabernacles on the stem. The other ornamented font of the period, at Porton, differs significantly in shape from the Wilton and Woodford examples; the bowl is chamfered back in its lower part, instead of being straight-sided. The font at Laverstock, though plain except for a ring of moulding at the junction of bowl and stem, has the same profile and therefore could be of the same date.

The remaining four polygonal fonts share a distinctive, slimmer shape resembling a modern egg-cup. They have small bowls with rounded bases and, except for the former font at Chitterne All Saints, which appears to have had fleurons on its base, they bear only bands of moulding as ornament. With the font at Nunton this simplicity is carried to extremes: it has no mouldings at all except for a broad band below the rim, and the sides of the bowl continue unbroken into the base. Possibly this radical simplification of the traditional form is an indication of post-Reformation date.

One further stone fitting to be mentioned is the pulpit at Berwick St James. It originally cantilevered out from the north wall of the nave and was entered from behind, through the north chapel. It is not an elaborate piece; the sides have trefoil-headed panels enclosing shields which are now and perhaps always have been blank. The present heavily corbelled base is an addition.

91. Berwick St James: N side of nave, showing former arrangement of corbelled pulpit, archway to N chapel and entrance to rood loft, *Buckler c.* 1805.
92. Idmiston: rood stair.

94

95

93. Standlynch: niche to S of chancel arch.
94. Winterslow: late medieval fragment of sculpture.
95. Standlynch: carved panel (restored) depicting the symbols of the Passion.

Excepting the roof corbels discussed above, few surviving fragments of late medieval figurative sculpture in the area are impressive works of art but some are of iconographic interest. Above the door at Standlynch are three crudely carved panels, *ex situ*, one of which depicts God the Father holding the crucified Christ between his legs and another the symbols of the Passion. A more substantial and more enigmatic piece is a loose fragment in Winterslow church, which shows, beneath a projecting gabled canopy, a bearded male head cut off at the chin by waves, with hands raised to his temples as if to a crown, possibly an image of God the Father. More conventional carvings include two Crucifixions with St Mary and St John: one is in the east gable of the chancel of Stapleford church, perhaps *in situ*; the other, probably a cross head in origin, was found in the 19th century in a cottage wall and is now housed in Shrewton church. On the sides it has the curious feature of giant single figures, perhaps of patron saints.

Some of the architectural sculpture is of a higher standard. As well as the arch of the tomb at Chitterne St Mary, already mentioned, there is fine carving in the two niches flanking the chancel arch of Standlynch where, under the crocketed nodding ogees of the tabernacles, are concealed miniature lierne vaults. Less elaborate niches were used to decorate the splays of the east window of Bulford.

Two-dimensional decoration was not neglected although little is now discernible. Stained glass in the area has not survived well.[54] The most notable pieces are those reset in the Decorated window on the north side of Amesbury chancel, which include the upper part of a crowned female saint. The glass was probably designed for the late 15th-century east window. At Durnford church is preserved a Crucifixus and part of a figure of St Nicholas, and at Chitterne St Mary, an Ox of St Luke, one of a set of Evangelist symbols originally in the upper tracery lights of the east window of Chitterne All Saints. These are of unexceptional 15th-century workmanship, using mostly yellow staining but with some ruby and blue. The late medieval English panels included in the great collection of stained glass in the church of St Mary and St Nicholas, Wilton (Appendix 3), are not original to the area.

Of the wall-paintings of the area even less is visible although evidence survives of their existence in at least fifteen churches. Only one narrative scene is recorded, the Last Judgement over the chancel arch at Winterslow; elsewhere all the paintings are of single saints, notably St Christopher. His image, invariably opposite the principal

96. Chitterne, All Saints: details from former church including, bottom right, part of traceried head of E window with stained glass of Evangelist symbols, *Kemm* 1860 (*see* also 97).

door of the church, can still just be made out at Durnford and Bulford, but watercolour sketches also preserve the appearance of paintings of the saint at Idmiston and Durrington. That at Durrington was noted by John Aubrey as very large (Jackson 1862, 357).[55] The only traces of a general decorative scheme are in the east part of the nave at Durnford and were probably associated with the rood; the ceilure over the rood still had distinctive decoration in the 19th century. On the east splay of the window to the west of the rood stair is the outline of a painted ogee-headed niche, which perhaps originally had an image set before it, and above the chancel arch behind the rood is an indistinct pattern of red, blue and yellow rosettes.

Late medieval funeral monuments remain in greater number than wall paintings in south-east Wiltshire, although the two brasses of any size, at West Grimstead and Winterbourne Earls, survive only as indents. Britford and Chitterne St Mary have

98

97. Chitterne, St Mary: S window. Stained glass fragment of the Ox of St Luke from E window of former church of All Saints (*see* p. 123).
98. Amesbury: stained glass in N window of chancel, *Kemm* 1863.

99

100

99. Britford: 15th-century tomb, N wall of chancel.
100. Chitterne, St Mary: tomb, N wall of chancel, before removal of tomb chest, *Buckler* 1805 (*see* also 277).

ogee canopies associated with tomb chests but both were altered in the 19th century: the latter lost its tomb chest and the arch at Britford was scraped and reset freestanding. The Britford tomb chest acquired notoriety through its mistaken identification by Sir Richard Colt Hoare (1835, 54–5) as the tomb of the Duke of Buckingham who was executed in Salisbury in 1483. It is a pretentious but clumsily executed work, ornamented on its south face with six ogee niches enclosing statues of saints and on its west face with two angels holding shields. It has been suggested that arch and tomb chest are of different periods and do not belong together, but there is no serious stylistic discrepancy between them.[56] The arch of the tomb at Chitterne St Mary is a more refined object despite resetting in the 19th century. Its mouldings and fleuron decoration suggest a date in the latter part of the 15th century.

THE POST-REFORMATION PERIOD

The Sixteenth Century. The Reformation had little effect on the fabric of the churches of south-east Wiltshire. At Durnford, for instance, there was no break in continuity and the fabric and furnishings of the medieval building were adapted to the new forms of worship with a minimum of alteration. The parish churches of the area were not richly endowed with chantries nor did they contain shrines or relics to be condemned as superstitious. There is little evidence of wilful iconoclasm, except perhaps in the case of the corbel of the west tower arch at Homington, where the head below has had its face and chin planed away.

The monastic houses were dissolved without any difficulty.[57] At Wilton and Amesbury the nuns' churches and most of their quarters were demolished with speed. At Ivychurch the whole monastic complex including the north aisle of the church was transformed into a house; here the local inhabitants did suffer a loss, since the rights of the villagers of Whaddon to use the church as the parish church, acknowledged by the Royal Commissioners at the Dissolution, did not prevent its suppression within a decade.[58]

Even such obvious changes as the removal of rood lofts and the covering over of religious pictures were not carried out with fanatical rigour. The destruction of the roods did not include the screens, which, as already mentioned, survived in many churches of the area until the mid 19th century. The wall paintings were concealed not only with plain whitewash but often also with black-letter texts in decorative borders (for instance on the south wall of Bulford chancel), so that church interiors did not present the austere monochrome appearance that they do today. The walls round the chancel arches at Bulford, Durnford and Winterbourne Gunner bear

101. Homington: defaced corbel head, W tower arch.

44

palimpsests of wall paintings, with layer added upon layer from the 15th to the 18th century. It was not until the mid 19th century that two-thirds of the wall paintings then surviving were destroyed.

Major refittings and reconstructions were not undertaken until the 17th century, but ecclesiastical activity was not lacking in a diocese which boasted Jewell as bishop from 1560–71 and Richard Hooker as one of its incumbents. Until its recent theft a copy of Jewell's *Works* remained, in obedience to Elizabethan injunctions, chained to the (later) lectern at Durnford. Pious tradition connects the construction of the north transverse 'aisle' at Boscombe, which is indeed a building of *c.* 1600, with the crowds attracted by the sermons of Richard Hooker while he was rector of the parish from 1591–5.

The most urgent requirement, so far as church furnishings were concerned, was the provision of suitable church plate; the depredations of Edward VI's Commissioners and the successive doctrinal changes had either denuded the parishes of all vessels for the administration of Communion or left them with vessels of obsolete type and size. In the area of the Till and Wylye valleys a deliberate effort seems to have been made to retain traditional plate, for it can hardly be coincidence that most of the pre-Reformation examples in Wiltshire are to be found here, such as the 13th-century chalice of Berwick St James (in the British Museum since the 19th century) and the paten of 1506 still in use at Orcheston St Mary. In the diocese of Salisbury as a whole, 1576 seems to have been the year when a concerted effort was made to ensure that parishes had the required paten and deep Communion cup, necessary when the laity received in both kinds, although no definite instruction to this effect is extant (Pevsner 1975, 38). Plate of this kind and of this year survives at Rollestone and Woodford. Parishes would also have needed to provide themselves with the other furnishing of liturgical contention, the Communion table. No certain Elizabethan examples can, however, be identified.

In the absence of documentary evidence it is hard to distinguish structural work of the later 16th century either from earlier work in the century or from 17th-century work, since rebuildings continued to be in the Perpendicular style. The north wall of the nave of the former church at Winterbourne Earls had allegedly been rebuilt in 1553, an unusual year for church building, but it was still wholly Gothic in style (Colt Hoare 1837, 99). Without a date-stone or documentary date, a feature such as the east window of Whiteparish, which has slightly cusped panel tracery and a transom dividing the tracery from the main lights, cannot be assigned with confidence to any more precise period than *c.* 1550 to *c.* 1650. Perhaps attributable to the latter part of the 16th century are the mullioned windows and round-headed doorways (typical of those in contemporary secular buildings) which were once, as Buckler's drawings show, to be found in churches of the area. The simple two-light, mullioned east window formerly at Winterbourne Gunner was probably of this period.[59]

Money was available for routine repair or small alterations since the pre-Reformation tradition that almost every will included a small bequest to the church fabric survived until at least the reign of James I (Symonds 1910, 33–4).

The Seventeenth Century. With the new century and new dynasty, enthusiasm for rebuilding and refurbishing churches increased again to such a degree that, as regards fittings at least, it rivalled the generous patronage of the later Middle Ages. It can hardly be chance that nearly all the dated Stuart woodwork belongs to the first third of the century. The Civil War and Interregnum enforced a pause of twenty years in church building although there was no break in regular maintenance. After this an interest in ecclesiastical work revived, reaching its climax in the building of the fine church at Farley in 1690.

The Commonwealth period provides one invaluable insight into the parish life of the century through the parochial survey undertaken by Parliament in 1650 with the assistance of local witnesses (Bodington 1919 *passim*). The survey, despite being concerned with financial rather than pastoral matters, reveals not only the relative values of the different livings but also something of the attitudes of local people towards their places of worship. The recommendations for the reform of the numbers and siting of churches anticipate those of the 19th and 20th centuries: Nunton should be taken from Downton and united with Odstock, a reform of geographical commonsense which took another 250 years to accomplish; Rollestone, Shrewton and Maddington should be brought together into one parish, again a rationalisation not achieved until modern times. Fourteen changes were proposed in the organisation of parishes, which would have involved the abandonment of thirteen of the existing medieval churches and the construction of three new ones. In only one instance, at Bulford, was a request included to retain a church and then only because it lay on a 'thorough fare to the West', and not for any aesthetic or sentimental reasons.

It is only from the 17th century onwards that documentary evidence survives recording the reasons for alterations to the fabric of churches. They were, first, the desire for more accommodation, especially for the leading families of a parish, and secondly, the need for repairs after damage such as fire or storm had wrecked a building in part or completely.[60] Victorian rebuilding, however, removed much of the work of the period, as for instance at Maddington church which had been very largely reconstructed between 1600 and 1700. In about 1603 the north wall of the nave was rebuilt some 18 in. (0.46 m) further north, thus necessitating the construction of a new roof in a revealing mixture of styles: essentially a pointed, ceiled barrel roof but including the medieval feature of hammer beams used decoratively rather than functionally and brought up to date by the addition of Jacobean pendants. At the same time the north porch was built or rebuilt, again with a mixture of medieval forms

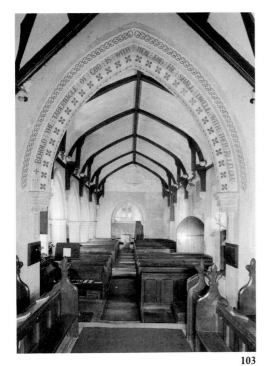

104

105

106

103. Maddington: interior looking W from chancel.
104. Maddington: plaster cartouche, W wall of nave.
105. Berwick St James: datestone on W tower.
106. Farley: Communion plate of 1689, given by Sir Stephen Fox.

(the four-centred arch and the mouldings of the doorway) and contemporary features (a decorated plaster ceiling and a straight-headed mullioned window). This modification of the north side of the nave may have been due to structural problems but the alterations on the south side were the result, on the one hand, of the threatened or actual collapse of the south-east angle of the tower and, on the other, of a need for more seating. The south wall and the southern half of the west wall of the tower were rebuilt in good ashlar, but the medieval mouldings were preserved, a care which was also observed with the west respond of the arcade and the south respond of the tower arch. The windows of the south aisle and of the (later) projecting 'transept' were, however, of the domestic mullioned type. Indeed, the whole idea of the relatively long and narrow transverse aisle to house pews fronting the pulpit is as much a product of its time as the strapwork of the plaster cartouche bearing the date of 1637 on the west wall of the nave and perhaps marking the completion of the repairs.

All the early 17th-century work at Maddington is traditionally associated with the Tooker family, which was the principal family in the parish from c. 1560– c. 1660, and whose arms decorated the corner vanes on the tower pinnacles. This assumption of a major role by the lay patron was continued by the next lord of the manor, Sir Stephen Fox. He rebuilt the chancel and the parsonage and almost certainly gave the splendid mid 17th-century set of plate.[61] The profits of the rectory, which had been appropriated by Amesbury Priory, were now returned by Sir Stephen to a charitable purpose, that of supporting the new hospital at Farley.

In the latter part of the 17th century some major works of restoration and repair were undertaken, as well as the building of a whole new church to replace the ancient chapel of Farley. In 1670 the west tower of Berwick St James, which had fallen down c. 1650 (see p.109), was rebuilt from the foundations. The design probably imitated the general lines of the medieval tower but the openings were given simple rounded heads. The upper part of the tower at Stapleford was similarly rebuilt in 1674. The closeness in date and the use of the identical type of window-opening and of commemorative inscription in both buildings suggest that the same masons were employed.

108. Standlynch: former font.

The upper stages of many of the towers in the area appear to have been reconstructed in the 17th century, though little documentary evidence survives in support of this. The towers of Maddington and Odstock have already been mentioned; the upper stage of Durrington is probably a work of repair following the storm of 1693 which was noted (by a later hand) in the manuscript of Aubrey's *Wiltshire Notes* as blowing down the whole church (Jackson 1862, 357). The solid parapet and pyramid pinnacles carved with strapwork could well date from *c.* 1700.

Much of this concern with towers must be the result of the interest taken by parishes in their bells. The 17th and 18th centuries were the age of local bell-foundries; Wiltshire could draw on those in Salisbury, Aldbourne, Bristol and elsewhere. Salisbury founders, particularly John Wallis and, later, the Tosier family, were the most active in the area. Some massive bell-frames survive, for example that at Tilshead, which must be associated with the provision of a new ring of three bells in 1764. Perhaps the unusual beehive form of roof to the tower is also of that date.

These various works of repair show not only the continuity of parochial involvement with the church fabric but also a stylistic continuity with no sudden change from Gothic to Classical forms. There was no deliberate revivalism but rather a settled attachment to old forms and a slow acceptance of new. When Standlynch chapel was restored by the Buckland family in 1677 mullioned and transomed windows and plaster coving were inserted in the side walls but the west wall with its traceried window was kept, with the addition of a cartouche of the Buckland arms and a date-stone. Medieval windows were re-used in the new north wall of Maddington nave, although they were replaced by mullions in the south aisles of Downton and Whiteparish. Even in the Classical and relatively sophisticated church of Farley, the priest's doorway in the south wall of the chancel has a four-centred head, in contrast to the pedimented doorways of the nave and tower.

Traditional fittings also acquired new forms only slowly. The font at Standlynch, probably installed as part of the 1677 restoration, has slender proportions and an ogee curve to the bowl, so representing a transition between the late medieval 'egg-cup' form of font and the baluster fonts of the 18th century.

Font covers were required by the bishop for every church: either none had survived in the area from before the Reformation or none was considered worth retaining. There seems to have been a preference for the crown form of design in which volutes rise from the rim of the cover to a central baluster. The most elaborate example is at Winterbourne Stoke where the volutes are interspersed with balusters and pawns, but more typical are the simpler examples to be found at Rollestone, Farley and, formerly, at Winterbourne Dauntsey and Winterbourne Earls. The crude quality of the Boscombe cover may help to explain why these covers were often discarded in the 19th century.

The provision of Communion rails was another example of episcopal determination to retain some protection for the Sacraments. Rails, consisting of standard rows of balusters (e.g. Tilshead), were common here as elsewhere, but there appear to have been several other designs for rails. The most striking is that found at Berwick St James, Durnford, Stratford Tony and the church of St Mary at Wilton, at all of which the newel balusters were stressed by being surmounted above the rail by pawn-like finials and, at the two first-named, by projecting claw feet.[62] Another form was the pierced splat, either used on its own as at Bulford and formerly at Winterbourne Earls and Chitterne All Saints, or interspaced with turned balusters as at Durnford, Wilton and Maddington.

The remaining 17th-century furnishings, such as pulpits, pews, Communion tables and chests, are discussed together since not only are many of the same decorative motifs shared among them but also the extent of the refurnishing of churches is thereby made apparent. The tentative suggestions made here about the possible existence of local schools serve as a reminder that this woodwork is among the best surviving expressions of the craftsmanship of the region (Chinnery 1979, 444).

Pulpits should be considered first, because they were usually the most substantial furnishings provided for a church, an unsurprising prominence in view of the value placed on preaching in contemporary religious life. They also help to date furnishings having similar decoration, since they are often carved with their dates of construction. Unfortunately none of the pulpits in the area has survived unaltered; most have been cut down and reset and all but two have lost their sounding-boards. The pulpit from St Mary's Wilton, the least altered, is not in its original church but has been moved to Wylye.

The most common decorative motif on the panels is arcading with a blind arch to each panel; basically the Renaissance scheme of two pilasters supporting a round-headed arch. It was used on the Durnford pulpit of 1619 and it still formed the principal element in the Farley pulpit of c. 1690. Arcading might frame figures (Durrington), fronds of foliage (Chitterne St Mary) or stylised trees (Britford). Figurative carving, whether of full length cherubs or merely cherub heads, is unsophisticated even on the more ambitious pulpits of Wilton and Britford and is sometimes decidedly primitive, as in the four male figures (possibly the Evangelists) at Durrington.[63] The other favoured motif is symmetrical, stylised foliage which may have been introduced earlier than arcading since it is free from any elements of strapwork: it appears on the Odstock pulpit which has a reputed date of 1580. But different decorative patterns were often used together on the same pulpit; Durrington, for example, has stylised foliage on its upper panels and arcading on the lower.

Stylised foliage recurs on the other formerly prominent fitting; the panelled private pews, which, though once universal, have either been broken up and in part re-used or completely destroyed. The most elaborate that can still be reconstructed are the two manorial pews of Durrington, which included not only coats-of-arms but, on one,

109

110

109. Winterbourne Stoke: font cover.
110. Boscombe: early medieval font with 17th-century cover.

111. Durrington: former pew, now screen in tower arch.

112. Durnford: interior looking E, showing 17th and 18th-century furnishings, *G. Rennard* 1830.

113. Odstock: 17th-century chairs.

114. Cholderton: 17th-century Communion table.

115. South Newton: chest, 1703.

116. Nunton: coffin stool, 1736.

117. Durnford: coffin stool.

the date 1634. Their main decorative motif was symmetrical foliage centred on that common Jacobean ornament, the rosette or the pie. Such richness was probably unusual. The commonest design for pews, which continued to be used well into the 18th century, consisted of plain panels with moulded rails and a screen of dwarf balusters round the top, ornament being confined to a band of half pies (Fugglestone) or a running 'S' (Alderbury).

The open seating of the ordinary parishioners tended, as the 17th century proceeded, to acquire some of the characteristics of the pews, in particular their high-panelled sides. At Durnford the late medieval West Country type of bench having rectangular ends carved with tracery survived alongside benches with plain ends of the same size, moulded and stopped in the 17th-century manner; in the 18th century all the benches were built up with deal panelling to form box-pews.[64] At Durrington much of the carved work now incorporated in the 19th-century seating seems authentically Stuart, but it is impossible to reconstruct the original design of the benches, as opposed to the pews.

Five early Stuart chairs survive (although some of their elements have been renewed, e.g. at Porton, *see* p.179): two in the church at Odstock; two at Porton, one of which is from Idmiston church; and one at Chitterne St Mary. The commonest decorative motifs used for the backs are arcading and symmetrical foliage. They may come from a local workshop, at least in the case of the chairs at Porton and the Odstock chair with segmental top, since they share similar motifs with other woodwork in the area: the arrangement of four tendrils found in the Odstock chairback is repeated in the lower panels of the West Grimstead pulpit; the arcading of the Idmiston chairback is a less skilful version of that found on the Durnford pulpit (Chinnery 1979, 450–4). Examples of later 'Stuart' chairs, particularly those of a Charles II type, appear to be 19th-century copies, but some may incorporate 17th-century fragments.

Coffin stools remained virtually unaltered in their essential elements right through the 17th and 18th centuries. There are two dated examples in the area: at Nunton, 1736, and at Alderbury, 1778. The scalloped upper rail of the Durnford stool and the elaborately turned legs of the pair at Orcheston St George suggest that these stools, at least, are earlier.

The 17th-century Communion tables are not elaborate. That at Cholderton has intersecting semi-circles along the upper rail and decorated cup-and-cover legs, but the execution of the motifs is not sophisticated. More typical of the area is the table at West Grimstead which has half pies along the upper rail and bellied baluster legs, or that from the former church of Winterbourne Dauntsey, which has cable moulding on the rail and simplified cup-and-cover legs. Several tables were crudely altered in the 19th century either by trimming the top, as at Bulford and Orcheston St George, or by the insertion of a panelled board between the legs to form a frontal, as at Rollestone. Not all the tables now housed in churches were intended for ecclesiastical use. The very long refectory table with barley-sugar legs in the south transept of Amesbury was given to the church in the 1950s[65] and the fine mid 17th-century gateleg table in Woodford church may also be secular in origin.

The post-medieval chests preserved in the churches of the region vary in type from the iron-bound plank chest at Durnford, probably of the 16th century, to such plain examples as the unpanelled chest at South Newton which bears the date 1703 and the churchwardens' initials. The chests at Downton and Stratford Tony are of a simple form, with panels in moulded frames which die abruptly against the lower rails.[66]

From the Reformation to the Civil War the funerary monuments of the area were of three types: wall monuments with conventional kneeling effigies; tablets, whether plain or framed; and brasses. The three examples of the first type, at Idmiston, Wilton and West Dean, are not outstanding for their figure carving, but that at West Dean to John Evelyn I (+ 1627) has a rich and architecturally sophisticated marble setting which can be attributed to the workshop of Nicholas Stone. The small tablets have little artistic ambition for all the quaintness or piety of their inscriptions. The most remarkable series is the set of six in Winterslow church to various members of the Thistlethwayte family. The design of the tablets appears to have been conceived c. 1640, although the deaths commemorated range from 1587 to 1715. The tablets have simple stone frames clearly intended to be similar if not identical to each other with, in most cases, a relatively large achievement-of-arms above. This last feature presumably gives the motive for the whole project; family pride is here demonstrated in a succession of small memorials instead of in the more usual display of a great mass of heraldry on one tomb.

The inscribed brass plates dating from this period hardly differ from the two surviving pre-Reformation examples. There are, however, four which incorporate depictions of the deceased, in two cases including the wife and children of the dead man as well as coats-of-arms and inscriptions. The brass plate at Durnford to Edward Younge (+ 1607) is set in the recess of a canopied tomb, as if in imitation of three-dimensional effigies. The latest figurative brass is that to the six-year-old George Evelyn, who died in 1641 and was buried in the chancel of West Dean church (Kite 1860, 90); but the last 17th-century brass to be found in the area is that to Matthew Nicholas, dean of St Paul's, who died just after the Restoration and was buried at Winterbourne Earls under a slab bearing two brass plates with finely engraved coats-of-arms as well as an inscription plate.[67] After this date the only use of a memorial brass, before its mid 19th-century revival, is the mid 18th-century plate to the Benson family in Newton Toney.

There seems no obvious reason why a patron should have chosen a memorial of brass rather than of stone. Cost does not appear to have been a decisive factor: John Coffer, (+ 1589) gentleman servant to the Earl of Pembroke, was commemorated by a brass in Wilton church, but Charles Hartshorne (+ 1644), who occupied an equivalent position in the household of Lord Gorges, by a stone tablet in Nunton.

In the latter part of the 17th century the simple tablet continued to be a popular form of memorial, although it could be enlarged and enhanced in status by the use of finer material or of a more elaborate frame as, for example, that erected at Whiteparish to Gyles Eyre where the marble slab is given dignity by the moulded frame and gadrooned base. In the same period there appeared a form of memorial which was to be much employed over the next hundred years: the architectural tablet, in which the frame consists of variations of a Classical aedicule. The late 17th and even early 18th-century examples in the area share the characteristic of two columns which, though supporting an entablature, flank an inscription slab of greater height than the columns. The architectural frame is recessed behind the inscription rather than, as later, integrated with it. The form could be used either for modest or for large and elaborate monuments. Its earliest occurrence on a relatively grand scale was in the Nicholas monument of 1662, at Winterbourne Earls; its use was continued, in a richer and more delicate version, in the monument of 1689 to Joan Buckland at Standlynch and culminated in the early 18th century with the Duncombe tomb at Downton and the three Fox tombs at Farley.[68] The Duncombe and Fox monuments still employ the basic architectural elements but emphasise the importance of the deceased by lavish use of cartouches-of-arms, flaming urns, lamps, swags of flowers, curtains and cherubs. The same type could be reduced, as in two of the Eyre monuments at Whiteparish, to a less pretentious level by the use of simpler stone and relief, not undercut, carving.

118

119

120

118. Standlynch: tablet, nave S wall, to Joan Buckland (+ 1689).

119. Whiteparish: 17th-century tablet, nave W wall, to Gyles Eyre.

120. Whiteparish: tablet in chancel, to Edward St Barbe (+ 1671).

121

122

123

121. Winterbourne Earls: memorial brass, reset on nave N wall, to Matthew Nicholas (+ 1661).

122. Wilton, St Mary and St Nicholas: memorial brass (formerly in St Mary's) reset on nave N wall, to John Coffer (+ 1589).

123. Winterslow: tablet, S aisle, to Gabriell Pile (+ 1639).

The use of figure sculpture in these 17th-century monuments is confined to the Evelyn and Pierrepont tombs at West Dean, except for a bust of Lady Fox incorporated in her tomb at Farley. Robert Pierrepont is shown full length in his shroud but otherwise the figures are presented as busts. The earliest bust, that of Elizabeth Tyrell (+ 1629), perhaps attributable to Nicholas Stone, has delicately rendered features and clothing;[69] that of Lady Fox, of the end of the century, is broadly carved and posed in inappropriate *deshabille*. In the tomb at West Dean, to John Evelyn II (+ 1685), a bust of the deceased is set within a pedimented aedicule inserted directly in the side of a sarcophagus. Two almost life-size allegorical figures sit on the lid of the sarcophagus. The design cannot easily be attributed but may stem from the circle of Quellin and Nost. The monument to Evelyn's son-in-law, Robert Pierrepont (+ 1669), can, however, be assigned with some confidence to John Bushnell (*see* Whinney 1964, 42). It is typical of Bushnell's Baroque style to employ the dramatic conceit that the doors of the central niche open to reveal the dead man as he rises at the summons of an angel at the Last Trump. It is also possible that the treatment of the architecture of the tomb as a tripartite altar piece could have been inspired by Italian examples seen by Bushnell during the years he worked abroad.

The Eighteenth Century. Although no churches in the area were built or completely reconstructed in the 18th century, it was not the age of utter neglect often pictured. Two restorations, one at Boscombe in 1709 and the other at Homington in 1794, help to illustrate both the continuity of parish life and the subtle change over the century in attitudes towards the church fabric. Both restorations were led by the clergy rather than by grand benefactors and both concerned villages of modest size and importance. At Boscombe the walls and the roof of the church were repaired, the pews refitted and the pulpit reset and better lit by a new window. The restoration was completed by the purchase of a new Communion set of Britannia silver. The total cost was about £75 the greater part of which was raised by the incumbent from 'Persons of Quality . . . most of them living in and near London'.[70] The tenor of the work is conservative and yet substantial. All worthwhile earlier work was retained and the new additions were of good quality. The inhabitants of Homington, with a more complex church including aisles and a tower, no doubt faced a more expensive task in its repair. Even so, the

124

125

124. West Dean, Evelyn Chapel: monument, reset on S wall, to Elizabeth Tyrell (+ 1629).
125. Farley: portrait bust from monument in N chapel, to Elizabeth, Lady Fox (+ 1696).

126

127

128

WEST DEAN, EVELYN CHAPEL

126. Monument, E wall, to Robert Pierrepont (+ 1669), showing doors open.
127. Monument, E wall, to Robert Pierrepont, showing doors closed.
128. Monument, N wall, to John Evelyn II (+ 1685).

approach adopted was noticeably more radical and less respectful of antiquity than that at Boscombe. The bells and the old lead and glass were sold and three windows in the chancel were blocked but a new entrance was contrived at the west end and the whole church received new pews. By means of the sales of the materials and with some help from Lord Radnor, the local community was put to no greater expense than the obtaining of the Faculty.[71]

Typical 18th-century repairs were the rebuilding of gables (Coombe Bissett) or aisles (Whiteparish). Such repairs are still recognisable by their use of brick, either on its own or mixed with stone, a breach with tradition which grew more frequent as time went by. Gothic reminiscences faded. There was one striking use of Classical forms: the refacing of the south front of the Amesbury south transept in 1721 with neat round-headed windows and doorway, crowned by an *oeil de boeuf* in the gable. The north and south walls of the nave of Stratford Tony were recased during the period in alternate bands of brick and flint, but whereas the windows on the south side were given curious arched heads, perhaps to suggest Gothic forms, the blind windows on the north were built with conventional segmental heads. Again, the contrast at Whiteparish between the 17th-century south aisle and the 18th-century north aisle is instructive; the latter follows contemporary domestic building types, with brick walls and wooden, not stone, window-frames. Wooden casements are a typical 18th-century insertion in many churches, particularly when, as at Durnford, they light the gallery and the pulpit. Rustic simplicity can even appear revolutionary: the unadorned brick tower of West Grimstead church, erected not later than *c.* 1800, anticipates the progressive architecture of the early 20th century.[72]

The only ambitious work was that undertaken by the aristocracy when they wished to house their dead or to enhance their view. At St Mary's, Wilton the original chancel, which did not project beyond the aisles, was lengthened by one bay in 1751, chiefly so that the earls of Pembroke might have a burial chamber below. The new

129. Whiteparish: exterior from SW, showing former 17th-century S aisle, *Buckler* 1805 (*see* also 483).

56

130. Amesbury: exterior from SE, showing church before Butterfield's restoration in 1852–3, *Buckler c.* 1805 (*see* also 224).

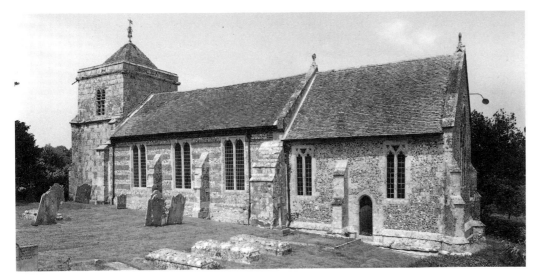

131. Stratford Tony: exterior from SE.

132. Whiteparish: exterior from N showing former 18th-century N aisle, *F.M.B.* 1869.

east window and the ribbed plaster vault are in a simple but elegant Gothick. The bishop remarked when granting a faculty for the building that he had 'personally viewed' it and found it not only a 'great ornament and beauty to the church' but also 'of great benefit and advantage' to the parishioners (DRO Faculties vol. 3, 53). The same motive prompted the Pleydell-Bouverie family, when raised to the earldom of Radnor in 1765, to add a great two-storied mortuary chamber to Britford church, neighbouring and over-topping the chancel. The parish benefitted from the simultaneous rebuilding of the rest of the church; the west wall and the crossing-tower were completely reconstructed and the chancel refitted and refenestrated. In the 1790s the Radnors extended their munificence to the church at Downton with more questionable results. They had inherited a share in the local 'empire' developed by Anthony Duncombe, Lord Feversham, who had already caused the chancel of the church to be transformed into a family mausoleum (though the successive monuments by the Scheemakers, father and son, ironically mark the failure of Feversham's attempts to found a dynasty). The second Earl of Radnor, son-in-law to Lord Feversham, prompted and largely paid for the heightening of the crossing tower in stuccoed brick and its crowning with tall stone pinnacles (a gesture perhaps motivated as much by a desire to gain local goodwill in a hotly contested Parliamentary seat as by genuine asethetic feeling); the base of the tower was unable to bear the added strain, however, and the addition was removed after only seventy years.[73]

Georgian fittings have mostly disappeared. Only the sounding-board survives from what must have been a fine pulpit at Downton, and it has suffered from being turned upside down and made into a table. At Chitterne All Saints the font cover from the former church, dating from 1767, was transferred to the Victorian church where it surmounts the font from St Mary's, but the gadrooned early 18th-century font of Britford church was cast out in the 1873 restoration and transported to South Australia. Only the neat baluster font at Fugglestone continues in use.

Slightly more numerous than fittings are Georgian Royal Arms, though not as striking as the large, boldly painted, Stuart panels (of which that at Bulford, of 1666, preserves its decorated frame). In the first half of the 18th century there appears to have been a preference for carving the Arms in wood rather than depicting them on a painted panel. The example in Wilsford church probably dates from c. 1720, to judge from the scrolls at its base, and another at Newton Toney is one of the comparatively few from the reign of William III.[74] In the reign of George III there was a return to pictorial display of the Royal Arms, but painted on canvas rather than panel. Those at Woodford and Fugglestone, both of before 1801, show the advance of restrained, neo-Classical taste, with the decoration around the motto changing from scrolls at Woodford to garlands of husks at Fugglestone, but the large painting of the Arms of 1805 at Tilshead is reminiscent of Stuart work in its size and exuberance. The remaining four Royal Arms in the area are all Victorian and show the diverse ways in which this traditional feature could be treated before being finally abandoned: Boscombe has a conventional canvas of late Georgian type; Chitterne All Saints a sculptured group in plaster or artificial stone; the church of St Mary and St Nicholas, Wilton a panel of stained glass; and Cholderton a rich representation in floor tiles.

The hatchments of the area are mostly of the type and date of the late Georgian Royal Arms. The most spirited in treatment are the five in Bulford church to members of the Duke and Southby families. Many hatchments perished during the restorations of the 19th century; a large number for the Eyre family are shown in views of the nave of Whiteparish before 1869. At Amesbury, hatchments in the chancel, for the third Duke of Queensberry and his Duchess Kitty, were discarded in 1852–3.

133

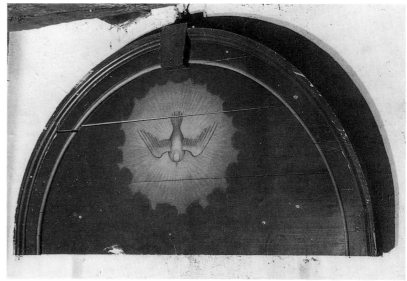

134

135

133. Bulford: Royal Arms of 1666.
134. Durnford: arched head of former Commandment tables, now in tower (*see* also 112).
135. Tilshead: Royal Arms of 1805.
136. Bulford: hatchment with arms of Southby family.
137. Winterbourne Gunner: Commandment table of 1787.

136

CHAP. XX

V.
HONOUR thy father and thy mother, that thy days may be long in the land which the Lord thy God giveth thee.

VI.
THOU shalt do no murder.

VII.
THOU shalt not commit adultery.

VIII.
THOU shalt not steal.

IX.
THOU shalt not bear false witness against thy neighbour.

X.
THOU shalt not covet thy neighbours house, thou shalt not covet thy neighbours wife, nor his servant, nor his maid, nor his ox, nor his ass, nor any thing that is his.

I BELIEVE in God the Father Almighty, Maker of heaven and earth: And in Jesus Christ his only Son our Lord, Who was conceived by the Holy Ghost, Born of the Virgin Mary, Suffered under Pontius Pilate, was crucified, dead, and buried, He descended into hell; The third day he rose again from the dead. He ascended into heaven, And sitteth on the right hand of God the Father Almighty; From thence he shall come to judge the quick and the dead.

I Believe in the Holy Ghost; The holy Catholick Church; The Communion of Saints; The forgiveness of sins; The resurrection of the body, And the life everlasting, Amen.

Placed up in 1787.
Rev.d Cha.s Coleman, Rector. Edw.d Kelsey, Churchwarden.

137

Commandment tables of the Georgian period survive painted directly on the wall above the chancel arch at Bulford and, more conventionally, on two panels at Winterbourne Gunner dated 1787. The only survivor of the more elaborate compositions, such as can occasionally be glimpsed in the mid 19th-century interior views by Kemm, is at Durnford. The arched 'Glory' which once surmounted the central panel of a triptych inscribed with the Commandment tables and placed over the chancel arch, now hangs in filthy condition, high up within the tower.

The dominant position of the landowning classes at this period is even more clearly demonstrated in the various collections of major monuments than in the church building schemes discussed earlier. The Herberts at Wilton, the Foxes at Farley, the Duncombes at Downton and, less elevated, the Michells at Chitterne All Saints, the Bowles at Idmiston and the Eyres at Whiteparish and Landford, all commemorated their dead with substantial memorials. Only the Pleydell-Bouveries failed to commission any tombs of importance in the area in spite of the great mausoleum they built at Britford.

The major monuments of the 18th century are attributable to specific artists. In the middle of the century, Peter Scheemakers executed two monuments and his son Thomas at least one for the family of Lord Feversham, and Roubiliac designed one to the ninth Earl, the 'Architect Earl', of Pembroke (+ 1750). Those produced by the Scheemakers are not exceptional, although the delicate carving of a Classically draped woman mourning over an urn on the tomb of Margaret, Lady Feversham (+ 1755) gives poignancy to what was to become a stock image, as, for instance, in the tablet to Phillis Rooke (+ 1793) at Chitterne All Saints. However, Roubiliac's monument to Lord Pembroke at Wilton, for which he was paid £150, is a masterly composition of a simple base in carefully contrasting marbles bearing a version of the powerful bust he had recently sculpted of the earl.[75] The other outstanding memorial of those years is that to Commodore Mathew Michell (+ 1752) at Chitterne All Saints, unsigned but in the style of Sir Henry Cheere. The white marble inscription is flanked by trophies and, below, an elaborate apron in *giallo* marble encloses a relief of a sea battle framed by shells and bullrushes.

The tombs of the neo-Classical period in south-east Wiltshire are of particular quality. The free-standing sarcophagus in the antique style designed by James Wyatt for the tenth Earl of Pembroke (+ 1794) and carved by the elder Westmacott is outstanding in the refinement of its proportions and its detailing.[76] Contemporary with it but in great contrast is the monument by Rossi commemorating the earl's daughter-in-law, Lady Herbert (+ 1793), and her eldest son who died shortly before her; whereas the earl's tomb is a public statement of social position and cultivated taste, that to Lady Herbert expresses a private grief.[77] The relief on the Rossi monument, the subtle *schiacciato* technique of which matches the delicacy of its sentiment, depicts the mother and child ascending to the heavens while mourning allegorical figures below veil their faces. Lady Herbert's husband (+ 1827), who became eleventh earl, was also commemorated by a relief, but it is larger and of a general subject. In fact the sculptor, the younger Westmacott, had already used this composition of a Classically draped rustic family in a roundel for the tomb to Lord Bridgewater (+ 1824) at Little Gaddesden, Hertfordshire (Penny 1977, 195–6). Westmacott designed the other two important early 19th-century monuments in the area; that to the second Lord Ilchester (+ 1802) at Farley, and that to John Thomas Batt (+ 1831) at Nunton. The first includes a sensitive relief of Charity as a mother with playing children. The second has almost life-size figures of Faith and Hope carved in bold relief, with the inscription below flanked by two allegorical medallions of Law and Philosophy. Another productive workshop of the period, that of the

138

139

138. Wilton, St Mary and St Nicholas: monument, S apse, by J.C.F. Rossi, to Elizabeth, Lady Herbert (+ 1793). Formerly in St Mary's.

139. Chitterne, All Saints: monument to Commodore Mathew Michell (+ 1752), moved into tower from former church 1877.

140. Wilton, St Mary and St Nicholas: detail of monument, S apse, by R. Westmacott junior, to 11th Earl of Pembroke (+ 1827). Formerly in St Mary's.

141. Wilton, St Mary
and St Nicholas: monu-
ment, S apse, by L.F.
Roubiliac, to 9th Earl of
Pembroke   (+ 1749).
Formerly in St Mary's.

142

143

144

younger John Bacon, contributed two monuments of which one, to Sir Charles Malet (+ 1817) at Newton Toney, has a conventional draped urn but the other, of 1820 and in Britford church, is designed in the form of an open folio book in order to show the descent of the Jervoise family, for many years lords of the manor of Britford.

While the great monuments were carved in London, the majority of memorials must have been made locally. The first Salisbury masons to sign their works as a matter of course were the Osmonds, but they did not become established until the early 19th century. The earliest documentary reference to a designer of a non-aristocratic tomb concerns the tablet of 1765 to Kitty Wansborough (and her mother) at Shrewton which her father is recorded as ordering in Salisbury for £27 4s. 0d. from 'Langley',[78] presumably the Langley of Salisbury who was paid for mason's work at Wilton House in 1744 (Wilton House Book 1733–49; 24 May 1744). The tablet has a fussy but technically skilful decoration of drapes and garlands which suggests that Salisbury workshops were capable of work of high quality. The two tablets signed by the younger Richard Earlsman, of Salisbury (Wilsford, c. 1783, and 1794) and the two signed by F. Brown, also of Salisbury (Nunton, c. 1765; West Dean, c. 1800), do not, however, indicate more than average skill.

It is possible that in the 17th and the early 18th century the use of freestone for a tablet indicates that it was carved locally and the use of marble that it was not, but by the mid to late 18th century marble was employed for almost every monument. In the remoter villages where freestone was still used in the late 18th century, even for three relatively ambitious tablets (Tilshead, the Edwards family, 1778; Maddington, the Gilbert family, 1783; West Grimstead, William and Hannah Hebbard, c. 1792), their design is notably old-fashioned. One memorial that must surely be of local origin is

142. Britford: tablet, N transept, commemorating Jervoise family, 1820.
143. Wilsford: tablet, nave S wall, by R. Earlsman junior, to Robert Duke, 1794.
144. Shrewton: tablet, S aisle, by Langley, to Elizabeth and Catherine Wansborough, 1765.

145   146   147

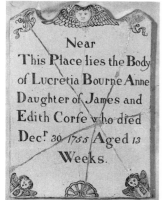

148

145. Landford: tablet, S chapel, to Elizabeth Eyre (+ 1758).
146. Bulford: tablet, N 'aisle', to Matthew Devenish (+ 1811).
147. Woodford: tablet, S aisle, to Edward Polhill (+ 1759).
148. Amesbury: ceramic tablet, now in chancel, to Lucretia Corfe (+ 1755).

the small ceramic tablet, simply a tile, to the infant daughter of James and Edith Corfe (Amesbury, c. 1755), although no other examples have survived.

The architectural tablet of the kind developed in the late 17th century (see above p. 52), continued in demand until c. 1780. The finest example is that to Elizabeth Eyre (+ 1758) at Landford where not only the apron but the faces of the Corinthian pilasters are carved with fruit and flowers. An unornamented but still distinguished version with Doric pilasters can be found at Fugglestone (1771) and another, almost identical to the Fugglestone tablet although of much later date, at St Mary's, Wilton. At Durnford, on the south side of the chancel, is a monument with a complete Doric aedicule erected c. 1750 to John Younge by his kinsman Edward Younge. For his own memorial, which he had erected during his lifetime, in 1771, on the north side of the chancel, he preferred the reduced type in which the flanking pilasters were omitted and the pediment placed over the central, projecting panel containing the inscription. The two 18th-century tablets in Maddington church are of a similar design; the Woodroffe memorial of c. 1750 is of marble and decorated with a cherub head and drapery swag, whereas that erected to members of the Gilbert family in 1783 is a less sophisticated version in freestone. By 1800 the original inspiration of the type had become so remote that the latest in date, the memorial to Matthew Devenish (+ 1811) in Bulford church, resembles more a looking-glass frame than a piece of Classical architecture.

The most characteristic form of memorial in the 18th century was the crowned tablet, a type in which the frame, if any, is subsidiary to the decorative elements above the inscription. Although it had been used in the late 17th century, as in the St Barbe memorial at Whiteparish, only in the next century did it rival and eventually surpass the architectural tablet in popularity, developing during the century from an alternative of equal status to the architectural tablet (as in the memorial to Edward Polhill (+ 1759) at Woodford) into a more ordinary form in which a simple tablet was placed on a larger ground. Decorative elements, such as cherub heads and coats-of-arms, could then be inserted on the ground at no great expense, especially as they were often just painted rather than engraved on the stone. In the standard monuments of *c.* 1800 the crown usually consisted merely of an urn or cartouche-of-arms, but in more expensive designs the decoration was sometimes elaborated with drapes round the urn and the inscription or with swags and medallions in the apron.

Both the architectural and the crowned tablet are essentially rectilinear. Three other types current during the 18th century were of more eccentric forms: the curvilinear or shaped, the oval, and the pyramidal. The shaped is the earliest in date. The first example in the area, the monument to Peregrine Thistlethwayte (+ 1694/5) in Winterslow church, is comparatively simple in design compared with its companion, to Dorothea Thistlethwayte (+ 1715), which successfully incorporates cherubs' heads and drapes to enrich the curved outline of the tablet. The shaped tablet appears to have fallen out of fashion by the middle of the century. The large example at Winterbourne Gunner of *c.* 1753 is unsophisticated and those of *c.* 1762 (Downton) and *c.* 1771 (Winterslow) are small in size and crude in design.

An interesting version of the shaped tablet exists in the area, where it may have been a local development. There are three medium-sized tablets with shaped heads and bases and sunk decorative surrounds, dating between *c.* 1702 (Alderbury) and *c.* 1755 (West Grimstead), i.e. within the limits of general fashion for shaped tablets. The finest, that to Robert Goldisborough (+ 1735) in Shrewton church, has a border

150. Alderbury: tablet, now in S chancel 'chapel', to Thomas Stringer (+ 1702).

149. Winterslow: tablet, N aisle, to Dorothea Thistlethwayte (+ 1715).

151. Shrewton: tablet, S aisle, to Robert Goldisborough (+ 1735).

which includes not only stylised fruit and flowers but also the rural emblems of scythes, sheaves of corn, guns and powder flasks.

Oval tablets date from *c.* 1757 when they rapidly became popular both as a substitute for plain rectangular tablets, an example being the undecorated white tablet erected to Charles James Fox in his family church at Farley, and as larger memorials (which were often developed into crowned tablets) such as the memorial to Susanna Skinner (+ 1805) at Winterbourne Earls, which shows how well the oval could be combined with the equally popular crossed fronds and wreaths. An oval inscription was sometimes set as the major element on a rectilinear ground of plain or veined marble, as on the tablet to Thomas Michell (+ 1757) at Chitterne All Saints.

The pyramidal tablet, like the oval tablet of the second half of the 18th century, was derived from major monuments which have a pyramid rising from a sarcophagus base, like those of the Duncombes at Downton. It could be used either as a plain tablet, with the inscription written directly on the pyramid, or the pyramid could form the ground on which a more conventionally shaped inscription was placed, thus resembling the crowned tablet. At Landford and Whiteparish there are two pairs of contemporary tablets which show the variations possible within the pyramidal type. On those to John Eyre and to Henry and Harriott Eyre, all of whom died in 1799, a crowning pyramid was employed as the ground on which to display the family arms with rich carving on the apron below. An earlier pair, to Robert and to Jane Eyre, of *c.* 1775, are of starker form with the black pyramid and plain shaped base relieved only by a white inscription and a band of wave decoration.

Floor slabs have not been included in this volume; they were recorded for each parish in the successive volumes of Colt Hoare's *Modern Wiltshire*, before the removals and repavings of the Victorian era caused the destruction of many of them. There remain, however, some fine examples of the standard 17th and 18th-century type of black marble slab, graced with coats-of-arms and good lettering, at Durrington (to the Moore family) and at Bulford.

152

153

152. Winterbourne Earls: tablet, now on S wall, by King, to Susanna Skinner (+ 1805).
153. Whiteparish: tablet, now on W wall nave, to Henry and Harriott Eyre (both died in 1799).

154

155

Grave slabs and churchyard monuments have also not been recorded comprehensively in this survey. Seventeenth-century headstones, such as those to John Saph and his wife at Stapleford, are small with shaped heads and no carved decoration. Two 18th-century headstones at Winterbourne Gunner show how the conventional motifs of skulls or floral garlands, seemingly introduced *c*. 1700, were treated more competently as the century advanced; on the stone to John [? Hunt] who died in 1723 the carving is very crude but on that to Jenny Brown, thirty years later, the flowers are recognisably naturalistic.

It is probably right to assume a general social division in this period between the propertied classes, who were buried within the church, and the rest, who were buried outside. By *c*. 1800, however, the presence of large and ornate chest tombs[79] in some churchyards, such as those to William Cooper (+ 1804) and John Bently (+ 1810) at Tilshead, shows that those who could afford substantial monuments were by then being interred outside. In contrast, there are the servants' memorials set up within a church, notably for the retainers of the Harris family at Durnford; they do not pretend to any ornament. By the Victorian era motives of hygiene regarding burials within a building meant that for some prominent landowners a memorial tablet was set up within the church in addition to a substantial tomb over the grave in the churchyard. Examples are to be found at Winterbourne Gunner and Wilsford (Frances Turner, + 1842) and (Giles Loder, + 1857).

The Nineteenth Century. In the first few decades of the 19th century there was a quickening of church life at parish level. The office of rural dean was revived in 1811. Another sign of concern for efficient administration was the effort in 1813 to make every parish in the area order a cast-iron strong-box to hold the parish registers. The boxes were manufactured by the smith William Henbest at Bramshaw, now just across the Hampshire border but at that time still part of Wiltshire (Elliot 1971, 42). They share a standard design and inscription '1813, W.H. Bramshaw Foundry' and survive in almost every church.

Some of the early 19th-century alterations to the fabric of buildings are in the plain utilitarian spirit of the time. Transverse aisles in stock brick were added to the

156

154. Tilshead: chest tomb in churchyard to William Cooper (+ 1804).
155. Bulford: floor slab, nave, commemorating Sarah Axford (+ 1733).
156. Bulford: cast-iron parish strong-box, 1813.

churches of Pitton and Bulford; at Winterbourne Stoke, which had already lost its north transept in the 17th or 18th century, the chancel and nave were remodelled in 1838–9 in a very unambitious style of Gothic. The wooden Y tracery inserted in some of the windows of the church of West Grimstead in a restoration of 1837 has some charm, but that formerly in the east window of Bulford must have looked all it was; a cheap job.

Already by the 1830s, however, there was church building in and around the area undertaken in a different spirit.[80] To the west of the area, the nave and tower at Fisherton Delamere were rebuilt in 1834 in a good paraphrase of the original medieval fabric and the church at Bishopstone was restored with care by the scholarly incumbent. Within the area, the chancel and south porch of Orcheston St Mary were rebuilt from the ground in 1832 and the east and south elevations of the building remodelled in a rustic version of Salisbury Cathedral's lancet style. The chancel and the new font and altar were supplied by the 'liberality and taste' of the rector, a former Fellow of Clare College, Cambridge, and the inhabitants, with the help of the Incorporated Church Building Society, paid for the remainder (*Br. Mag.* 1836, 263). On the other side of Salisbury the chapel of St Mary, Redlynch, was built in 1837 to serve the south-east part of the sprawling parish of Downton. It was the first church since the Middle Ages to be built on a new site and in an area which had never possessed any church or chapel.[81] It was designed in an unpretentious Perpendicular-Gothic style, except for the ogee bellcote on the W gable. The architect is not known for certain but was probably James Dean, since the building shares many of the characteristics of his work at Orcheston St Mary, particularly the design of the nave roof and the panels that frame the east window.[82] Most notably, both churches possess stone altars with boldly traceried front panels, a feature which less than ten years later would have been prohibited as popish. An article of July 1834 in the *British Magazine*, describing the work at Orcheston, shows that such altars were a deliberate proto-Tractarian attempt to restore 'decent ornament' and 'imposing ceremonial' by turning away from the 'mean and crazy spider-legged tables . . . in the days of Cromwell . . . substituted . . . for the former altars' (*Br. Mag.* 1836, 264).

These buildings of the 1830s are significant harbingers of the Victorian Revival. The increasing concern for medieval correctness, the influence of individual patrons, often ecclesiastics determined to improve standards of religion and taste rather than merely satisfy practical needs, and the introduction of fittings with a polemical liturgical message were all to be regular characteristics of church building over the next thirty years.

The church building in the area during the following decade of the 1840s was in its mixture of traditions and styles the most interesting of the century. The restoration of the church at Tilshead in 1845 by Thomas Henry Wyatt and David Brandon, a partnership which was to dominate church building in the area for the next thirty years, was not treated in the stereotyped fashion of the architects' later work. Features were retained typical of earlier restoration schemes, such as the combination in the new stained glass of crudely coloured pictorial scenes and displays of heraldry commemorating contributors to the restoration fund. In the Bourne valley there is an interesting contrast between the painstaking rebuilding in the late 1840s of the tiny church at Allington by its incumbent and the local Salisbury architect, J.R. Fisher, censured by contemporaries as inadequate and uninspired, and the wholesale replacement of the medieval church at neighbouring Newton Toney in 1844 by an economical design by Wyatt and Brandon which incorporated only a few relics of the original (Mozley 1885, 344–5).

The two most distinguished 19th-century churches in the area were begun in the same year, 1841, ostensibly to the designs of the same architect, T.H. Wyatt, and for patrons who had known each other at Oriel College, Oxford: at Wilton for the Hon. Sydney Herbert and at Cholderton for the Rev. Thomas Mozley.[83] The complete difference between the two buildings and their great superiority in quality to any other design by T.H. Wyatt suggest that the creative force behind their design belonged to the patrons, not to the architect. This is confirmed by Mozley in his *Reminiscences, chiefly of Oriel College and the Oxford Movement.* 'Herbert and I both probably had the same reasons for our choice. We both intended to have our own way as much as possible, and make a convenience of the poor architect. We both expected to invite criticism, perhaps rebuke, and thought that a man so well placed as Wyatt would be able to smooth matters for us and carry us through little difficulties. Then he was very neutral and eclectic in his style, condescending sometimes to no style at all when his patrons were so inclined' (Mozley 1882, 2, 159).

158

159

158. Redlynch, St Mary: interior of chancel looking E, showing original stone Holy Table.
159. Tilshead: stained glass of 1846, S aisle window.

The Italian Romanesque basilica of Wilton can hardly differ more from the Perpendicular 'college chapel' of Cholderton, but they have in common the same excellence of craftsmanship and, indeed, involved some of the same craftsmen. They are also comparable in that they incorporate major medieval features in keeping with the style of each church: Wilton possesses the Cosmatesque 'Shrine of Capocci' of 1256, from S. Maria Maggiore in Rome, which Herbert bought from the Horace Walpole collection at Strawberry Hill; Cholderton has a great 15th-century hammer-beam roof, which Mozley brought from Ipswich. Indeed the Cholderton roof was not only the determining factor in establishing the form and proportions of the church but was itself a declaration of ecclesiological principle.[84]

Both the Cholderton and Wilton church reflect the religious and social viewpoints of their founders. Both were parish churches, yet the whole process of condemning the old church, then designing, building and paying for the new building was taken over in the one case by the parson and in the other by the squire. The feelings of the average parishioner at being thus organised are not recorded. The townspeople of Wilton could not have withstood the *de facto* earl of Pembroke (the titular earl lived abroad and let Wilton to his half-brother Sidney)[85] but at Cholderton, Mozley, who was neither aristocratic nor rich, had many difficulties with the local landowners. The Dowager Countess Nelson, otherwise a devoted churchwoman, refused to contribute because, while she was in favour of repairing or enlarging the existing building, she would 'not help sweep it away and to put in its place a building quite unlike any other English village church'.[86]

The exotic style of these churches did not extend to their liturgical arrangement, although their restraint in this respect was perhaps due to the dislike of the then bishop, Denison, of any Romanising stone altars or rood screens. The essentials of any Anglican church of the 1840s were all present: the wooden Holy Table; inscriptions of the Commandments, Lord's Prayer and Creed; painted texts on the walls; and the Royal Arms – though this feature was concealed at Cholderton in the tiling of the antechapel floor and at Wilton in the stained glass of the central oculus of the rose window. Wilton even retained a west gallery and charity-boards. Compared with the Tractarian Mozley, brother-in-law to the later Cardinal Newman, Sidney Herbert was firmly Protestant, yet Wilton in the 17th and 18th-century Continental woodwork of its fittings and in its medieval stained glass, contained many more images than did Cholderton. The complete array of contemporary stained glass at Cholderton was an addition to the original design introduced by Mozley's successor, but in its choice of subject it preserved the emphasis, traditional in Anglican stained glass, upon the Old Testament and the Miracles of Christ rather than on the saints and their lives (Winston 1867, **1**, 266).[87]

The great rebuilding phase of the mid 19th century, which, as already noted, entailed the demolition of thirteen churches and the radical restoration and extension of twenty-four more, can be treated in social as much as architectural terms. Except for Teulon's Alderbury, Butterfield's Landford and Pownall's East Grimstead, the mid Victorian and Victorianised churches are not of the first rank.

During this period and after, the life of south-east Wiltshire was dominated by three great families, the Herbert earls of Pembroke at Wilton House, the Pleydell-Bouverie earls of Radnor at Longford Castle, and the earls Nelson at Trafalgar House (the former Standlynch House). All three families actively promoted church restoration in their several territories.

The Herberts were the major influence in the Wylye valley. The building of the church of St Mary and St Nicholas, Wilton, was their most important and most costly achievement but they also largely financed the restoration of South Newton in 1862 and of Netherhampton in 1876–7, besides building a large new church at Bemerton.

160. Britford: exterior from NE showing Street's rebuilding of the Radnor mausoleum (*see* also 244).

For the most part they remained content with T.H. Wyatt as their architect.[88] The Radnors were less active at this time although in the last two decades of the 18th century they had aided restoration at Odstock, Homington and Downton, and also played a prominent part in the transformation of Salisbury Cathedral under James Wyatt. In the 19th century their activities were limited to Britford, where they allowed Street to reduce their mortuary chapel to a low bunker, and Alderbury, where they shared the cost of rebuilding with their neighbours, the Forts of Alderbury House and the Hervey-Bathursts of Clarendon Park. They later became the principal patrons of Alderbury church, redecorating the chancel with stained glass and sumptuous mosaic and tile work.

The role of the Radnor family as sponsors of matters ecclesiastical in the south-east part of the county was partly taken over by the newly established great family, the Nelsons. Although Standlynch was acquired on their behalf by parliamentary trustees in 1815, the dynastic misfortunes of the first earl losing his son and the second earl, the Rev. Thomas Bolton, dying in 1835 only a few months after succeeding to the title, meant that it remained for the third earl to confirm the family's prominence in the area. This he achieved partly because of his very long life (he lived until 1913) and his involvement in public, especially church, affairs, but chiefly through the influence of his mother, Frances Elizabeth Eyre, who was sole heiress to the great estates in the area belonging to her branch of the Eyre family. Her marriage to the second earl gave the Nelsons the local base and connections they lacked and the Eyres the title they sought.

Both the dowager countess and the third earl were enthusiastic church builders and restorers who, because they had High Church leanings, came to prefer Butterfield to T.H. Wyatt as their architect. Wyatt had been employed to build the new church at Charlton All Saints, erected by the earl in his youth to serve the congregation on both banks of the Avon, which had for centuries used Standlynch chapel, but in the 1860s it was Butterfield who restored the chapel, by then firmly private, as well as designing secular works for the earl, such as a bowling green shelter (Thompson 1971, 407–8). Through the influence of the dowager countess, Butterfield was later commissioned to restore the nave and aisles of Whiteparish church and to rebuild Landford church

entirely, preserving the Eyre vault as the foundation of the south aisle but 'skying' their monuments with apparent disrespect.

Other prominent families in the area, such as the Malets at Newton Toney and the Antrobus family at Amesbury, also played their expected role in prompting church rebuilding. In an almost completely agricultural society suffering serious economic hardship the contributions of landowners were essential to any scheme of church building or restoration of even the cheaper kind costing about £1,000 (*see* Table 3 for details of restorations).

Of the architects active in the area during this period, the busiest was Thomas Henry Wyatt. He restored eleven of the churches and built anew four more. Yet the cruel summary by Mozley, quoted earlier, is hard to gainsay. The chief aesthetic virtue of Wyatt's buildings, unlike those of some of his greater contemporaries, is that they have a traditional scale in keeping with their surroundings. The church at Charlton All Saints, perhaps his best, was designed in 'Early English of the most simple character' and succeeds in being an 'unpretentious village church', enhancing but not obtruding on the neighbouring houses (*Builder* 1851, 286). He also, as Newman and Pevsner have pointed out, was prepared to design in late medieval styles at a time when they were anathema to the purists (Pevsner 1972, 19). His most glaring faults are, first, his drastic rearrangement of original fabric especially when, as at Chitterne All Saints and Winterbourne Earls, he arbitrarily inserted features from two old churches into his new one, and, secondly, his insensitivity to detail: the openings of the tower at Nunton are in an astonishingly coarse Gothic for 1853. His lack of imagination when not prompted by more gifted clients and his use of a large staff of assistants meant that certain features became stereotyped, notably the arrangement of the roof in alternating major and minor trusses with corbels correspondingly alternating in height. The naturalistic carving of such corbels, could, however, be of a high standard, as at South Newton.

In spite of the dominance of T.H. Wyatt, such major Victorian architects as Street, Pearson and particularly Butterfield all worked on churches in the area. Butterfield's treatment of Amesbury in 1852–3 is a classic example of High Victorian restoration. The later medieval work of the east and west ends was as ruthlessly condemned as the early Georgian of the south transept in favour of the First Pointed style, and a brand new stair tower was confidently placed in the north-east angle of the crossing; yet only fifty years later the crossing nearly collapsed and the whole church needed primary repairs such as proper foundations and drainage. Internally almost every fitting was removed, including the monuments, and burnt or smashed to pieces, to be replaced by woodwork of a strongly individual Gothic. While Butterfield was undoubtedly under local pressure, especially from the incumbent, he cannot be absolved from all responsibility.[89] Landford, his only completely new church in the area, may be accepted with less reservation. The west front with its central buttress and bellcote is well sited on the brow of a hill, but the profile of the building is kept discreet by the low, sweeping roofs of the aisles. Internally the fittings and polychromy are carefully balanced to produce a unified effect.

Pearson is represented by his restoration of the important church of Idmiston and the replacement of the old chapel at Porton. Both show his characteristic interest in detailing but lack any particular atmosphere or sensitivity to the landscape (Quiney 1979, 258, 270). The restoration of Britford by Street, though correct and highly regarded at the time, is strangely dull.

More interesting are the works of two of the less famous architects of the period, F.H. Pownall and S.S. Teulon. Pownall was commissioned, perhaps through family interest, to rebuild first the chapel of East Grimstead and then, ten years later, the mother church of West Dean.[90] In those ten years he moved from the pure Middle Pointed of the chapel to an almost 'rogue Gothic' for the new parish church. Teulon, at Alderbury, followed the High Victorian line more directly, perhaps because he was working very much under the eyes of the great. His prominent steeple was designed primarily to be viewed from the Longford Castle estate to the west, but when seen from the east it also formed the climax of a careful composition of related gables. Like Butterfield he used polychromy: flint and brown heathstone externally; red and black brick inside.

The chance personal connections of particular incumbents led to some architects from other parts of England being employed in the area. J.W. Hugall, from Pontefract, restored and enlarged Durrington (and Figheldean to the north)[91] and J. Fowler, of Louth in Lincolnshire, rebuilt the chancel and repaired the nave of Odstock. More distinguished and conscientious was the work at Stapleford by William Slater, much of whose practice lay in Northamptonshire. He managed to repair and re-order the greater part of the building without compromising its complicated history by more than the alteration of the west window.

The Victorian fittings of the area are (except at Cholderton and the church of St Mary and St Nicholas, Wilton) unremarkable individually yet form an impressive unity in many churches. The major loss sustained over the last century has been the decoration of the sanctuary (upon which Victorian architects lavished most attention), changed aesthetic and liturgical attitudes having led to the dismantling or concealment of the paintings and coloured stone or woodwork which enriched the east end. The outstanding example of this is the chancel of Britford church where Street compensated for the austerity of his restoration of the fabric with a colourful east wall decorated with Spanish tiles, mosaic panels of the Evangelist symbols and praying angels flanking the stained-glass window.[92] Butterfield provided idiosyncratic stencilling and tiles for the east wall at Amesbury and a reredos of coloured marbles at Landford, though, significantly, the Landford reredos was a replacement, some twenty-five years after the consecration of the church, of the original tin Commandment Tables. Such enrichment of the east end conforms to a standard pattern whereby the texts preferred in the middle of the century, even at Wilton and Cholderton, gave way later to more elaborate architectural treatments incorporating sacred scenes and symbols. A typical example is the wooden reredos at Pitton which encloses paintings of the Apostles on a gold ground.

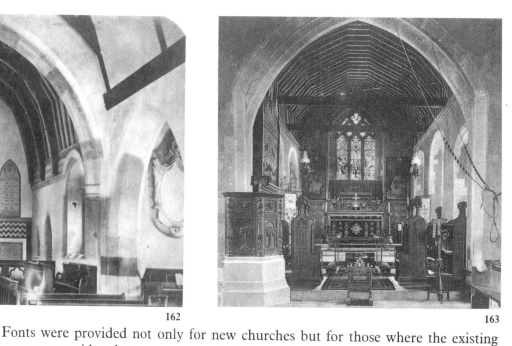

162

163

164

Fonts were provided not only for new churches but for those where the existing fonts were considered too worn or rude. The original fonts of eleven churches were removed, although those of Amesbury, Tilshead and Cholderton have since been returned, and at Amesbury and Tilshead it is their Victorian replacements which have now vanished.[93] In the 1830s and 1840s churches such as Orcheston St George and Orcheston St Mary acquired polygonal 'Perpendicular' fonts, whose slender dimensions show their Georgian ancestry in spite of the ecclesiological pretensions of their Gothic design. Of the fonts designed by architects, rather than taken from commercial catalogues, those of Butterfield are, again, the most interesting (Netherhampton, Whiteparish and, by attribution, Charlton). The 'Romanesque' font designs of Hugall at Durrington and Wyatt at Shrewton are bizarre rather than convincing, but the strangest font of all is at the church of St Mary and St Nicholas, Wilton, where an Italian Renaissance bowl is married to a Baroque base by a stem decorated with Victorian *sgraffito* work.

Victorian pulpits are more numerous than fonts although less original in their design. Corresponding to the 'Perpendicular' fonts are the panelled stone pulpits of the same era at Tilshead, Coombe Bissett and Maddington. After the 1840s it became more usual to place a wooden frame on a stone base, a treatment unfortunately extended to the wooden pulpits of the 17th century, but, with the exception of the boldly unconventional wooden pulpit by Butterfield at Amesbury, the best designs were still in stone. The pulpit of 1857 at Laverstock, though of the 1840s type, has excellent carving by Hewett, one of the master craftsmen assembled for Wilton. That at Stapleford, presumably designed by Slater, is more sophisticated, with narrow green marble bands picking up the greensand banding of the Romanesque arcades. Some pulpits stand outside the pattern: Wilton, with numerous supporting columns like the 13th-century pulpits at Pistoia or Pisa; and Winterslow, a clever pastiche of 16th and 17th-century elements.

The tiling provided for the churches of the area conformed to the standard Victorian patterns. The usual supplier prescribed by architects was the firm of Minton, which produced a minor masterpiece in the floor of Cholderton church, where the different stages of the progress to the east end are marked by different colour schemes which subtly become less vivid towards the sanctuary. The design was shown at the Great Exhibition of 1851.

162. Landford: interior looking E; chancel furnishings photographed before installation of present reredos in 1879.
163. Britford: interior of chancel looking E, photographed soon after Street's restoration of 1872–3.
164. Orcheston St George: font *c.* 1833.

Stained glass of the period is better considered in terms of the series of windows provided for certain churches than as individual works of art. The churches of Cholderton and Landford were both entirely glazed according to set programmes during the 1850s. The glass at Cholderton was drawn from three workshops of varying skill but that at Landford was supplied exclusively by Lavers, Barraud and Westlake, who gave a complimentary window in return. The technically competent but uninspired series installed by the Nelsons at Standlynch and by the Malets at Newton Toney date from the end of the century. Stylistically, the glass in the area developed from the crude (and now faded) pictorial type of the Tilshead scenes of the mid 1840s to the vigorous but angular medievalising of Hardman's 'transept' window at Alderbury of ten years later, and culminated in the masterly east windows designed by Kempe for Stratford Tony and Pitton. In colour, too, the subtle greens and golds of these later windows mark a great progression from the harsher colours used, for instance, at Laverstock in the 1850s in the multi-coloured fragments that formed their set of 'fruit salad' windows.

165

166

167

168

165. Durrington: font by J.W. Hugall of 1850.
166. Charlton: font, probably by Butterfield, c. 1864.
167. Laverstock: stained glass in E window S aisle, by Ward & Co., c. 1858.
168. Stapleford: pulpit by W. Slater, of 1861.

170

Other Victorian fittings do not merit individual mention, although their accumulation, to the last embroidered binding and brass vase, is tellingly documented for Cholderton (Barrow 1889, 25–8) and Landford (MS Parish Book from 1857). More distinctive are some of the items of functional metalwork. The hinges of the main north door at Odstock, the elaborate hinges, lock plate and sliding cover for the south door at Durrington or the heating grilles in the floor at Wilton, are all of quality.

The most important supplier of church monuments was the firm of Osmond. It could provide examples of every size and to suit every pocket, in designs of either Gothic or Classical style, that remained unchanged into the 20th century. The major monuments in the area by Osmond are Gothic, but they are not of outstanding quality. Their detailing has a bloated quality which led Pugin to term them Osmond's 'blisters' (Ferrey 1978, 76). Even the most ambitious design, the great tabernacled tomb to the second Earl Nelson at Standlynch, lacks interest for all the accuracy of its carving. T.H. Wyatt looked elsewhere, to J.B. Philip, for the execution of the recumbent effigies and tomb chests he designed for the founders of Wilton church, Lord Herbert of Lea and his mother, but these are of greater historical than artistic interest. The use of brass tablets was revived, especially for clerics and their families. There are good though unexceptional examples at Berwick St James, to Emma Lakin, wife of the incumbent (+ 1873), and at Durrington to Richard Webb (+ 1862), incumbent there for forty years and instigator of the restoration of the church.

The Twentieth Century. In this century contributions toward the fabric of churches have been very modest although the treatment of church interiors, especially of 19th-century decoration and furnishings, has often been drastic. It is fitting that the one turn-of-the-century building, St Birinus, Morgan's Vale, should have been designed by C.E. Ponting, the Marlborough architect who dominated both local church studies and restorations in the late Victorian and Edwardian era. Otherwise the only completely new church in the area is the garrison church at Bulford, a sizable

169. Odstock: metalwork on N door.
170. Wilton, St Mary and St Nicholas: tomb in chancel of Sidney Herbert, Lord Herbert of Lea (+ 1861), designed by T.H. Wyatt and executed by J.B. Philip (*see* also 517).

but conventional design of the 1920s by Blount. The most considerable additions to any church were the north aisle and vestry added to Nunton in 1933 by Randoll Blacking of Salisbury. These are self-effacing, but more positive expressions of the taste of the period can be seen in the contemporary re-ordering and furnishing of the sanctuary and of the south chancel chapel, in particular the glass in the two east windows by Christopher Webb. Other glass of similar type and period, by Ninian Comper, was installed at Woodford. A series of wealthy parishioners at Wilsford in the early part of the century contributed not only interesting medieval and 18th-century metalwork to the church but also contemporary monuments by Eric Gill and Rex Whistler.

Since the Second World War new building has been confined to vestries connected with but kept carefully distinct from the south side of the chancels of Durrington and Whiteparish and to an extension of the hall/chapel at the west end of Laverstock.[94] Chancels were refurnished at Coombe Bissett in 1961 and Winterslow in 1975.

The main task in the 20th century has, however, been the maintenance of the existing church buildings of the area rather than the erection of new. The Edwardian restorations at Bulford and Durnford churches may be seen as late examples of the great 19th-century renovation campaign although they were conducted with much greater sensitivity. At the same time Amesbury required a further major restoration, which involved reflooring the entire church, underpinning foundations and repairing and even partly rebuilding the piers of the crossing and of the south arcade. Orcheston St Mary needed major works of repair in 1964–5. Today repairs, the costs of which runs ahead of inflation, inevitably constitute an ever-increasing burden on the congregations of the area but the great majority are still used for religious worship.

171

172

171. Wilsford: tablet, nave N wall, by Eric Gill, to Wynlayne Lodge (+ 1922).
172. Wilsford: gravestone (in churchyard) by Rex Whistler, to Pamela, Lady Grey (+ 1928).

NOTES

1. A small excavation was carried out in 1958 in the angle of the nave and N transept of Britford church (G.E. Chambers, 'The Pre-Conquest Church of St Peter at Britford', *WAM* 57, 1960, 212–3): two inconclusive excavations have been made outside the NW corner of the nave of Amesbury in 1920 and 1978.

2. The church of St Oswald in Exeter Street, Salisbury, by A.W.N. Pugin is treated in RCHM, *City of Salisbury* (1980) 44–5. The chapel at Standlynch (p. 191) was used for Roman Catholic worship from 1914 to 1949. A Roman Catholic chapel was licensed at Wilbury House, Newton Toney, in 1797, but it does not appear to have functioned for long, if at all. (VCH *Wilts.* 3, 1956, 91).

3. *See* p. vii for correlation between individual churches and civil parishes.

4. *See* Table 1 for full list of patrons. Winterbourne Dauntsey formed part of the prebend of Chute and Chisenbury, while Winterbourne Earls only became a prebend by exchange after the Dissolution.

5. This does not include the very small and unpretentious chapel of St John, erected in the eastern part of Winterslow in 1860.

6. For a fuller discussion of the sources *see* pp. 3–4.

7. The objections to the identification of the present parish church of Amesbury with the former priory church are set out in Appendix 1.

8. The pencil drawings, now held as BL Add MSS 36390–2, were the originals from which the finished watercolours were made. The great majority of the views appear to have been drawn in 1805 but isolated drawings, e.g. of Amesbury, vary in date from 1803 to 1811.

9. The only apparent exception is the font at Berwick St James which was drawn up as having a square bowl, whereas it now has a similar but round bowl. In the original note book drawing (BL Add MS 36392 fol.120 v) Buckler drew the round sides of the bowl too sharply, so possibly he later mistook the shape as square.

10. Sets of his watercolours exist in Salisbury Museum and in Libr. of the Wilts. Archaeol. Soc. in Devizes. *See* E.H. Goddard ed., 'The Kemm Drawings of Wiltshire', *WAM* 45 (1932) 254–67.

11. The 19th-century archives of the ICBS are divided between the libraries of the Soc. Antiq., London, and of Lambeth Palace.

12. Even at Amesbury, ashlar was confined to the S wall, above sill height, and possibly, as in the 19th-century rebuilding, the E wall.

13. Square Roman brick tile had been used in the Anglo-Saxon porticus arches of Britford. It may possibly have been brought from the Roman villa at Rockbourne (Hants.) where brick tiles of similar form and dimensions were used in the piers of the hypocaust.

14. It was said to be 61 ft (18.60 m) high, and was demolished in 1541, with the aid of pulleys, ropes and gunpowder: Longleat MSS 6524, 6526.

15. A view of 1820 (BL Maps 34 g 1 vol.6 fol.56) suggests that the lantern was not large.

16. The W walls of the present transepts at Britford appear to incorporate Saxon work but the plan of the eastern parts of the Saxon church is unknown.

17. Saxon work survives in two other nearby Hants. churches, Little Somborne and Middle Wallop.

18. The first, timber, church of the abbey is said to have been rebuilt in stone by queen Edith, wife of the Confessor; VCH *Wilts.* 3 (1956) 232.

19. Ralegh Radford considers minster status for Breamore 'a legitimate deduction'. C.A.R. Radford, 'Pre-Conquest Minster Churches', *Archaeol. J.* **130** (1973) 127.

20. The two arches visible above the S window of the tower possibly indicate the presence of an early opening, although the arches and the whole external face of the tower are of much later date.

21. Work of the Saxo-Norman Overlap period survives not far away in the nave door and windows of Quarley (Hants.) and in the tympanum at Knook to the W up the Wylye valley.

22. At Tilshead and Allington the imposts on the W face of the chancel arches are returned on to the nave walls; they are simply decorated. The Nunton imposts have been re-used in a later arch.

23. The W tower of Winterbourne Gunner may also be of 12th-century origin although its openings are Perpendicular.

24. A carved tympanum is preserved in the church of Little Langford to the W of Stapleford.

25. The term is that used by A. Borg, 'The Development of Chevron Ornament', *J. Br. Archaeol. Assoc.* ser 3, **30** (1967) 136.

26. In the present doorway the opening has been raised and cut into the lintel: the original form is shown by Buckler.

27. A county-wide typology of medieval fonts before Victorian restoration could be made using the drawings by Buckler now in Devizes Museum; vol.8 fols 1–31.

28. The font formerly installed in the chapel of St John's Hospital, Wilton but recently sold, could also have been originally of tub form.

29. The form of decoration of the Tilshead font was paralleled in the font at Imber, the next parish but one to the W.

30. Personal communication from Prof. G. Zarnecki.

31. The figures were removed in 1982 for conservation and exhibition and are now on permanent loan to the Victoria & Albert Museum, London. Conservation revealed that the St Peter was carved in the reverse of an unfinished cross slab.

32. The simple 14th-century sedilia at Britford reputedly had Purbeck seats when revealed in 1873.

33. The patronage of Berwick St James belonged to Mottisfont Priory.

34. Other examples survive at Winterbourne Stoke and Fugglestone. They may have been inspired by the double aumbry in the N wall of the NE chapel of Salisbury Cathedral.

35. A variation of this type of respond with a triplet of slender but quite short shafts around a central core, with linked capitals, either carved or moulded, is found in churches of the Wylye and Till valleys, e.g. Winterbourne Stoke, Shrewton, Steeple Langford and Fisherton De la Mere.

36. The truncated tower of Bulford church may never have risen to any great height, in spite of its thick walls. Possibly it carried a timber belfry.

37. For a further discussion of the significance of the respond for the connection between church and priory, *see* Appendix 1.

38. Other evidence for the dating of the arches was obscured by the 14th-century alterations to the crossing.

39. Tracings from the paintings survive in the Salisbury Museum.

40. There is no surviving evidence of sedilia in the chancel at Amesbury in spite of its 13th and early 14th-century date. The elaborately moulded recess to the N of the altar is a blocked doorway.

41. This paragraph is based on a text kindly provided by Mrs Elizabeth Eames.

42. Tiles were uncovered *in situ* to the N of Amesbury Abbey House in 1860–1, and again in 1981, when further *ex situ* tiles of the same design were excavated to the NE of the house.

43. The simplicity of the West Dean mouldings is unfortunate in that they belong to the only securely dated building in the area.

44. The only example of 13th-century Geometric tracery is the fine two-light window in the E gable of the Amesbury transept chapel.

45. This appears to have remained a favourite form of belfry opening until the 16th or even 17th century.

46. The Perpendicular walls were built plumb, although the unbuttressed Romanesque walls were already leaning outwards.

47. The external doors to tower stairs are in general Victorian, e.g. Coombe Bissett, Durrington.

48. Other unusual features are the W buttresses at Odstock (with projecting 'toe' at the foot) and Durnford (corbelled in to support the upper stages, rather than being set back on top of a string course).

49. Tracery panelling is a common Perpendicular feature in Wilts. and Dorset churches, e.g. Sherborne Abbey.

50. Some of the detailing may be the creation of the Edwardian restoration when the roof was unceiled.

51. Other intact examples are in the churches of St Martin's, Salisbury and St George's, Harnham.

52. The faculty drawings by T.H. Wyatt (DRO 10/19) show that the original intention was to install the screen intact.

53. The photograph and the drawing, by R. Kemm, are in Salisbury Museum.

54. I am grateful to Miss Jill Kerr for her comments on the stained glass of the area.

55. The painting concealed the Romanesque doorway into the N aisle. Late medieval paintings of single saints similarly covered the 13th-century paintings in Winterbourne Dauntsey church.

56. Similar foliate crockets are found on the arch to the Perpendicular tomb recess in the N aisle of Great Wishford church, across the river from South Newton.

57. The hospitals of St Giles and St John at Wilton survived the Dissolution but the original buildings of St Giles have been completely destroyed.

58. It may be significant that in 1544 the property was sold to Lord Hertford, later the Protector Somerset, who had already been very brisk in dismantling the priory church of Amesbury.

59. It has been suggested that straight-headed mullioned windows are typical features of Elizabethan church work: J. Simmons, 'Brooke Church, Rutland, with Notes on Elizabethan Church Building', *Trans Leics. Archaeol. Hist. Soc.* 35, 1959, 41. Renaissance details first appear in the area in a late 16th-century tomb at Odstock, later re-used for members of the Webb family in the 18th century.

60. Such disasters must have afflicted churches in the area in earlier times, but were not recorded.

61. Fox also presented a set of contemporary plate to the church he rebuilt at Farley (*see* Illus. 106).

62. A fragment of the old Wilton rails survives at Wylye, adapted as the front of the prayer desk at the foot of the pulpit stairs.

63. The motifs and the carving of the Britford pulpit are so close to those of the former Wilton pulpit that they must come from the same workshop (possibly that of the Beckhams) at about the same date.

64. It is unclear how much of the original design of the benches has survived their conversion into box-pews and then the dismantling of that arrangement in 1883.

65. The table appears to be essentially Victorian but probably incorporates earlier woodwork.

66. Some of the 17th-century chests, like the tables, may not be original furnishings. The four-panel chest at Woodford was given to the church in the early 20th century.

67. This was in addition to a wall monument.

68. All these monuments are unsigned. The Duncombe monument can be attributed to James Hardy who had executed a monument to Duncombe's daughter five years earlier at Horsham (Sussex). MS notes by Mrs Esdaile, on deposit in NMR.

69. Nicholas Stone supplied a very similar portrait bust for the monument to Lady Katharine Paston (+ 1636) in Oxnead church, Norfolk (I owe this comparison to Mr Adam White).

70. Note on last page of Boscombe Church Register 1696–1782 (WRO 1068–21).

71. Dean and Chapter Records 61: Court Records, Non-contentious (P. Stewart, ed., *Diocese of Salisbury: Guide to the Records of the Bishop . . .* , 1973, 112): Note of 1796 in Homington Church Register 1755–1813, (WRO 538–2).

72. The use of headers in darker brick to produce a hint of diaper in the S wall may indicate that the tower dates from earlier in the 18th century.

73. Bills of 1810–14 for surveys by Daniel Alexander of the tower and the tower arches and for extensive repairs to the church survive in the Muniment Room, Longford Castle.

74. There is another at Great Wishford.

75. The signed bill for the monument is in the Estate Office, Wilton House.

76. The lions claw feet of the sarcophagus were not replaced when the monument was moved in 1946, but they are preserved in the crypt.

77. Lady Herbert died in childbirth but her baby lived, only to die five years later, when an extra inscription was added at the foot of the monument.

78. Bristol Univ. Libr: Account Book of Robert Wansborough 1759–1769 (DH 25/100), entry for 10 Dec. 1765.

79. This type of tomb resembles a large furniture chest: it is a relatively common feature of 18th and 19th-century graveyards though not church interiors. Unlike a tomb chest it does not form part of a larger composition.

80. The 1830s were a time of economic distress and social strife in Wiltshire: *Br. Mag.* **9**, (1836) 258.

81. The 17th-century church at Farley replaced a medieval chapel.

82. Although John Oxenberry Jane signed the certificate of completion required by the ICBS, the plan of Orcheston St Mary is signed by James Dean, 'architect': ICBS papers on deposit in Lambeth Palace Libr.

83. Although Wyatt and Brandon were theoretically in partnership from *c.* 1840 to *c.* 1860, Wyatt was the dominant figure, in Wilts. at least. Any share by Brandon in the design of Wilton church was denied in Wyatt's obituary (*Builder* **39** (1880) 193) and he was never mentioned by Mozley in connection with Cholderton.

84. Flat, ceiled roofs were considered to be marks of uninspired worship; open roofs, of medieval fervour. T. Mozley 'Open Roofs', *Br. Critic & Q. Theol. Rev.* (1841) *passim*, and *Remains, Chiefly of Oriel College and the Oxford Movement* (1885) 164.

85. The account books of the Wilton churchwardens, on deposit in the WRO, Trowbridge, record a unanimous vote of thanks to Sidney Herbert at a meeting held on 5 April 1841 to consider Herbert's offer of a new church.

86. Cutting from *Salisbury and Winchester J.* of 1889 in the Wiltshire Collections of Canon Jackson, Libr. of the Soc. Antiq. London (vol.2, fol.115).

87. The original intention had been to have two simple stained glass windows which Mrs Mozley, Newman's sister, ordered from Willement.

88. T.H. Wyatt also altered the private chapel in Wilton House created by James Wyatt.

89. Butterfield also built a small chapel for Amesbury cemetery, demolished in 1970.

90. A family connection is suggested by the name of the then rector of West Dean (also in charge of East Grimstead), George Pownall Glossop, whose family paid for its rebuilding. Some fragments from the medieval church have been re-used in the new church, others are now garden ornaments at Tower House, West Dean.

91. Hugall moved during this period to Cheltenham.

92. The angels may have been additions to Street's design.

93. The Amesbury font by Butterfield was given in 1914 to the temporary garrison church at Bulford but it is not the 19th-century font now installed in the church of 1920–7. *See* also T. Cocke, 'The William Butterfield Font from Amesbury Church', *WAM* **79** (1985) 248–50.

94. The lavatories in these buildings are the first to be installed in an Anglican church in the area.

TABLES

TABLE 1   PATRONAGE AND EARLIEST MENTION OF CHURCHES

Place	Modern dedication	Status	Patron	Earliest mention
Alderbury	St Mary	Vicarage by 1291	The king. Given to the Dean and Chapter of Salisbury 1107 × 1122.[1] Appropriated for the treasurer of Salisbury Chapter by 1291.	Domesday Book
Allington	St John Baptist	Rectory	Successive lay patrons.	1291 Taxatio
Amesbury	St Mary and St Melor	Rectory served by chaplains before the Reformation and perpetual curates after	The king until *c.* 1177, then Amesbury Priory. Post Dissolution— Lord Hertford. Dean and Chapter of Windsor.	*c.* 1177 Confirmation of refoundation charter of Amesbury Priory by Henry II. (VCH 1956, 244)
Berwick St James	St James	Vicarage by 1406	Mottisfont Abbey. Appropriated church *c.* 1406. Post Dissolution— Sandys family until *c.* 1638. Successive lay patrons.	1291 Taxatio
Boscombe	St Andrew	Rectory	St Neots Priory (Hunts.) *c.* 1175. Bishop of Salisbury by *c.* 1225.	*c.* 1175 Grant to St Neots Priory (Gorham 1820, cxxxv)
Britford	St Peter	Vicarage	Given to Salisbury Chapter 1107 × 1122.[2] Dean and Chapter of Salisbury.	Domesday Book
Bulford	St Leonard	Rectory served by chaplains before the Reformation and by perpetual curates after	The king. Amesbury Priory *c.* 1177. Post Dissolution— Successive lords of the manor.	Domesday Book
Chitterne	All Saints	Vicarage	Given to Vaux College, Salisbury, 1268. Post Dissolution— Successive lay patrons	Vaux grant. (VCH 1956, 370)
Chitterne	St Mary	Vicarage by 1291	Appropriated to Dean and Chapter of Salisbury by 1291.	1291 Taxatio
Cholderton	St Nicholas	Rectory	St Neots Priory (Hunts.) until *c.* 1449. Successive lay patrons. To Oriel College, Oxford in 1693.	*c.* 1175 Grant to St Neots Priory. (Gorham 1820, cxxxvi)
Coombe Bissett	St Michael	Vicarage	Given to Salisbury Chapter 1107 × 1122.[3] Prebend of Coombe and Harnham.	Domesday Book
Downton	St Lawrence	Vicarage from 1383	Bishop of Winchester. Appropriated to Winchester College 1382.	Domesday Book
Durnford	St Andrew	Vicarage	Given to Salisbury Chapter before 1147. Prebend of Durnford.	*c.* 1147 in Register of St Osmund as gift from Walter de Tuny. (VCH 1956, 159)

Place	Modern dedication	Status	Patron	Earliest mention
Durrington	All Saints	Rectory served by chaplains before the Reformation and by perpetual curates after	The king. Amesbury Priory c. 1177. Post Dissolution— Dean and Chapter of Winchester.	?1179 Confirmation of refoundation charter of Amesbury Priory by Henry II. (VCH 1956, 244)
East Grimstead	Holy Trinity	Dependent chapelry	Chapel dependent on West Dean.	
Farley	All Saints	Dependent chapelry	Chapel dependent on Alderbury until 1874.	
Fugglestone	St Peter	Rectory (united with Bemerton 1291–1972)	Abbess of Wilton. Post Dissolution— Earls of Pembroke.	1291 Taxatio
Homington	St Mary	Vicarage	Dean and Chapter of Salisbury by 1291.	1291 Taxatio
Idmiston	All Saints	Vicarage by 1282	Bishop of Winchester until c. 1500, then Bishop of Salisbury. Rectory appropriated to Dean and Chapter of Salisbury by 1282.	1282 in Register of St Osmund. (VCH 1956, 168)
Landford	St Andrew	Rectory	Successive lay patrons.	1291 Taxatio
Laverstock	St Andrew	Vicarage by c. 1225	Bishop of Salisbury. Appropriated to Vicars' Choral of Salisbury Cathedral.	c. 1225 Grant by Bishop Poore. (VCH 1956, 168)
Maddington	St Mary	Rectory served by chaplains before the Reformation and by perpetual curates after	Amesbury Priory. Post Dissolution— Successive lords of the manor.	c. 1177 Confirmation of refoundation charter of Amesbury Priory by Henry II. (VCH 1956, 244)
Netherhampton	St Katherine	Dependent chapelry	Chapel dependent on rector or abbess of Wilton. Post Dissolution— Earls of Pembroke.	
Newton Toney	St Andrew	Rectory	Successive lay patrons. Queens' College, Cambridge c. 1660.	1291 Taxatio
Nunton	St Andrew	Dependent chapelry	Chapel dependent on Downton until 1915.	
Odstock	St Mary	Rectory	Successive lay patrons.	1291 Taxatio
Orcheston	St George	Rectory	Successive lay patrons including Fitz Alan earls of Arundel c. 1420–1580.	Abortive grant to St Peter's Abbey, Gloucester before 1200. (RS 33, 1, 207–8)
Orcheston	St Mary	Rectory	Successive lay patrons. Clare College, Cambridge 1730.	1291 Taxatio
Pitton	St Peter	Dependent chapelry	Chapel dependent on Alderbury until 1874.	
Porton	St Nicholas	Dependent chapelry	Chapel dependent on Idmiston.	

Place	Modern dedication	Status	Patron	Earliest mention
Redlynch	St Birinus		Church, 1894–6, district assigned 1915.	
Redlynch	St Mary		Church, 1839, district assigned 1841.	
Rollestone	St Andrew	Rectory	Priory of St John of Jerusalem by *c.* 1300. Post Dissolution— Crown.	1291 Taxatio
Shrewton	St Mary	Vicarage	Earls of Salisbury by *c.* 1200. Appropriated by Countess Ela to Lacock Abbey 1241. Post Dissolution— Bishop of Salisbury.	1236 Grant to Lacock Abbey. (VCH 1956, 305)
South Newton	St Andrew	Vicarage	Prebend dependent on the abbess of Wilton. Appropriated to abbey 1449. Post Dissolution— Earls of Pembroke.	1291 Taxatio
Standlynch	St Mary	Dependent chapelry	Chapel dependent on Downton until joined with Charlton in separate district 1851.	1147 Agreement on tithes. (VCH 1980, 71)
Stapleford	St Mary	Vicarage by 1444	Allegedly given to Salisbury Chapter in early 12th century, but Esturmy (Seymour) by *c.* 1300. Given to Easton Priory (Wilts.) 1444 and appropriated to priory. Post Dissolution— Seymour family. Dean and Chapter of Windsor *c.* 1660.	*c.* 1130 Charter of Henry I[4] (VCH 1956, 159)
Stratford Tony	St Mary and St Lawrence	Rectory	Abbey of Lyre (Évreux) administered by priory of Wareham. Transferred as alien priory to Sheen Priory in 1414. Post Dissolution— Crown until 1560. Hyde family until 1718. College of Corpus Christi Oxford 1757.	1291 Taxatio
Tilshead	St Thomas of Canterbury	Vicarage by 1291	The king. Appropriated to Ivychurch Priory by 1291. Post Dissolution— Crown.	Domesday Book
West Dean	St Mary	Rectory	Successive lay patrons.	1291 Taxatio
West Grimstead	St John	Rectory	Successive lay patrons.	1291 Taxatio
Whiteparish	All Saints	Vicarage by 1305	College of St Edmund, Salisbury by 1339. Post Dissolution— Successive lay patrons.	1339 Grant to St Edmund's College. (VCH 1956, 386)
Wilsford	St Michael	Vicarage by *c.* 1140	Dean and Chapter of Salisbury by 1091. Appropriated to prebend by *c.* 1140. Combined with Woodford to form single prebend in gift of bishop of Salisbury by *c.* 1225. Prebend of Wilsford and Woodford.	1091 in Register of St Osmund; foundation charter of Salisbury Cathedral. (VCH 1956, 157)

Place	Modern dedication	Status	Patron	Earliest mention
Wilton	St Mary	Rectory	Abbess of Wilton. Post Dissolution— Earls of Pembroke.	1291 Taxatio
Winterbourne Dauntsey	St Edward	Vicarage	Prebend of Chute and Chisenbury by by c. 1300.	Jones 1879, 373
Winterbourne Earls	St Michael	Vicarage from 1553	Successive earls of Lincoln, Warren and Salisbury. Appropriated as prebend by Salisbury Chapter in exchange for Ratfyn prebend in 1542/5.	1291 Taxatio
Winterbourne Gunner	St Mary	Rectory	Successive lay patrons.	1291 Taxatio
Winterbourne Stoke	St Peter	Vicarage by c. 1250	The king. Abbey of Jumièges c. 1080. Administered by Hayling Priory. Given as alien priory to Sheen Priory 1416 and appropriated to it. Post Dissolution— Successive lay patrons.	Domesday Book
Winterslow	All Saints	Rectory	Given to Amesbury Priory in 1199. By 1304 belonged to lord of manor. Inherited in turn by Despenser, York, Beauchamp, Neville families.	1199 Grant by Amiria, sister of Hugh Pantulph. (VCH 1956, 245)
Woodford	All Saints	Vicarage	Appropriated to prebend by 1187. Prebend of Wilsford and Woodford.	1187 Pipe Roll. (VCH 1962, 220)

1. *Regista Regum Anglo–Normannorum*, ed. C. Johnson and H.A. Cronne (1956) **2**, no. 1291.   2. *ibid.*   3. *ibid.*
4. The charters supporting the grant (*Reg. Regum Anglo–Normannorum* **3**, no. 788 and note; *Reg. St Osmund* **1**, 201) are probably spurious.

Sources recurring under *Earliest mention*:
Domesday Book: translation of Domesday survey of Wiltshire as published in VCH *Wiltshire* **2** (1955) 113–68.
Register of St Osmund: *The Register of St Osmund*, Rolls Series [78], ed. W.H. Rich Jones, **1** (1883).
1291 Taxatio: *Taxatio Ecclesiastica Angliae et Walliae, auctoritate Papae Nicholae IV circa 1291*, eds. S. Ayscough and J. Coley (1802), Publications of Record Commission.

TABLE 2   CHURCHES AND CHAPELS DESTROYED OR DISUSED AND NOT INCLUDED IN THE SURVEY

Monastic churches or chapels	Amesbury: Fontevraultine priory church of St Mary and St Melor. Wilton: Benedictine nunnery church of St Edith; Dominican Friary★; Hospital of St Giles; Hospital of St Mary Magdalene.
Parish churches	West Dean, Hants: All Saints Wilton: St Edward; St Mary (West Street); Holy Trinity; St Michael (Kingsbury); St Michael (South Street); St Nicholas (West Street); St Nicholas in Atrio. St Peter, Bulbridge; St Andrew, Ditchampton; St James, Washern.
Free chapels[1]	Abbeston (St James), Whiteparish; Asserton★, Berwick St James; Barn Court★, Whiteparish; Chitterne All Saints (St Andrew); Lake★, Wilsford; Testwood★, Whiteparish; Whaddon★, Alderbury; Whelpley (St Leonard), Whiteparish★; Witherington, Downton.
Domestic chapels	Clarendon Palace: All Saints (principal chapel); King's chapel★; Queen's chapel★. Longford Castle★. Wilton House★.

★ Dedication unknown

1. The free chapels of Wilts. (*see* J.E. Jackson, 'Ancient Chapels, &, in Co. Wilts.', *WAM* **10**, 1867, 253–322) were subordinate buildings erected in the 12th century or later to serve outlying parts of the parish.

TABLE 3   DOCUMENTED NINETEENTH AND EARLY TWENTIETH-CENTURY RESTORATIONS

Building	Date	Cost★	Architect	Patron/Promoter	Source
ALDERBURY St Mary (new building)	1857–8	£2,500	S.S. Teulon	Cost shared between Lord Radnor, Sir Frederick Hervey-Bathurst and George Fort	DRO Faculties 6/9.
	1891	—	E. Dorran	? Lord Radnor	*Salisbury Diocesan Gaz.* Nov. 1891.
	1902–3	£720	S. Greenwood	Parish	Churchwardens' accounts 1851–1922.
	1911–12	£200	S. Gambier Perry	Lord Radnor	DRO Faculties 45/3.
ALLINGTON St John Baptist	1847–51	£1,007	F.R. Fisher	Rev. William Gray (curate-in-charge)	DRO Faculties 3/22.
AMESBURY St Mary and St Melor	1852–3	£3,220	W. Butterfield	Sir Edmund Antrobus (paid ¾ cost)	DRO Faculties 1550–30.
	1904–5	£2,500	D.B. Blow	Parish (tower and crossing)	*Wilts. County Mirror* 8 Dec. 1905.
	1907	—	C.E. Ponting	Dean & Chapter of Salisbury (chancel)	*Wilts. County Mirror* 19 Dec. 1907.
BERWICK ST JAMES St James	*c.* 1848	—	—	—	Churchwardens' Presentment 21 Dec. 1847
BRITFORD St Peter	1872–3 (plans 1869)	£2,000	G.E. Street	Parish, aided by Lord Radnor	DRO Faculties 20/10. *Salisbury and Winchester J.* 19 July 1873.
BULFORD St Leonard	1902	£300	C.E. Ponting	War Office (chancel)	*Wilts. County Mirror* 9 May 1902.
	1903–10	£840	C.E. Ponting	Parish (nave and tower)	WRO 517/25.
CHARLTON All Saints (new building)	1851 (plans 1849)	£1,500	T.H. Wyatt	Lord Nelson (in part)	ICBS Lambeth. *Builder* 9, 1851, 286.
CHITTERNE All Saints (new building)	1861–2	£1,850	T.H. Wyatt	Parish	DRO Faculties 10/19.
CHOLDERTON St Nicholas (new building)	1841–50	£5,000	T.H. Wyatt	Rev. T. Mozley (incumbent)	WRO 1293/5. Mozley 1882, 163–73.
COOMBE BISSETT St Michael	1810	£110	—	Parish, by rate	ICBS Lambeth.
	1844–5	£1,041	T.H. Wyatt	Parish, by subscription	ICBS Lambeth.
DOWNTON St Lawrence	1812–14	£700	D. Alexander	Lord Radnor (in part)	Longford Castle muniment room.
	1859–60	£2,400	T.H. Wyatt	Winchester College (chancel)	DRO Faculties 7/8, 8/17.

Building	Date	Cost*	Architect	Patron/Promoter	Source
DURNFORD St Andrew	1891	—	—	Ecclesiastical Commissioners (chancel)	*Salisbury Diocesan Gaz.* June 1891.
	1903–4	£1,300	C.E. Ponting	Parish	*Salisbury Diocesan Gaz.* Aug. 1903, Sept. 1904.
DURRINGTON All Saints	1850–1	£1,200	J.W. Hugall	Rev. R. Webb (incumbent)	DRO Faculties 4/18.
EAST GRIMSTEAD Holy Trinity (new building)	1856–8	£800–£1,000	F.H. Pownall	Glossop family	DRO Faculties 6/6.
FARLEY All Saints	1874	£600	E. Christian	Hon. Amelia Fox-Strangways (in part)	DRO Faculties 22/7.
HOMINGTON St Mary	1860	£740	T.H. Wyatt	Parish	DRO Faculties 9/2.
IDMISTON All Saints	1865–7 (plans 1857–8 and 1862–3)	£1,700	J.L. Pearson	Parish	DRO Faculties 15/9. Quiney 1979, 258.
LANDFORD St Andrew (new building)	1857–8	£1,490	W. Butterfield	Dowager Lady Nelson	DRO Faculties 7/5.
LAVERSTOCK St Andrew (new building)	1857	£1,860	T.H. Wyatt	Rev. C.H. Townsend (curate-in-charge)	DRO Faculties 7/3.
MADDINGTON St Mary	1843 (nave roof)	£96	—	—	ICBS Lambeth.
	1846–7 (nave)	£330	T.H. Wyatt	—	ICBS Lambeth.
	1853 (chancel)	—	? T.H. Wyatt	Maton family (lay impropriator)	WRO 1336/59.
NETHERHAMPTON St Katherine	1876	£1,900	W. Butterfield	Lord Pembroke (in part)	DRO Faculties 24/11.
NEWTON TONEY St Andrew (new building)	1843–4	£1,100	T.H. Wyatt	Parish	DRO Faculties 3/6.
NUNTON St Andrew	1853–4	£1,000	T.H. Wyatt	Parish	DRO Faculties 5/10.
ODSTOCK St Mary	1869 (chancel)	£220	J. Fowler	Rev. P. Miles (incumbent)	DRO Mortgages 1869, 189.
	1871–2	—	J. Fowler	Rev. P. Miles	Miles 1976, 2.
ORCHESTON St George	1833	£210	? J. Dean	Rev. G.P. Lowther (incumbent)	ICBS Lambeth.
	1858	—	—	Mills family	Tablet in church.
	1883	£180	—	Parish	DRO Faculties 29/5.
ORCHESTON St Mary	1832–3	£450	? J. Dean	Rev. E.T. Bidwell (incumbent)	ICBS Lambeth.
	1865 (plans 1860)	£250	—	Parish	DRO Faculties 14/3.

Building	Date	Cost*	Architect	Patron/Promoter	Source
PITTON St Peter	1879–80	£1,500	E. Christian	Lord Ilchester (gave ⅓)	DRO Faculties 27/6.
PORTON St Nicholas (new building)	1876–7	£1,467	J.L. Pearson	Parish	DRO Faculties 24/17.
REDLYNCH St Birinus (new building)	1894–6	£2,000	C.E. Ponting	Bequest from Rev. E.A. Ferryman (local landowner)	Redlynch church chest: memo of 28 Sept. 1894.
REDLYNCH St Mary (new building)	1835–7	£1,611	? J. Dean	Rev. L. Clarke (vicar of Downton)	ICBS Lambeth.
SHREWTON St Mary	1854–5	£1,900	T.H. Wyatt	Parish	DRO Faculties 5/13.
SOUTH NEWTON St Andrew	1821–2	£350	—	Parish rate and Lord Pembroke	ICBS Lambeth.
	1861–2	£1,500	T.H. Wyatt	Lord Pembroke and Lady Herbert of Lea	DRO Faculties 10/15.
STANDLYNCH St Mary	1846	—	(?) T.H. Wyatt	Lord Nelson	*Ecclesiologist* **6**, 1846, 195.
	c. 1860	—	W. Butterfield	Lord Nelson	Thompson 1971, 407–8.
STAPLEFORD St Mary	1861	£970	W. Slater	Lord Ashburton and H. Danby Seymour (gave ½)	DRO Faculties 10/17.
	1869 (chancel)	—	E. Christian	Ecclesiastical Commissioners	Church notes.
TILSHEAD St Thomas of Canterbury	1845–6	£700	T.H. Wyatt	Rev. J.H. Johnson (incumbent)	DRO Faculties 3/12.
WEST DEAN Evelyn Chapel	1868	£350	J. Crook	William Evelyn	WRO 120/21.
WEST DEAN St Mary (new building)	1864–6	£2,578	F.H. Pownall	Thomas Baring (gave site and £1,000)	WRO 120/29.
WEST GRIMSTEAD St John	c. 1835	—	—	(?) Hervey-Bathurst family	Colt Hoare 1837, 204.
WHITEPARISH All Saints	1869 (excluding chancel)	£1,900	W. Butterfield	Dowager Lady Nelson (in part)	DRO Faculties 18/2.
WILSFORD St Michael	1856–7	£1,600	T.H. Wyatt	Giles Loder (impropriate rector)	DRO Faculties 6/15.
WILTON St Mary and St Nicholas (new building)	1841–5	£30,000 (fabric alone)	T.H. Wyatt	Hon. Sidney Herbert and Dowager Lady Pembroke	Gordon 1906, 99. *Salisbury and Winchester J.* 11 Oct. 1845.
WILTON St Mary	1871–2	—	—	—	*Salisbury and Winchester J.* 6 Jan. 1872.

Building	Date	Cost*	Architect	Patron/Promoter	Source
WILTON St Peter, Fugglestone	1840	£205	J.H. Hakewill	Lord Pembroke and William Woodcock (churchwarden)	WRO 930/15.
WINTERBOURNE EARLS St Michael (new building)	1867–8	£3,100	T.H. Wyatt	Parish	DRO Faculties 16/4.
WINTERBOURNE STOKE St Peter	1838–9	£580	T. Crook	Lord Ashburton (chancel)	ICBS Lambeth.
	1880–1	£930	W. Crook	Lord Ashburton (gave ¾)	Memo in church baptism register 1813–97.
WINTERSLOW All Saints	1849–50	£1,500	T.H. Wyatt	Rev. E. Luard (incumbent)	DRO Faculties 4/4.
WOODFORD All Saints	1845	£1,500	T.H. Wyatt	Rev. R.M. Chatfield (incumbent) and Giles Loder (lay impropriator; gave ⅓)	ICBS Lambeth.

* Where sources disagree on cost, the figure given is the highest.

TABLE 4   ROMANESQUE ORNAMENT

	Beading	Chevron (vertical)	Chevron (sawtooth)	Dogtooth	Lozenge	Mask	Star	Zigzag
Doorways	Allington (fragment)	Winterbourne Stoke (N side)	Allington (fragment)	Coombe Bissett	Allington (fragment)	Durnford (N side)	Landford	Winterbourne Stoke (S side)
	Durnford (S side)		Berwick St James	Stapleford	Berwick St James	South Newton	South Newton	
	Woodford		Durnford (2: N and S sides)		Durnford (2: N and S sides)	Stapleford	Winterbourne Stoke (2: N and S sides)	
			Laverstock		Durrington			
			Stapleford		Landford			
			Woodford		Winterbourne Earls			
					Winterbourne Stoke			
					Woodford			
Arcade or chancel arches	Allington		Durnford Stapleford	Stapleford		Stapleford	Nunton	

88

TYPOLOGIES
(names are italicised where the feature in question has disappeared and followed by a
question mark if the form of the original feature has been obscured)

TABLE 5   ROMANESQUE DOORWAYS (*see* pp. 16–17)

Open tympana	Coombe Bissett; Durrington (?); Landford; Orcheston St George (?); Stapleford; Wilsford; *Winterbourne Earls*; Winterbourne Stoke, N side **174, 393, 177, 524, 176**
Closed tympana	Berwick St James, N side; Durnford, (2) N and S sides; South Newton; Winterbourne Stoke, S side; Woodford **173, 571, 441, 176**
Roll-moulded arches	Landford; Stratford Tony (?); *Winterbourne Earls*; Winterbourne Stoke, S side **174, 17, 524, 176**
Arches of chevron	Berwick St James, N side; Durnford, (2) N and S sides; Laverstock; Stapleford; Winterbourne Stoke, N side; Woodford **173, 571, 358, 177, 176, 175**

173. Berwick St James: N doorway.

174. Landford: Romanesque N doorway, reset in present church.

175. Woodford: S doorway.

176. Winterbourne Stoke: N doorway (L) before addition of N porch and S doorway (R), *Buckler* 1805.

177. Stapleford: S doorway.

TABLE 6   MEDIEVAL FONTS (*see* pp. 17–18, 41)

Tub	*Netherhampton*; West Dean; West Grimstead; Wilton, St John's Hospital; Winterbourne Gunner; Winterslow **18, 470, 497, 180, 178**
Deep bowl and roll	Boscombe; Newton Toney; *Shrewton*; Winterbourne Stoke **110, 379, 179, 535**
Shallow bowl and roll	Pitton; Rollestone; Stratford Tony **409–10, 182, 181**
Straight-sided bowl	Allington; Berwick St James; Odstock **183, 235, 6**
Bowl with decorated sides	Chitterne St Mary; Durnford; Stapleford; Tilshead **265, 571, 184, 185**
Bowl with decorated base	Cholderton **279**
Table	Bulford **186**
Table with blind arches	Amesbury; Downton **231**
Round table with moulded bowl and shafts for base	Coombe Bissett **187**
Polygonal bowl with shafted base	South Newton
Polygonal bowl	Idmiston; *Maddington* **188, 367**
Polygonal bowl with decorated panels	*Wilton, St Mary*; Woodford **189, 190**
Polygonal bowl with rounded base	*Chitterne All Saints*; Nunton; Wilsford; Winterbourne Earls **191, 192, 527**
Polygonal bowl with chamfered base	*Durrington*; Laverstock; Porton **193, 195, 194**

178. Winterslow.
179. Shrewton: *Buckler c.* 1805.
180. Winterbourne Gunner.
181. Stratford Tony.
182. Rollestone.
183. Allington.

178

179

180

181

182

183

184

185

186

187

188

189

190

191

192

193

194

195

TABLE 7   ROMANESQUE ARCADES AND ARCHES (*see* p. 14)

Romanesque arcades	Rectangular piers with imposts	Fugglestone (?); Nunton, chancel aisle; Tilshead; Winterslow, S arcade **329, 12, 13, 544**
	Round piers with square capitals	Coombe Bissett; Downton; Shrewton, S respond; Stapleford; Wilton, St John's Hospital; Winterbourne Gunner (now with later, polygonal shaft) **15, 197, 530**
	Round piers and round capitals	Durrington; Ivychurch; Whiteparish; Winterslow, N arcade **343–4, 14, 544**
Tower or chancel arches	With imposts	Allington; Bulford; Nunton; Wilsford **222, 102, 12**
	With imposts and order	Durnford **304**

196. Coombe Bissett: S arcade from N.

197. Stapleford: interior looking E, showing Romanesque arcade.

92

TABLE 8   Piscinae, Recesses and Stoups (piscinae unless otherwise stated) (*see* pp. 20–21)

Round headed	Durrington, S aisle; Nunton, S aisle **12**
Chamfered two-centred arch	Amesbury (twin openings, two drains); Coombe Bissett (twin openings, one drain); Durrington; Homington, chancel; Idmiston, chancel; Maddington; *Winterbourne Dauntsey* **229, 230, 519**
Trefoil with pointed lobes	Berwick St James; Shrewton; Stapleford [recess]; Stratford Tony; West Grimstead; Wilton, St John's Hospital; Woodford **199, 200, 456, 28, 461, 547**
Trefoil with round lobes	Bulford [piscina and stoup]; Downton, N transept; Durnford [stoup]; Idmiston, N aisle; Odstock; *Winterbourne Dauntsey* [stoup]; Winterbourne Stoke, S transept **519**
Cinquefoil with round lobes	*Winterbourne Dauntsey* **519**
'Double decker'	Fugglestone; West Dean; Winterbourne Stoke (?) **201, 45, 471**
Simple ogee	Britford, N aisle; Homington, N aisle **202**
Ogee trefoil	Britford, S transept; Stapleford, S transept; Stapleford, chancel; Tilshead, S aisle **43, 43, 203**
Triangular head	Amesbury, S aisle [stoup]; Idmiston, S aisle
Round-lobed trefoil under hood mould	Amesbury, S aisle **204**
Sill	Orcheston St George; Pitton **29**
Pillar	Allington
Angle	Wilton, St Mary

198   **199**   **200**   **201**

202   **203**   **204**

198. Maddington: piscina, chancel.
199. Berwick St James: piscina, S chapel.
200. Shrewton: piscina, chancel.
201. Fugglestone: 'double decker' piscina and aumbry, chancel.
202. Britford: piscina, N transept.
203. Tilshead: piscina, S aisle.
204. Amesbury: piscina, S aisle.

Arcading	Britford (with trees); Chitterne St Mary (with simple fronds); Durnford (dated 1619); Durrington (with figures); Farley; Wilton, St Mary (with trees and dated 1628) **254, 208, 307, 312, 320, 207**
Pie	Boscombe (dated 1633) **242**
Symmetrical foliage	Odstock (dated 1580); West Grimstead; Winterbourne Earls (formerly Imber); Winterbourne Stoke **206, 480 523, 205**
Fielded panelling	Stratford Tony **460**

The pulpits of Chitterne All Saints and Winterbourne Dauntsey (both destroyed) were also carved.

205

206

207

208

205. Winterbourne Stoke: pulpit (base largely 19th century).
206. Odstock: pulpit (19th-century base).
207. Wilton, St Mary: pulpit and sounding-board, now in Wylye church.
208. Chitterne: pulpit formerly in St Mary's, now in All Saints (19th-century base).
209. Berwick St James: Communion rails.
210. Rollestone: Communion rails and 17th-century Communion table incorporating 19th-century carved panels.

TABLE 10	SEVENTEENTH-CENTURY COMMUNION RAILS
Balusters	Alderbury (?); Berwick St James; *Chitterne St Mary*; Farley; Fugglestone; Rollestone; Tilshead; Winterbourne Stoke **209, 88, 327, 210**
Baluster and splat	Durnford; Maddington; Wilton, St Mary **211, 212, 501**
Splat	Bulford; *Chitterne All Saints*; *Winterbourne Earls* **74, 528**
With 'pawn' finials	Berwick St James; Durnford; Stratford Tony; Wilton, St Mary **209, 211, 462, 501**

209

211. Durnford: Communion rails.

212. Maddington: former Communion rails, now screen.

210

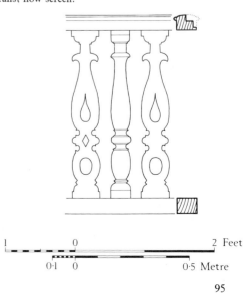

Building	Subject and Date	Illustration	Condition	Literature
ALLINGTON St John Baptist	St Christopher on N wall of nave, opposite S door: 15th-century	None	Disappeared by mid 19th century	Parish notes of 1867 (compiled for Rev. J. Wilkinson), Devizes Museum
AMESBURY St Mary and St Melor	Single figure, ? St Melor, on *c.* 1500 strengthening of SW crossing pier. Probably uncovered *c.* 1905	One in church guide book by E.J. Windley (q.v.)	Barely visible	Windley 1917, 26
BERWICK ST JAMES St James	Ascension on E wall: ? 13th-century	None	No longer visible	Tristram 1950, 506
BOSCOMBE St Andrew	Black-letter text on N wall of nave: 16th-century	RCHM photograph	Adequate	
BULFORD St Leonard	Extensive remains on W face chancel arch, including 14th-century female saint's head and 18th-century Commandment tables	RCHM photograph	Reasonable	
	Fragment of black-letter text on S wall chancel: 16th-century	RCHM photograph	Reasonable	
DOWNTON St Lawrence	Throughout church 'traces of red and yellow wall painting of slight execution but good taste', discovered in 1860 restoration: date unknown	RCHM photograph	Covered up or destroyed, except for fragment on the W wall of the N transept exposed in 1983 and consisting of masonry-outlining and a border of foliage	Parish notes of 1861, Devizes Museum
	? The Nativity, discovered 1890: date unknown	Reputed to be in parish magazine of December 1890	Covered up or destroyed	Parish magazine for 1890 (not traced)
DURNFORD St Andrew	Foliage on walls of nave: 12th or 13th-century	RCHM photograph	Reasonable	Salmon 1939, 144–6
	Masonry-outlining and crocket flourishes on E wall chancel: 13th-century	RCHM photograph	Worn	
	Decorative painting around rood stair and over chancel arch: 15th-century	RCHM photograph	Worn	
	St Christopher, to E of nave S door: 15th-century	RCHM photograph	Worn	
DURRINGTON All Saints	Very large figure of St Christopher on N wall nave: 15th-century	Drawing in MS account of 1850/1 restoration by J.W. Hugall	Destroyed in 1850	Jackson 1862, 357 Ponting 1904, 287
IDMISTON All Saints 213	St Christopher, found 1866 on S wall of S aisle: 15th-century	Watercolour of *c.* 1866 by R.C. Kemm (copies at Devizes and Salisbury museums)	Probably destroyed in 1867	

213. Idmiston: wall painting of St Christopher, formerly on S wall, *Kemm* 1866.

Building	Subject and Date	Illustration	Condition	Literature
IVYCHURCH Ivychurch Priory	Last Supper on E wall refectory: 13th-century	Tracings (now lost) made and exhibited at Soc. of Antiq. London Coloured drawings now in Salisbury Museum (RCHM photograph)	Destroyed 1889	Nightingale 1891b, 352–5
PITTON St Peter	St George: date unknown	None	Destroyed c. 1880	Colt Hoare 1837, 207 Keyser 1883, 321
STAPLEFORD St Mary **215**	Foliage painting in soffits of Romanesque S arcade: 13th-century	RCHM photograph	Reasonable	
WEST DEAN St Mary (old church)	Masonry-outlining in chancel and nave arcades: ? 13th-century	RCHM photograph of nave arcade painting	Chancel painting destroyed c. 1867. Fragment in nave arcade revealed and visible	Master 1885, 287
WILSFORD St Michael	St Christopher, uncovered c. 1830 (2 successive versions painted on top of each other): late medieval	Engraving in Duke (1837)	Probably destroyed 1856	Duke 1837, 560–7
	St Michael and the Devil	None	Probably destroyed 1856	Duke 1837, 568
	St George and the Dragon	None	Probably destroyed 1856	Duke 1837, 568
WINTERBOURNE DAUNTSEY St Edward **42, 214**	Virtually complete cycle of Life of Christ: 13th-century	Photographs survive but tracings (formerly in Salisbury Museum) now lost	Destroyed 1867	Borenius 1932, 397–401
WINTERBOURNE EARLS St Michaels	God the Father and the Son, over inner S door: said to be Norman	None	Destroyed 1867	Borenius 1932, 402–4
	On N wall nave, St Christopher, and St Michael, also, decorative painting on chancel window splay: probably late medieval	None	Destroyed 1867	Borenius 1932, 402–4
WINTERBOURNE GUNNER St Mary	Extensive remains, mainly of texts, around chancel arch and on N wall of nave: 16th to 18th-century	RCHM photograph	Only some by chancel arch exposed	
WINTERSLOW All Saints	Last Judgement over W face chancel arch: probably late medieval	Drawings and an engraving made in 1849 (copy in Devizes Museum)	Destroyed in 1850	Ponting 1910, 19
	Masonry-outlining in chancel window splay: probably 13th-century	Visible in watercolour of 1849 by John Luard	Destroyed in 1850	
WOODFORD All Saints	St Christopher, discovered in 1845 restoration on N wall: probably late medieval	None	Almost certainly destroyed c. 1845.	Parish notes of 1861, Devizes Museum

214. Winterbourne Dauntsey: wall painting of the Resurrection and the Harrowing of Hell, photographed before destruction in 1867 (*see* also 42).

215. Stapleford: decorative painting in soffit of nave arcade arch.

216. Exterior from W.

DESCRIPTIVE ACCOUNTS OF INDIVIDUAL BUILDINGS

ALDERBURY

St Mary   SU 182269   *Civil Parish of Alderbury*

The present church was built in 1857 to the designs of S.S. Teulon at the joint expense of Lord Radnor of Longford Castle, Sir Frederick Hervey-Bathurst of Clarendon Park and George Fort of Alderbury House. The exterior is of uncoursed and unknapped flint rubble with Bath stone dressings and heathstone voussoirs to the windows, the interior is of brick with voussoirs in red, white and black. The style of the detailing is Middle Pointed, with Geometrical tracery in the windows and naturalistic carving of the roof corbels and the capitals of the chancel arch. In 1891 the sanctuary was redecorated with rich tile and mosaic work; the chancel and the W end were re-arranged in 1912 by S. Gambier Parry. In 1902–3 the church was extensively repaired (*see* Table 3).

The former church, which occupied the same site, consisted at time of demolition of a nave, perhaps early medieval in origin, a chancel with Perpendicular windows, a stump of a W tower with a weatherboarded belfry and a post-Reformation S porch.

Teulon's original fittings include a stone pulpit with small mosaic inlays and a polygonal font with traceried sides. The Communion rails are made up from the cresting of the screen designed by G.G. Scott for Salisbury Cathedral in 1870 and removed from there a century later. The balustered rails of 17th/18th-century style, in front of the choir stalls, are too long to have been used as Communion rails in the former chancel and were probably introduced by Gambier Parry. Definitely from the old church are the pair of coffin stools inscribed with the date 1778, the simple 17th-century panelling (from a former pew) now used to screen off the tower vestry, and two stone tablets. The first tablet, now polychrome, bears the date 1612 and the arms (incorrectly painted) and initials of Richard Goldstone and his wife Margaret (*née* Ryves). The second is a memorial to Thomas Stringer and his wife Jane (+ 1702, + 1740) and is in the form of a shaped tablet with decorative border in sunk relief. The stained glass includes windows of *c.* 1857 by Hardman, in the S 'transept', and of *c.* 1879 by Halliday, in the sanctuary.

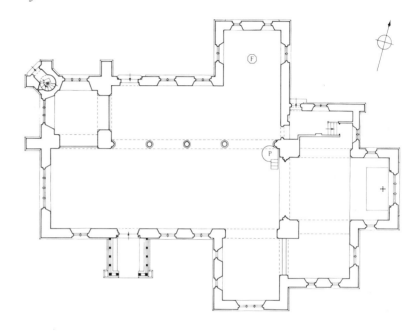

10   0   10   20   30   40   50   60 *Feet*

Metres *1* 0   5   10   15   20   **217**

218. Interior looking E.

ALLINGTON

St John the Baptist   su 204395   *Civil Parish of Allington*

The church was rebuilt according to a faculty plan dated 1847, but not reconsecrated until 1851. The plans were by F.R. Fisher of Salisbury but the main responsibility for the rebuilding lay with the curate, William Grey, who scrupulously reproduced all the detailing of the original fabric except for the tower, where the timber belfry was replaced by masonry. The walls of the church are of coursed knapped flint irregularly chequered with freestone. Dressings are of freestone.

Evidence for the existence of a Romanesque church on the site includes the imposts of the chancel arch, which are continued on the W face as a decorative band as far as the side walls of the nave, and the fragment of a decorated arch, perhaps of a doorway, now built into the N wall of the nave. Until 1850 the church was essentially of the 13th century, with lancet side-windows, a pillar piscina and a sedile in the chancel. The E window and the doorways and windows of the nave were, however, Perpendicular.

The font, a replica of the original, has a round bowl decorated with blind arcading in shallow relief; the carved and pierced cover is mid 19th century. In the E reveal of the chancel SW window is a stone recess, possibly a credence shelf. Wooden furnishings comprise a 16th-century plank chest and a 17th-century oak bench with simply moulded ends. The major Victorian feature of the church is the painted decoration of the chancel, of *c.* 1876.

220

222   **221**

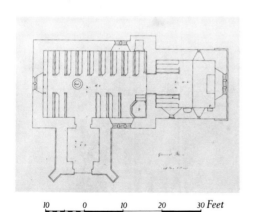

219

219. Plan from faculty, 1847.
220. Exterior from SE.
221. Exterior from SE, *Buckler* 1805.
222. Interior looking E.

AMESBURY

ST MARY AND ST MELOR   SU 152414   *Civil Parish of Amesbury*

The problems concerning the relationship of the church to the Saxon Benedictine abbey of Amesbury and to its successor, the priory of the Order of Fontrevault founded by Henry II, are discussed in Appendix 1. No pre-Conquest masonry has been traced in the fabric of the present building, although preserved in the church are two Saxon cross-heads the larger of which was discovered under the chancel floor in 1907. The 12th-century nave is of its original width and height; it was probably always unaisled. The crossing, transept and chancel are of one mid 13th-century design and build; the earlier plan of the eastern part of the church is unknown but may well have been cruciform. There were three transeptual chapels; one on the S, and on the N two, the northernmost of which still survives. In the first quarter of the 14th century two four-light traceried windows were inserted in the chancel; in the late 15th century a S aisle was added and the existing church remodelled with large Perpendicular E and W windows and new roofs and furnishings. In 1721 the S front of the S transept was given Classical round-headed windows and doorway but otherwise the church remained substantially unaltered until the restoration of 1852–3 by William Butterfield, when most of the post 14th-century work in the church, including all the furnishings and monuments, was removed. A heating chamber (now demolished) and a stair-tower were built in the angle between chancel and N transept, and new furnishings provided. In the early 20th century the architects C.E. Ponting and Detmar Blow undertook a further fundamental restoration not only in order to repair the roofs and the floors, but also to underpin and ventilate the foundations and to rebuild the piers of the crossing and the S aisle. Some of the furnishings removed from the

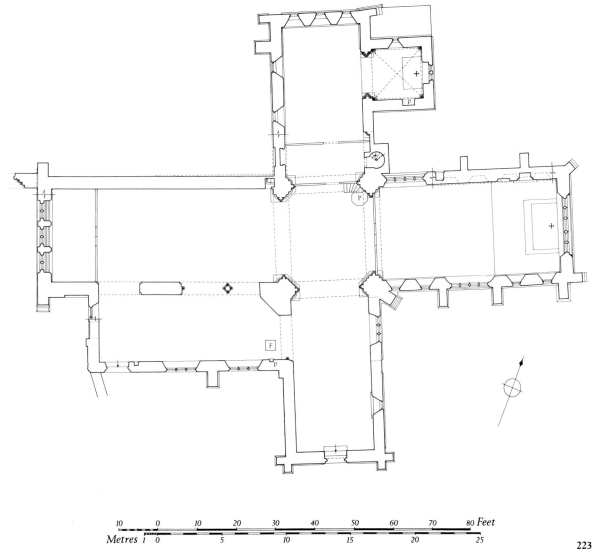

10   0   10   20   30   40   50   60   70   80 Feet

Metres 1 0   5   10   15   20   25

223

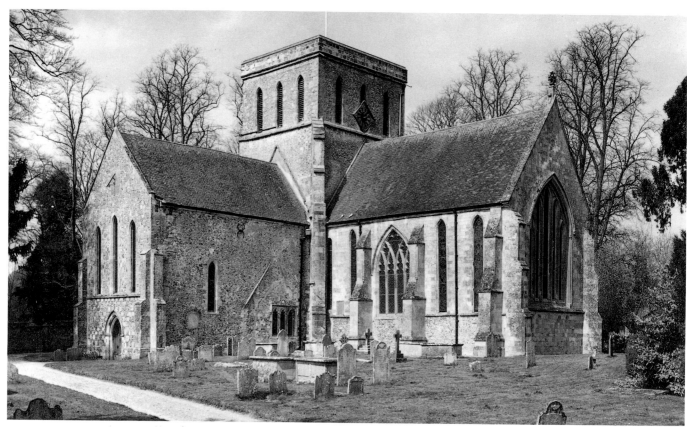

224.   Exterior from SE (*see* also 130).

225.   Exterior from NE.

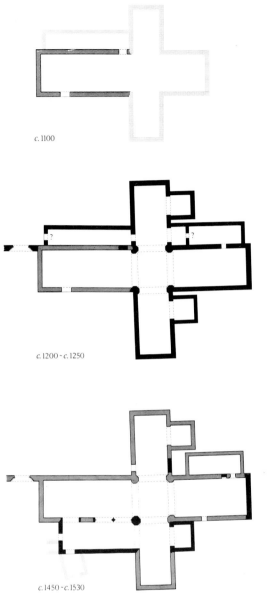

c. 1100

c. 1200 - c. 1250

c. 1450 - c. 1530

226.   Development.

orders and a pinnacled canopy above, enclosing a trefoil; some of the detail is Victorian. The building to the N was presumably used as a vestry, at least in part; an aumbry belonging to it survives in the outer face of the N wall of the chancel. The two four-light Decorated windows in the side walls of the chancel have fully developed tracery, reticulated in the N window and of dagger form in the S (*see* p.28). The late medieval roof, which resembled that of the nave, was replaced in 1852. The only part of the Perpendicular E window to survive is the pair of corbels that served as stops to its hood-mould and which now support a credence table. They are in the form of half-length angels, each clad in contemporary clothes and bearing a shield. The stained glass depicting a crowned female saint, now in the traceried N window, dates from the 15th century and may have come from the former E window.

The crossing and crossing tower are of the same 13th-century build. The crossing is spacious: each of its four arches is of three chamfered orders the inner of which springs from triple shafts with a single moulded capital. The low tower, although completely reconstructed in the early 20th century, has the same external appearance it had when Buckler drew it in 1803.

The transepts still have their original lancet windows except for those in the S wall of the S transept, reconstructed in the mid 19th century (*WAM* **17**, 1876, 16). Roofs of both transepts are of the ceiled wagon form and date from *c.* 1500, but the carved detail differs: the N transept roof has figures of angels on the wall plate and bosses with foliate crosses on the rib intersections; the S transept roof has similar bosses but more elaborate figures on the wall plate, including crowned heads and a man-eating monster.

The chapel on the E side of the N transept has a richly traceried two-light window of *c.* 1300 in the E gable, although the chapel as a whole appears to

church in 1852 were reinstated. Further repair, especially of roofs, has been necessary since the Second World War.

The chancel is mostly ashlar but the body of the church is of flint rubble with stone dressings (the S aisle has some brick tile mixed at random with the flint work).

The chancel is substantially Early English. The lancet windows in the side walls are original, but those in the E wall are of 1853. The lower parts of the lancet windows in the N wall are blocked where a building formerly abutted. This building was entered from the chancel through a small contemporary doorway to the W, which has a hood-mould and stiff-leaf stops, and through a larger and more elaborate doorway of *c.* 1300 near the E end. The latter doorway has an arch of three

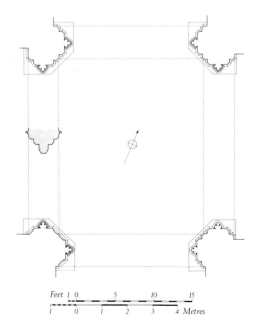

Feet 1 0   5   10   15

1   0   1   2   3   4 Metres

227.   Plan of crossing with arch profile.

228. Base of Romanesque respond now embedded in N wall of nave.

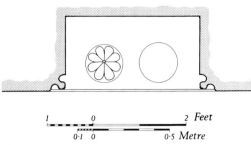
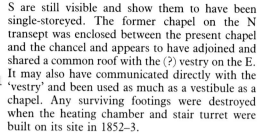

229. Plan of double piscina in N transept chapel.

date from *c.* 1250: possibly the building has been heightened. The chapel has a quadripartite stone vault carried on angle-shafts with stiff-leaf capitals to the E and moulded capitals to the W. The double piscina has a hood-mould and stiff-leaf stops similar to those of the adjacent arch to the S. The chapel was restored for use as a vestry in 1852 and again in 1910 when it was refitted for worship (Windley 1917, 24). The openings to two further chapels that formerly flanked the chancel to N and

S are still visible and show them to have been single-storeyed. The former chapel on the N transept was enclosed between the present chapel and the chancel and appears to have adjoined and shared a common roof with the (?) vestry on the E. It may also have communicated directly with the 'vestry' and been used as much as a vestibule as a chapel. Any surviving footings were destroyed when the heating chamber and stair turret were built on its site in 1852–3.

The nave is of the second quarter of the 12th century. The base mouldings of the respond at the E end of the N wall, discovered in 1905 (*Wilts. County Mirror* 8 Dec. 1905), suggest an earlier date, but the relatively tall, wide clearstorey windows, blocked in the course of the 15th-century reconstruction, confirm the later dating. Corbel tables carved with beasts and grotesque heads run along both N and S walls. The presence of a clearstorey on both sides of the nave and the existence of the respond in the N wall have been taken as evidence of an aisled nave. However, the slight form of the respond and its position indicate that it belonged not to an arcade but to a single arch giving access to a lean-to building (the roof crease is still visible on the external face of the N wall of the nave and the W wall of the N transept) that was a subsidiary structure, not an aisle integral with the church. If there had been a Romanesque aisle on the S side, it would be strange if it were not re-used, at least in part, in the 15th-century S aisle. The plan of a wide unaisled nave lit from windows set high in the walls can be found in other local churches such as Durnford.

Nave, like chancel, was transformed in the 15th century when a new W window was inserted and a new roof constructed. The window was replaced in 1852 by one designed by Butterfield, but the elaborately decorated five-bay arch-braced roof survives: the spandrels between the transverse members of each truss are filled with tracery and the longitudinal members are all moulded; the corbels supporting the wall posts are of wood painted to resemble stone and are carved with heads; there are figurative and foliage designs along the wall plate and on the bosses. At the external NW angle of the nave is the E part of a portal of four recessed orders with stiff-leaf capitals of *c.* 1200. Although it was not moved when the W wall was largely rebuilt in 1852, its original relationship to the church is obscure; limited excavations to the W which took place in 1920 and 1978 have revealed foundations of walling but it is not clear to what buildings or to what date they belonged. Possibly the portal formed an entrance to an outer court of the priory precinct.

The late 15th-century S aisle appears to have been built as a new, virtually autonomous, structure. It has its own entrance and communicates

230. Interior of N transept chapel, looking E, showing rib vault and double piscina.

with the nave only through a two-bay arcade towards the E end and a single arch towards the W end. The NE corner of the aisle was blocked by a solid wall at an early stage, presumably to buttress the SW pier of the crossing. The arches to the aisle each have two hollow-chamfered orders and are borne by polygonal capitals ornamented with a double row of fleurons. The roof is of the ceiled wagon type with carved wooden bosses repainted in 1958. Three original fittings survive in the S wall: the SW door itself; a stoup by the E jamb of the W door, now containing a crowned female head from a 14th-century image or effigy; and, further to the E, a shallow trefoil-headed piscina with a credence shelf under a rounded hood-mould. The porch in front of the SW doorway was removed in the Victorian restoration; it appears to have been of late medieval or later date. In the W wall of the aisle the presence of a blocked doorway, and stubs of projecting masonry and a roof scar on the exterior, suggests that in the early 16th century an extension to the W, possibly including a turret, was begun but never completed.

The font has a square Purbeck bowl of *c.* 1200 decorated with blind arcading and resting on a late medieval square base with traceried panels on the sides. The font, recorded in this form by Buckler, was broken up in 1852 and only reinstated in 1907. The 15th-century chancel screen with moulded panelling below and traceried lights above, was likewise removed in 1852 and reinstated in 1907. In the S transept is preserved a 15th-century clock (recently returned to the church, where it had been in use until 1919) together with various pieces of medieval stonework excavated in 1860 to the N of the present mansion-house, on the site of the former priory. Almost all other fittings and monuments were destroyed in the 1852 restoration. Amongst the monuments retrieved, like the font, from under the chancel floor in 1907 is an inscribed brass plate of *c.* 1470, a large plain tablet of 1683 and a ceramic tile of *c.* 1755 commemorating an infant. Butterfield designed a complete array of fittings and furnishings, most of which survive, but his decoration of the E wall in marble and polychrome tiling is now concealed. On the N wall of the nave hangs a 19th-century hatchment to Sir Edmund Antrobus (+ 1870) and at the E end of the S aisle is a painting of the Crucifixion, perhaps Spanish and of the 17th century.

232. Mid and late 13th-century doorways (now blocked) at E end of N wall, chancel.

233

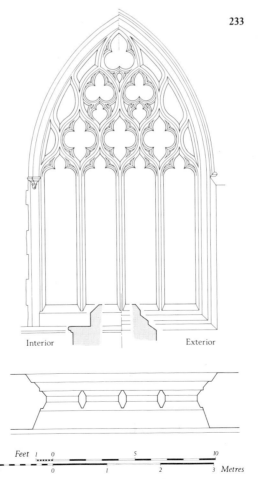

Interior　Exterior

231

231. Font, reinstated 1907.
233. Elevation and section of Decorated window on N side chancel.

Feet 1 0 5 10
1 0 1 2 3 Metres

234

236

235

234. Exterior from NE.
235. 13th-century font.
236. Interior looking E.

BERWICK ST JAMES

St James   su 072392   *Civil Parish of Berwick St James*

The nave of the church is Romanesque and preserves the two original N and S doorways. A chapel was added to the N in the early 13th century and rebuilt in the 15th century except for the arch to the nave. The chancel is mid 13th century but the continuously moulded chancel and tower arches are probably a century later. There was a major Perpendicular remodelling of the nave which involved the insertion of a clearstorey (defined externally by a broad, moulded string-course above and below the windows) and the construction of an arch-braced roof. A S chapel may have existed *c.* 1200 but the present structure was added shortly before the Reformation. The porch was built in the early 17th century; later in the century the medieval W tower fell and was rebuilt in 1670, still in a Gothic style (*see* below). The church was restored *c.* 1848.

The chancel and the lower parts of the nave are of flint rubble with freestone dressings. The nave clearstorey is ashlar, the side chapels, porch and tower are of chequered flint.

The original 13th-century features of the chancel remain almost intact, including lancet windows, symmetrically arranged in the side walls and stepped in the E wall, and an internal string-course broken to the W by two tall, thin lancets with trefoiled heads, of *c.* 1300. In their E reveals are small niches with chamfered and stopped jambs and slightly ogee heads, which might have been piscinae or recesses for lamps. The chancel roof is Victorian.

The nave is Romanesque in the lower, outward-leaning parts of the walls. The 15th-century addition of the clearstorey was built plumb. The S doorway is plain but the N doorway has shafts with scalloped capitals supporting an arch of a single order decorated with saw-tooth chevron. Carved decoration in the tympanum is confined to the lintel, but the courses of stone above are in contrasting greensand and buff stone as are the voussoirs of the arch. The door-opening was heightened and the lower part of the lintel cut away in the 19th century. On the N side of the nave, above and to the E of the arch to the N chapel, there was formerly a doorway to the rood loft, possibly re-used in part for the present doorway below. The opening of the W of the N chapel arch was intended for access to the 15th-century polygonal stone pulpit, which projected from the N wall of the nave until it was moved in the 19th century to the S side of the chancel arch and given additional mouldings. The 15th-century arch-braced roof was also restored in the 19th century; the wall posts stand on boldly carved head corbels.

The N chapel is plain except for the early 13th-century arch to the nave, which has a border

of dog-tooth on its S face and springs from simply-moulded imposts. The S chapel is even simpler and externally appears a late addition, but the presence of a piscina in the S wall shows it must antedate the Reformation. The arch to the nave is round headed and has imposts similar to those of the N chapel arch, but its width and arc suggest a rebuilding of *c.* 1600 rather than an original work of the 12th century.

The N porch is of *c.* 1600; in spite of its height it appears never to have had an upper storey. The W tower has an inscription under the parapet at the NW angle bearing the date 1670. The former tower, perhaps of the 14th century, had collapsed about thirty years before (Churchwardens' Presentment, Oct. 1662). The form of the new tower remains medieval although the heads of the windows are rounded and uncusped.

The two major medieval fittings are the pulpit and the 13th-century font, which has a plain round bowl and a water-holding base, probably original, to its stem. No trace remains of the medieval wall painting of the Ascension around the E window, recorded in the 19th century. A panelled chest, the Communion table and the Communion rails with principal balusters supported on long claw feet and prolonged above the rail into finials, survive from the 17th century. On either side of the E window is an early 19th-century pair of tablets by Osmond. In the E window of the chancel is stained glass by Burlison and Grylls, of *c.* 1873. Also in the chancel is a finely engraved memorial brass to Emma Lakin (+ 1873).

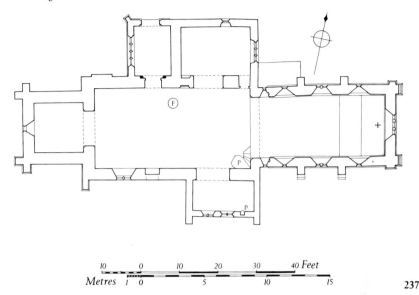

237

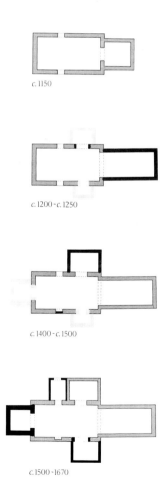

c. 1150

c. 1200 - *c.* 1250

c. 1400 - *c.* 1500

c. 1500 - 1670

238. Development.

239. Exterior from S.
240. Interior looking E.

BOSCOMBE

St Andrew   su 201386   *Civil Parish of Allington*

The plan of the church and part of the fabric may be of 12th-century origin but the only feature certainly of that date is the font. The nave windows and the chancel roof date from *c.* 1500; otherwise the present appearance of the building is largely the result of 17th and 18th-century contributions. A transverse N aisle was added *c.* 1600 and the pulpit installed thirty years later. In a major restoration of 1709 the church was refitted and repaved, the pulpit moved to its present position and a window inserted to light it. The E wall and window were rebuilt in 1755.

The building is of knapped flint rubble with stone dressings, with some use of brick in the E wall and N aisle.

The three-light E window of the chancel, although rebuilt in 1755, has a late medieval form, but the cusping of the heads of the lights is modern. The side windows are mullioned and straight headed. The four-centred N doorway is similar to the E doorway of the N aisle; both are probably of the early 17th century. The chancel roof is of ceiled wagon type with heavily moulded tie beams of *c.* 1500; the plaster was removed in the early 20th century.

The nave is lit by Perpendicular windows, each with two trefoiled lights, and an 18th-century casement window by the pulpit. The S doorway, of greensand and with a round arch, may be Romanesque but must be reset since it lacks any moulding beyond a narrow chamfer; it is also uncharacteristically central to the S wall. The 19th-century roof replaces one of ceiled wagon form.

The N aisle, of *c.* 1600, was built transverse to the nave. It is lit by a five-light mullioned and

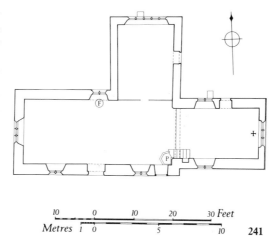

10   0   10   20   30 *Feet*

Metres 1   0   5   10   **241**

transomed window in the N wall and has been screened off in recent times with re-used panelling. The bellcote preserves the form shown in the Buckler drawing of 1805 but its sides are now shingled, not weatherboarded.

The Romanesque font has a rudely worked bowl and stem, and a roll moulding around the base of the bowl. The crude cover is probably of the 17th century. The pulpit, dated 1633, was reset and provided with a sounding-board in 1709. The box-pews are of the 18th century incorporating 17th-century elements. There is a fragment of a painted text on the N wall of the nave. The Royal Arms are early Victorian. There is one late 18th-century wall tablet on the E wall; the other tablets are early Victorian.

242. 17th-century pulpit with sounding-board, reset 1709.
243. N window of N transverse aisle.

244

245

246

244. Exterior from SE, *Buckler*
1805.
245. Interior of chancel looking E
(*see* also 163).
246. Interior of nave looking E
showing porticus arches.

BRITFORD

St Peter   SU 163284   *Civil Parish of Britford*

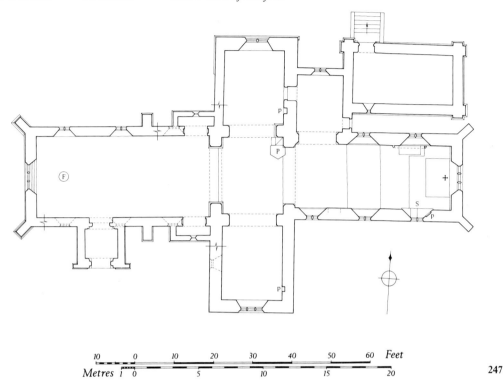

Feet							
10	0	10	20	30	40	50	60

Metres 1 0   5   10   15   20

247

The church is of Saxon origin. The fabric of the nave, at least in the lower parts of the N and S walls, is that of the church built in the 8th or 9th century. The original fenestration is lost and the archway or doorway at the W end of the S wall has been largely rebuilt, but the arches to the two former porticūs which flanked the eastern part of the nave are well preserved. The outline of the N porticus has been traced by excavation. Its E wall and probably also the E wall of the S porticus are incorporated in the W walls of the present transepts, but there is no evidence that these walls were prolonged into transepts in Saxon times. The form of the eastern arm of the Saxon church is unknown. There is no visible indication of a further stage of development until the 14th century when the present chancel and crossing were built, on a different axis from that of the nave. In 1764–5 the 2nd Viscount Folkestone (later 1st Earl of Radnor) of Longford Castle paid for an extensive repair and remodelling of the building, which involved a new W wall and W porch, a new crossing tower, Y-tracery windows and, to the N of the chancel, a large two-storied mausoleum for the Pleydell-Bouverie family. The Georgian appearance of the church was lost when in 1872–3 G.E. Street restored the church except for the tower: the windows were again given a medieval form; the entrance to the nave was removed from the W end to the re-opened Saxon S doorway; the mausoleum was lowered and shortened to allow for a vestry; and the porticus arches were unblocked.

Nearly all the furnishings were renewed. The tower was reconstructed in 1903 (*Salisbury & Winchester J*. 20 June and 26 Dec. 1903).

The early fabric of the church is of flint rubble and freestone with re-used Roman brick in the archways of both porticūs. The chancel and transepts are of flint with some rough chequering, but the tower, mausoleum and W front are of ashlar.

The chancel was built in the 14th century. The design of the tracery of the three-light Decorated E window is derived from tracery fragments found in 1872 during the removal of the Georgian masonry blocking the side windows. The two-light side windows are of similar design but lack tracery. The sedilia and piscina arranged within the splay of the SE window are also original features, although cut away in the 18th century and restored in the 19th. The late medieval wagon roof is now unceiled and has been given tie beams and a decorated wall plate. The vestry and organ chamber in the angle between the chancel and N transept were added in 1872.

The crossing has four equal arches, of two continuous chamfered orders, which support the 18th-century belfry. The 14th-century transepts both have contemporary piscinae. The S transept has a S window allegedly restored to its medieval form and, in the W wall, a wide squint now glazed. The roof is of the type and date of that of the chancel. In the N transept both the roof and N window are 19th century.

248

249

250

251

252

248. W jamb of N porticus archway.
249. E jamb of N porticus archway.
250. W jamb of S porticus archway.

251. N porticus archway; general
view from SW.
252. S porticus archway; general
view from N.

The nave is lit by high two-light windows of which only that to the E of the S porch is substantially medieval. Towards the E end of the nave are the openings to the former Saxon N and S porticūs. The arch to the N porticus is formed by stone panels set flush with the soffit and some brick tiles on edge; that to the S porticus is formed by brick tiles set radially in wide mortar beds. The design of the soffit of both archways consists of outer bands enclosing a recessed central strip. In the N archway, square stone panels set flush with the outer bands alternate with recessed brick tiles in the central strip, presumably for decorative effect. Sculpture is confined almost entirely to the E jamb of this archway; the outer bands are carved with vine scrolls and within the central strip are two carved panels, one with interlace the other with a rosette medallion. The W jamb has a single carved panel of interlace set in the central recessed strip. The projecting features of the central order at the base and springing of the N arch have yet to be explained. The brick voussoirs of the S arch enclose three plain stone panels. The external face of the doorway at the W end of the S wall is Victorian but the jambs and rear-arch are Saxon. The opening is taller than the archways of the porticūs and is undecorated; like the N porticus arch, the soffit is lined with thin stone slabs or panels, but it incorporates no brick tile. It may originally have opened into a further porticus or into a large S porch. The 18th-century nave roof has tie beams, king posts and raking struts with multiple purlins.

The font, designed by Street, is of 1873 and replaces one of the late 17th century now in Australia (Shortt 1964, 169). The cover is later. On the sill of the westernmost window on the N side of the chancel lies a late 13th-century miniature effigy of a male figure which was found in 1873 in the walling of the S transept (Anon. 1968, 5). Against the N wall of the chancel is a 15th-century monument consisting of a crocketed ogee arch (now, though not originally, freestanding) that frames a tomb chest. Neither the tomb chest, its slab, nor the arch necessarily belong together. The S and W faces of the tomb chest are decorated with ogee-headed niches: on the S face all but one contain images of saints; the two on the W face contain shields of unattributed arms. In the N transept are a number of early 19th-century wall tablets among which is a memorial of 1820 showing the descent of the Jervoise lords of the manor. It was designed by J. Bacon in the form of an open folio book.

The iron-bound chest in the N transept is probably of the 15th century. The richly carved pulpit, which is very similar to the former Wilton pulpit of 1628, has been reset on a Victorian stone base. Two of the bench ends in the chancel are of the late 15th century and are carved with a punning rebus. The box-pews in the S transept, belonging to the Earl of Radnor, remain from the 18th and early 19th-century furnishings of the church.

The *Radnor mausoleum*, to the N of the chancel, retains some 18th-century brickwork in the N, E and S walls, although the design of the exterior

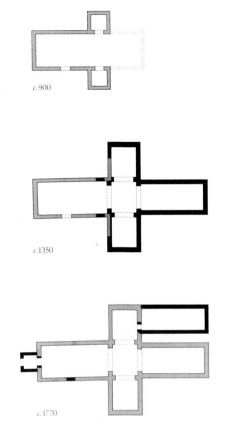

253. Development.

c.900

c.1350

c.1770

is by Street. Set into the E wall is a boldly carved achievement-of-arms of the Pleydell-Bouverie family carved by John Deval the Younger in 1779, and within the vault is a pious inscription of 1777 composed by the 2nd Earl of Radnor; both probably formed parts of the 'handsome pyramidical monument' to the Radnors in the original mausoleum (Gunnis 1971, 129).

254. Pulpit (19th-century base).

255

256 257

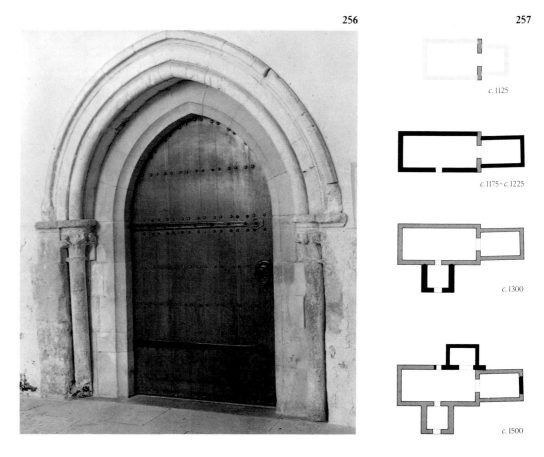

255. Exterior from SE.
256. S doorway.
257. Development.

c. 1125

c. 1175 - *c.* 1225

c. 1300

c. 1500

BULFORD

St Leonard   su 166437   *Civil Parish of Bulford*

The arch and wall between nave and chancel are of the 12th century but the nave and chancel themselves may be later since their datable features, such as the S doorway, are of the early 13th century. Possibly a church of *c.* 1100 was enlarged a century later, the original wall between nave and chancel being retained. During the second half of the 13th century the low but massive S tower-porch was constructed; it is not known whether it ever stood to a greater height. About 1500 the chancel was given a new roof and an E window set in an elaborate frame. The tower appears to have been reconstructed about a century later. In the mid 19th century a N chapel, probably of late medieval origin, was replaced by an 'aisle' of stock brick. C.E. Ponting rescued the church from advanced decay in a series of restorations from 1902 to 1910.

Most of the exterior is rendered but, like the tower, the W gable and the N aisle, it is probably of flint mixed with stone and, possibly, brick.

The chancel preserves its original form despite Perpendicular alterations. The corbel table, though restored, survives on both N and S walls; on the S, grotesque heads alternate with plain corbels. The westernmost window in the N wall is the only remaining lancet, but the Perpendicular windows on the S side have 13th-century rear-arches. The panel tracery of the E window is of 1902, reflecting the type but not the detail of the original (recorded by Buckler and subsequently destroyed in favour of intersecting wooden mullions). The splay decoration was not altered. The

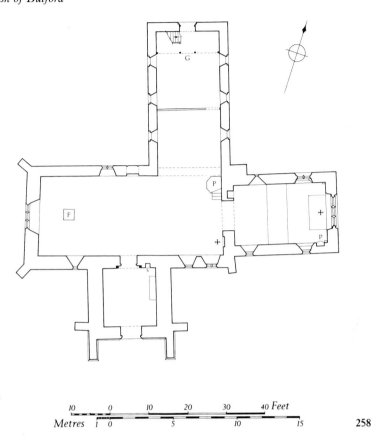

258

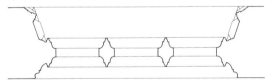

259. Section of E window.

jambs have two superimposed tabernacled niches; the soffit has tracery panels. Contemporary with the E window is the richly moulded arch-braced roof the E truss of which resembles a hammer beam as it lacks a tie – omitted in order to avoid blocking the window. The Romanesque chancel arch is low and narrow and has simple mouldings.

The nave has one lancet window in the S wall and a round-headed rear-arch to the Perpendicular N window. The W window and the pointed SE window have Decorated tracery; the latter window was presumably inserted to light the adjacent cinquefoiled niche to the S of the chancel arch. The straight-headed window adjacent to the SE window is post-medieval. The S doorway has a two-centred arch carried on shafts with stiff-leaf capitals; the plain N doorway is Perpendicular. The roof, which was originally ceiled, has tie beams, collars and double purlins; it is probably of the 17th century.

The present transverse N aisle, designed to front the pulpit, is of 1855. A buttress of the chapel it replaced survives in the angle between chancel and nave. The S tower preserves no medieval features except for one lancet opening on the W side. In the mid 17th century the S doorway with round head and pendant keystone was inserted, the E wall of the tower was reconstructed in brick and a new roof was framed.

The font is of the early medieval table type. How much it owes to the restoration of 1905, when it was re-placed in the church, succeeding one of 1739, is unclear. There is a piscina in the chancel and a stoup by the S door; both have trefoiled heads. The splat Communion rails are of the 17th century. Fragmentary wall paintings from before and after the Reformation survive in both chancel and nave. Commandment tables dating from the 18th century are painted over the chancel arch. There is a painted panel of the Royal Arms of 1666 surrounded by a marbled border. Five 18th and early 19th-century hatchments to the Duke and Southby families are hung in the church.

Memorials include a brass plate of *c.* 1811 and a number of 18th-century inscribed marble tomb slabs: in the chancel, to members of the Duke family; in the nave to Mary Beer (+ 1766) and Sarah Axford (+ 1733/4).

CHARLTON

ALL SAINTS   su 176241   *Civil Parish of Charlton*

The church, of brick with stone dressings, is in the First Pointed style. It was built in 1851 to the designs of T.H. Wyatt and largely at the expense of the 3rd Earl Nelson. The earl wished to provide a church for the inhabitants of both Charlton and Standlynch (on the E bank of the river Avon) who had previously worshipped in the chapel of Standlynch, by then assigned for the exclusive use of the household at Trafalgar (formerly Standlynch) House, the seat of Lord Nelson. It consists of a chancel and nave with a bellcote on the W gable and an organ chamber/vestry added to the N of the chancel in 1891. The polygonal marble font, perhaps designed by Butterfield, was given in memory of the Hon. Henry Nelson (+ 1863).

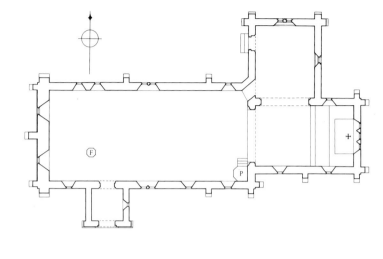

261.   Exterior from W.
262.   Interior looking W.

260

CHITTERNE

ALL SAINTS   ST 993441   *Civil Parish of Chitterne*

The present church of All Saints was built to replace the medieval churches which had served the two ancient parishes of the village: St Mary's to the W (*see* p. 123) and All Saints' to the E (*see* below). The chancels of both buildings were left standing to serve as mortuary chapels for their respective graveyards, but the chancel of All Saints' was demolished in 1877 and its graveyard is no longer in use (WRO 1109/4; Chitterne Vestry Book 1856–94).

The church was built in 1862, on a different site to the former church, to the designs of T.H. Wyatt. It has an apsed sanctuary, a wide, aisled nave, and a W tower. The windows of the N aisle are from the former church of All Saints; those of the S aisle are from the church of St Mary.

The major contemporary fitting is the plaster or artificial stone Royal Arms over the tower arch. The font of *c.* 1200 is from St Mary's, the cover (of 1767) from the former All Saints'. The much-worn angel corbel in the ringing chamber of the tower and two tiles in the sanctuary floor are from the former All Saints'. Also from the former church are the monuments to the Michell family, in the tower. These form a series dating from the mid 18th to the mid 19th century: there is one outstanding monument to Commodore Mathew Michell, of 1752; the rest are tablets of varying size and complexity. The 17th-century carved pulpit is from St Mary's, reset on a stone base. The low screen in front of the chancel is formed from the

263

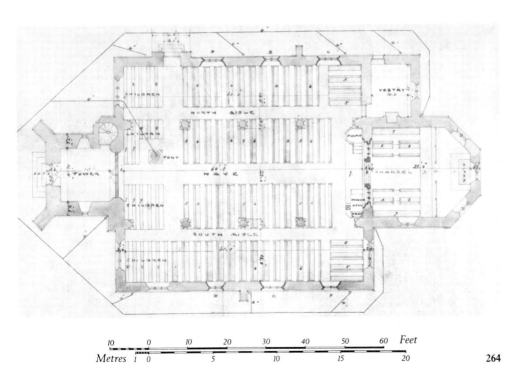

10   0   10   20   30   40   50   60   *Feet*

Metres   1   0   5   10   15   20   **264**

265

263. Exterior of present church from SE.

264. Plan of present church from faculty, 1861.

265. Font from St Mary's, now in present church of All Saints, with cover from former All Saints.

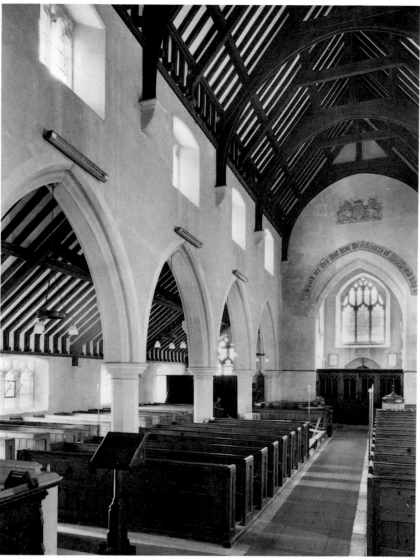

266. Interior of present church,
looking W.

tracery heads of the former stone screen in the chancel of St Mary's. The church also contains, as well as the monuments and fittings from the former church of All Saints and from St Mary's, some which cannot be assigned to either church: a 17th-century table and chest; four carved wooden panels of the 17th or 18th century (possibly from St Mary's); and a crudely carved head of uncertain date, in the belfry.

The former church of All Saints (ST 992444) can be reconstructed from plans and drawings executed prior to 1862 (WRO 10/19, Faculty plan; Colt Hoare 1824, 177) together with the evidence provided by re-used materials. The chancel was Early English with lancet windows, except for a three-light Perpendicular E window. Most of the openings of the nave and W tower were Perpendicular although the fabric appears to have been earlier; the N and S windows of the nave were re-used in the new church but the remaining windows and the ceiled barrel roof were destroyed. There was a plain N chapel probably of medieval origin and, to its W, a Classical building erected *c.* 1775 for the Michell family and comprising a mausoleum below and a pew above.

The font cover of 1767 (Goddard 1934, 393) is now in the present church but the late medieval font, the polygonal pulpit and the Communion rails of pierced splats have disappeared. The 15th-century stained glass depicting the Evangelist symbols, in the tracery lights of the E window, is also lost except for one fragment now in St Mary's. The Perpendicular niche with cinquefoiled head, formerly over the S doorway, was destroyed, but the angel corbel from the base of the niche is in the present tower. There were a number of medieval tiles including some heraldic tiles of the 15th century, but only two were reset in the present sanctuary floor. The monuments to the Michell family were transferred to the new church in 1877.

267

268

267, 268. Carved wooden panels in present church: depicting, (L) Faith (?) and foliate design and, (R), Moses (?) and foliate design.

269. Exterior of former church from SE, *Buckler* 1805.

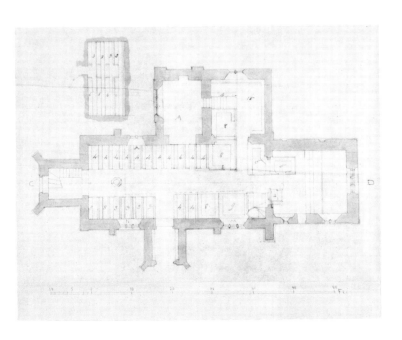

270. Plan of former church from faculty, 1861.

271

272

273

271. Exterior from SE before demolition of all but chancel, *Buckler*
c. 1805.
272. Exterior from NE.
273. Interior of chancel looking
SE (*see* also 88).

CHITTERNE

St Mary ST 989439 *Civil Parish of Chitterne*

Plans and drawings prior to 1862 (WRO 1109/4; Chitterne Vestry Book 1856–94) and the evidence provided by re-used materials allows reconstruction of the original church, which consisted of a chancel, nave, N chapel and S tower-porch. Only the chancel survives (*see* p. 119); it is of one build, probably of *c.* 1450, with windows all of the same type and tracery design, and with external walls of uniform flint chequer work. The W end of the chancel was formerly closed by a stone screen which had a continuously moulded central arch flanked by two traceried openings. The tracery heads were re-used in the present All Saints'. The rest of St Mary's also appears to have been Perpendicular including the nave roof and the arch to the N chapel, although the W and N windows of the nave were post-Reformation replacements. The windows of the N chapel and the S windows of the nave were re-used in the new All Saints'.

The 15th-century monument in the chancel is now set in the opening of the NE window and has been much restored. Originally it consisted of a tomb chest (now gone) under an ogee canopy crowned by a shield and helmet.

The font of *c.* 1200 which stood at the W end of the former nave, under the gallery, is in the parish church of All Saints but the cover, of the crown type with four volutes rising to a central baluster, was discarded. A fragment of the Ox of St Luke, set in a window in the S wall, is all that remains of the 15th-century stained glass originally in the former church of All Saints. The 17th-century carved pulpit is now in All Saints'. Fittings still in St Mary's include a Communion table and a chair, both of which probably date from *c.* 1700. There are tablets of the late 18th and the early 19th century attached to both internal and external walls.

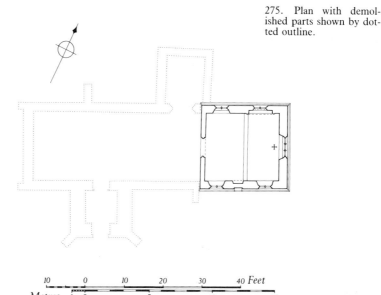

275. Plan with demolished parts shown by dotted outline.

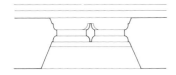

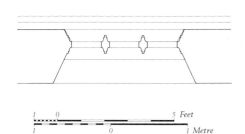

274. Section of chancel windows, side (top) and E (below).

277

276

276. Exterior from S.
277. Tomb on N wall (*see* also 100).

278

279

282

280

278. Tablet now at W end, to Anthony Cracherode (+ 1752).

279. Medieval font, disused since 1850.

280. Font and cover, 1850.

281. Exterior from SW before removal of belfry and pyramid cap.

282. Exterior from SE.

CHOLDERTON

St Nicholas   su 228424   *Civil Parish of Cholderton*

The present 19th-century building replaces a medieval church standing in the same churchyard but on a different site. It has none of the architectural features of its predecessor. The old building was very small and reputedly Saxon, although the recorded fenestration suggests an Early English chancel and Perpendicular nave. From the old church are the font of *c.* 1200, the 15th-century bell and the mid 17th-century Communion table. The memorials consist of a brass inscription-plate commemorating Cuthbert Rives or Reeves (+ 1594), a fine mid 18th-century tablet and a tablet of the early 19th century. Some of the fabric of the old church, including the windows, was re-used in the school building of 1851.

The architect of the new church was T.H. Wyatt but the inspiration for the design and the money for the construction came largely from the then rector, Thomas Mozley of Oriel College, Oxford, who was a convinced Tractarian. The form of the building was largely determined by the desire to incorporate a ten-bay hammer-beam roof from Suffolk, which Mozley bought in 1840: the style adopted was Perpendicular and the plan rectangular, with walls of sufficient height to accommodate large windows below the level of the wall posts of the roof. The foundation stone was laid in 1841 and the shell of the building was completed in 1847 in spite of a halt in construction lasting a year due to lack of funds. The church was consecrated in 1850.

The church is arranged like a college chapel: with an ante-chapel and without division between nave and sanctuary. It is built of small unknapped flints with dressings of Tisbury stone. The exterior

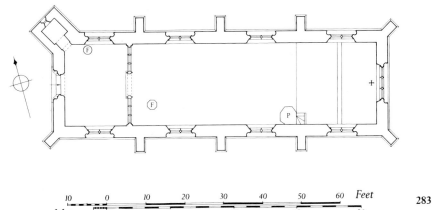

283

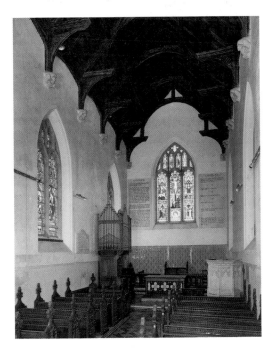

detail, such as the fleurons on the cornice and the head-stops to the windows, was carved on site by the masons from the contemporary church under construction at Wilton; some of the internal stonework, such as the font and the screen, was prepared at the Tisbury quarries. The oak bench-ends were carved with tracery and naturalistic detail by the Suffolk carpenters whom Mozley employed to repair and frame the roof. The floor tiles were made by Minton; their colour and size carefully graded from the W to the E end of the church.

The late medieval roof is original in its principal members but Mozley removed the tie beams, which he claimed had been inserted, and replaced the defective timbers and decorative spandrels (*see* Appendix 2).

The stained glass, which fills every window, is contemporary but was not part of the original design nor all from one maker. It was paid for by Mozley's successor James Frazer, later bishop of Manchester. Further adornment was provided by painted texts under the windows and a stencilled reredos; of these, only the Ten Commandments flanking the E window remain visible.

The structure and furnishings of the church have survived almost intact except for the bell turret where a squat wooden cage has recently been substituted for the original stone belfry and pyramidal cap.

284.   Interior looking E.
285.   Fleurons on eaves of S wall.

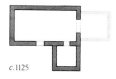

*c.*1125

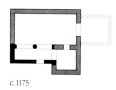

*c.*1175

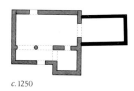

*c.*1250

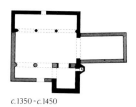

*c.*1350 ~ *c.*1450

*c.*1500

286.   Development.

287.   Exterior from SE.
288.   Interior looking E.

COOMBE BISSETT

St Michael and All Angels   su 108263   *Civil Parish of Coombe Bissett*

A church at Coombe Bissett is mentioned in Domesday, but the first stage of the present fabric probably dates from *c.* 1100 when the building consisted of a nave, a chancel and a chapel or tower to the S of the nave. The S arcade and aisle were added in the third quarter of the 12th century. The chancel, which is on a different alignment from that of the nave, was built in the mid 13th century. The present tower, at the E end of the S aisle, was begun during the 14th century and incorporates some Romanesque features in its lowest stage; the upper stages are of the 15th century. A major Perpendicular reconstruction of the rest of the church included the erection of a N aisle and, later, of a N chapel to the nave, a new roof and clearstorey to the nave and new windows in the chancel and the W end. Repairs to the roof and to the gables of the chancel and N chapel were made in the 18th century.

The restoration of the building by T.H. Wyatt in 1844–5 involved removal of earlier furnishings, the replacement of the roofs, the reconstruction of the S aisle and S porch and, as an afterthought, the rebuilding of the W end in order to enlarge the nave. An inscription records that the chancel was repaved and re-ordered in 1961.

The body of the church is of coursed flint rubble mixed irregularly with stone chequers; the tower and the aisle parapets are ashlar.

The chancel retains its 13th-century form, although only the windows on the N side and the S doorway remain from that period. The E and S windows are of *c.* 1500. In the S wall there is a piscina with a double opening and single drain, perhaps contemporary with the original building. The roof is Victorian.

The nave may preserve the Romanesque plan apart from the western extension of 1845; on the S side much of the Romanesque fabric survives including both the two-bay arcade to the W and the walling to the E, the latter pierced by an arch and remodelled in the late 14th century. The arcade has a circular pier and respond with scalloped capitals. The chancel arch was rebuilt with a wide stilted span, presumably at the same time as the upper stages of the tower since a single stair leads both to the tower and to the rood loft of which only the doorway survives. The roof is of 1845 but rests on corbel heads of Perpendicular date.

The three-bay N aisle has piers of conventional Perpendicular section and stilted four-centred arches: in the N wall, which is crowned externally by a battlemented and pinnacled parapet, there is a plain four-centred doorway and a three-light straight-headed window. The N chapel, though

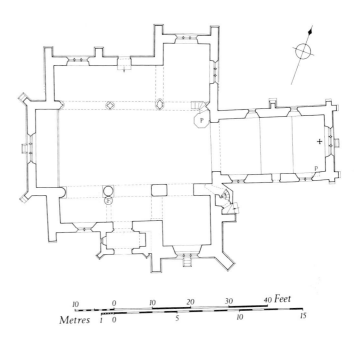

289

also of 15th or early 16th-century date and sharing the stylistic character of the aisle, is a later addition.

The S tower rises in three stages. The thick walls of its lowest stage probably incorporate a Romanesque structure: the crude S respond of the arch between S aisle and tower is probably an early feature and the arch from nave to tower appears to be cut through early masonry. The middle and upper stages of the tower are 15th century and were formerly capped by a short spire of wood and lead. The S aisle was rebuilt in 1845 re-using the battlemented parapet formerly on the S side of the nave. The greensand arch of the S doorway is of Romanesque origin but has been much rebuilt. The present S porch is of 1845, replacing one apparently of the 17th century.

The 13th-century font has a round, moulded bowl and four supporting shafts with capitals worked into the mouldings of the bowl. In the chancel is a late medieval altar slab, found in 1961. There are two chests; one of *c.* 1500 in the chancel, with a pitched lid and bound with iron, and another of the 18th century, in the nave. In the N chapel are three early 19th-century tablets and a 19th-century hatchment of the Becher family.

290

291

290. Exterior from NE showing extra stage added to tower 1791–1859, *Buckler* 1805 (*see* also 3).

291. Exterior from SE.

292. Development.

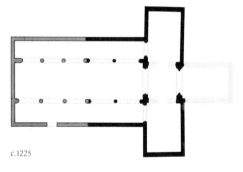

*c.*1100

*c.*1175

*c.*1225

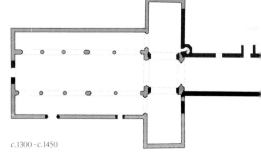

*c.*1300 - *c.*1450

DOWNTON

St Lawrence   su 181216   *Civil Parish of Downton*

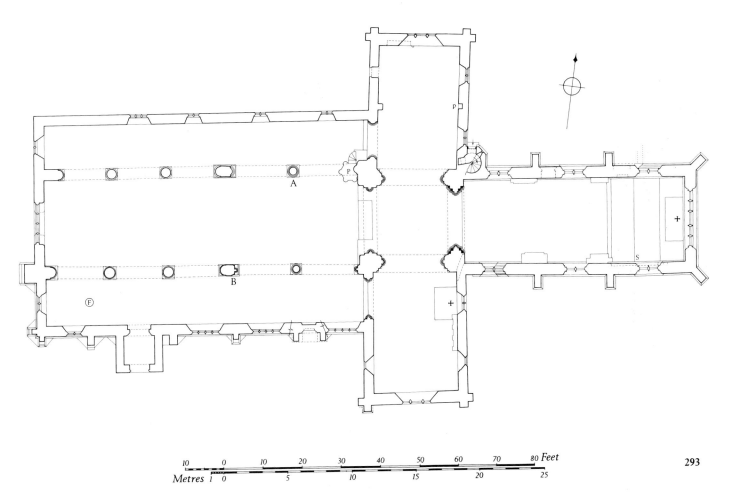

10   0   10   20   30   40   50   60   70   80 *Feet*

Metres 1   0   5   10   15   20   25

293

There was a church at Downton at the time of Domesday and almost certainly much earlier, since Downton was the chief settlement within the great Wiltshire estates granted to the bishop of Winchester soon after the foundation of the See. No standing part of the building recognisably survives from before the mid 12th century, but retention of earlier foundations may explain irregularities of plan such as the raking layout of the transepts and the uneven spacing of the nave arcades. Possibly the church of *c.* 1085 was cruciform and had a long nave, unaisled or with aisles extending westward from the crossing only halfway down the nave. In the second part of the 12th century the present aisled nave was begun from the W, but the N and S arcades are almost certainly the product of two distinct building campaigns. After a pause both aisles were continued E in the early 13th century, again as separate undertakings. The E and W crossing arches are mid 13th century as are the transepts, although differences in the size and layout of the latter suggest their reconstruction on older foundations rather than a new unified plan.

The chancel, begun perhaps *c.* 1275 and designed to be vaulted, was completed with a wooden roof *c.* 1300–20. During the second half of the 14th century there were alterations to three windows on the E side of the transepts, to the N and S crossing arches and to the doorways in the S aisle. Perpendicular work was confined to the W end of the nave. In the 17th century the S aisle was partly rebuilt, perhaps in 1648 when the S porch was erected. The crossing tower, in existence by at least the early 14th century, appears to have been rebuilt in the 17th century, and in 1791 it was heightened by an additional stage (later removed). Also of the 18th century were the brick parapets of which only that above the S aisle survives. In 1810–15 extensive work was carried out under the supervision of Daniel Alexander, much of it in the crossing to support the heightened tower.

The major 19th-century restoration took place in 1859–60 under T.H. Wyatt and D. Brandon: the N aisle was rebuilt, the tower was reduced to its original height (although the Georgian pinnacles were kept) and the post-medieval vestry between N transept and nave was removed; the interior was stripped of ceilings, panelling and most furnishings; in the chancel the medieval window tracery, string course and sedilia were reinstated. A restoration of 1890–1 included the replastering of the interior and the insertion of tracery in the W window (*Salisbury and Winchester J*. 1 Aug. 1891).

Nave and transepts are of roughly coursed rubble mixed with brown heathstone and freestone, the chancel is of coursed and finely knapped flint and the S aisle of coursed flint mixed with stone and brickwork. The tower is of mixed courses of flint rubble and heathstone; battlements and pinnacles are ashlar.

The chancel appears to have been built in two stages. A stone vault was probably intended at first since two angle shafts carried on head corbels survive in the E angles, but the executed design had a timber arch-braced roof. The present roof is a Victorian reconstruction, with the number of trusses doubled and the new trusses supported by corbels inserted into the window heads. The other corbels are original. The side windows are of two lights and have Decorated tracery of *c*. 1320. The

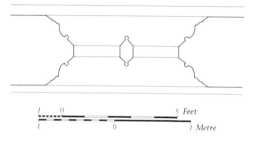

294.   Section of chancel side window.

tracery of most of the side windows was restored to accord with the original tracery surviving in the central windows; the tracery of the E window is not authentic. The W light of the westernmost window on the S side is dropped below a transom to allow for a low-side window which has had its original shutter restored. The sedilia are essentially contemporary with the chancel but the projecting parts, cut off when the walls were panelled in the 18th century, have been renewed and the original piscina in the easternmost bay has been replaced by a seat. There is a plain aumbry to the E. In the N wall are two doorways: the richly moulded one to the W was entered from the outside but the other gave access from the chancel into a passage, perhaps leading to a polygonal vestry, as at Enford, N of Salisbury. There is a squint through the SE crossing pier, probably to provide a view from the chancel to an altar in the S transept; a squint through the NE pier was discovered in the 19th century but again blocked.

The four arches of the crossing all have shafts and moulded capitals of mid 13th-century type but only those of the E arch are authentic. The W arch, though perhaps originally of the same character, was rebuilt and reduced in width in 1812 to carry the weight of the heightened tower. In 1859 the NW pier was completely reconstructed, the W arch widened again, and a brick relieving arch inserted above the opening. The N and S arches before restoration had simple continuously moulded responds and arches of 14th-century type. The crossing tower must have been erected before 1300 since its stair tower was refaced to correspond with the chancel; the openings in the tower are, however, late Perpendicular, probably of the 17th century. The extra stage, added in 1791, was 30 ft (9.14 m) in height

295.   Chancel side window.
296.   Nave S doorway.

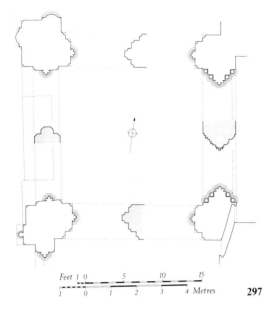

Feet 1 0   5   10   15
1 0 1 2 3 4 Metres   **297**

and built of stock brick stuccoed to imitate stone, with stone pinnacles and battlements which were retained and reset when the rest of the addition was removed in 1859.

The transepts appear to be substantially of the 13th century but they neither match one another in plan nor correspond in alignment with the crossing. Their plan may thus derive from an earlier phase of the building. Lancet windows survive in the W walls of both transepts and (one) in the E wall of the S transept. This last window is more elaborately moulded than the others. The other late 14th-century windows in the E walls are straight headed and traceried. The three-light windows in the N and S walls are post medieval. The roofs, which were unceiled in 1860, are of the 17th century. In the N transept there is a trefoil-headed piscina in the E wall, and in the N wall, an early 14th-century tomb recess which, though much defaced, has a pierced ogee cinquefoiled arch. The W doorway is Victorian. Above the W window a fragment of medieval wall painting has recently been exposed. In the S transept a post-medieval doorway which had been inserted under the S window was removed in 1860. The heavy stone parapet over the S wall is probably a 14th-century feature.

The nave arcades are of two periods. The two bays to the E are of the 13th century, the three to the W are 12th century. On each side a fragment of wall survives linking the E respond of the Romanesque arcade and the W respond of the Early English arcade. The Romanesque arcades have pointed arches of two unchamfered orders (the arches on the N being higher than those on the S) which may replace original round-headed arches. The arches are earlier than those to the E which have two chamfered orders. Slight differences occur in the detailing of the N and S Romanesque arcades, for instance in the scalloped capitals, and more fundamental differences in the bay spacing. The piers and the capitals of the Romanesque S arcade (except that of the W respond) were rebuilt in the 19th century in ashlar, unlike the greensand of the W arcade, but the position of the piers was not altered. In the Early English arcades to the E the moulded capitals and chamfered arches on both sides are similar, but the shafts of the N arcade are relatively broad and those on the S are tall and slender. This difference also occurs in the arches from each aisle into the respective transept: that on the N has broad responds and moulded capitals, corresponding to

298

299

297. Plan of crossing with arch profiles.
298. Interior of chancel looking E.
299. Interior of nave looking W from S transept.

300. Downton: carved funerary reliefs below monument in S transept to Sir Charles Duncombe (+ 1711).

301. Downton: detail from tomb on S wall of chancel by P. Scheemakers, to Margaret, Lady Feversham (+ 1755). (*See* also frontispiece.)

those of the N arcade; that on the S has slender shafts like those of the S arcade but bearing stiff-leaf capitals. The nave roof is reputed to have the original common rafters but the tie beams and king posts are Victorian. The catslide roof continuing down from the nave over the N aisle was not altered when the aisle was rebuilt in 1860. The S aisle has a flat roof of 17th or 18th-century date.

The nave has no clearstorey. The large four-light W window has Decorated tracery of 1891, designed by C.E. Ponting, reputedly on the basis of original fragments (*Salisbury and Winchester J*. 1 Aug. 1891). The original windows in the N aisle were cusped and straight headed, perhaps of the later 14th century: three new windows of the same type were inserted in 1860. At the W end of the S aisle there are windows of two cusped lights, with straight heads and hood moulds, of *c*. 1500. The three S aisle windows to the E of the S porch are of the 17th century. They still have hood-moulds and straight heads but the lights are not cusped. The W doorway of the nave, which has mouldings of an early 16th-century type, intrudes into the sill of the W window in such a way as to suggest the two were of one build. The main S doorway at the W end of the S aisle has a two-centred head and is continuously moulded; the door is contemporary with the doorway and both date from *c*. 1400. Further to the E is a small 14th-century doorway, with a projecting stone hood, perhaps an addition. There is a shallow niche above the doorway. The door itself is of the 17th century or earlier. The S porch was built in 1648, perhaps replacing an earlier one.

The font, of *c*. 1200, has a square Purbeck bowl with canted corners and shallow round-headed arches cut along the sides. The present pulpit is Victorian but the sounding-board from the late 18th-century pulpit survives transformed into a table. The only evidence of the rood screen are corbels for the rood beam on the E face of the easternmost arcade piers. Of the traces of medieval painting discovered during 19th-century repairs in various parts of the church, a fragment in the N transept has recently been exposed again. The principal mural decoration is the 19th-century Cross and Ten Commandments over the W crossing arch. There are two panels of late medieval stained glass, probably English, representing St Barbara and St Christopher, now in the easternmost window of the N aisle.

In the S transept there is, in addition to 18th-century and early 19th-century tablets of local interest, a large early 18th-century wall monument to Sir Charles Duncombe (+ 1711), possibly by James Hardy. The three-panelled carved stone screen below the tablet proper, although also 18th century and connected with the Duncombe family, seems not to be part of the original composition. In the chancel there are four major monuments of the mid 18th century: to Anthony Duncombe, the later Lord Feversham (+ 1763), his son (+ 1741) and two of his wives (+ 1755, + 1757). They are variously signed by or attributed to Peter Scheemakers or to his son, Thomas.

S of the church stands the shaft and base of a medieval cross.

DURNFORD

St Andrew   su 136383   *Civil Parish of Durnford*

The nave of the church is Romanesque; contemporary with it are chancel arch, N and S doorways and font, all richly carved. The similarity between several of the decorative motifs here and in the buildings of Bishop Roger at Old Sarum suggest a date of *c.* 1140 for this first building – the strip buttresses are a later addition. The chancel is mid 13th century, the tower probably later 13th century. The only later additions to the fabric are a rood stair turret on the N side of the nave (removed perhaps in the 18th century) and timber-framed N and S porches (the former replaced in brick in the early 19th century). Some painted decoration and many items of woodwork survive from the 15th and 17th centuries. The upper stage of the tower was rebuilt in the 17th century. Some windows were replaced by casements in the 18th century. The chancel was restored in 1890–1 and the body of the church was restored by C.E. Ponting in 1903–4. The nave furnishings were rearranged and to some extent reconstructed in 1883 (Kenworthy Brown 1944, 1).

The church is built largely of uncoursed flint rubble. The strip buttresses and parts of the N and S doorways are of greensand, the N porch and the repairs to the gables are of brick and the tower is ashlar.

The chancel remains substantially of the 13th century in spite of a 19th-century S doorway and much rebuilding of the N and S walls *c.* 1890. The E window is of three stepped lancets and the E wall

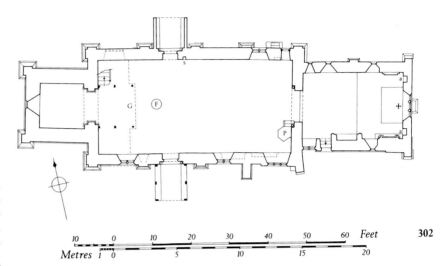

302

has painted decoration of masonry-outlining enlivened by hook-like flourishes; set into the wall to either side of the altar are two aumbries. Except for a two-light traceried window at the W end of the S wall the side windows are narrow deeply-splayed lancets. At the W end of the N wall is a 13th-century low-side window. The single-framed roof, originally ceiled to form a wagon type, is 14th or early 15th century. The tie beams are later.

303.   Exterior from SE.

304. Interior of nave looking E.

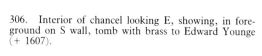

305. Tablet to Edward Younge on N wall chancel, 1771.

306. Interior of chancel looking E, showing, in foreground on S wall, tomb with brass to Edward Younge (+ 1607).

The nave is relatively tall and wide. The chancel arch is of one order carried on capitals carved with grotesque animals. The N and S doorways are of the same form but with scalloped capitals and tympana. The imposts to the jambs of the N doorway and the internal face of the E jamb of the S doorway are carved with decoration. The N door is dated 1677 and the S door 1714. The timber-framed S porch is probably 16th century; the 19th-century brick N porch incorporates some original timbers. The greensand strip buttresses, of Romanesque form, date from *c*. 1200 or later; a strip buttress on the S side of the nave blocks an original window and there is a similar buttress to the side of the Early English chancel. Other nave windows are late medieval or post-Reformation. The three-light window on the S side is of *c*. 1600; the wall over it was rebuilt in 1781 (inscription on wall). Associated with the two openings to the 15th-century rood stair are remains of contemporary wall painting. Wall paintings of the 15th and the 16th century survive over the chancel arch and by the S doorway, and decorative foliage painting, perhaps of the 13th century, is exposed in the W part of the nave. The roof is of the same wagon type as that of the chancel; ties have been inserted and the former ceiling, which was decorated above the rood, removed.

The W tower is probably of the later 13th century, i.e. the date of the tower arch. It has three stages: the uppermost is a 17th-century rebuilding with straight-headed openings; the middle stage is lit by two small oculi of uncertain date; the lowest stage has a window barred with a heavy metal grille. Preserved in the tower is a sheet of lead roofing inscribed with early 17th-century graffiti, probably from a spirelet which formerly sur-mounted the tower, also a fragment of the 18th-century Commandment Tables formerly over the chancel arch.

The only Romanesque fitting remaining is the carved font. Other stone features are the late medieval stoup by the N doorway and the two tomb recesses in the S wall of which that to the E has an ogee arch of the 14th century and the other a three-centred arch of *c*. 1500. There are a number of 15th or early 16th-century benches, some with traceried ends and some with simple moulded ends. The 17th-century furnishings include a pulpit of 1619, cut down but retaining its pulpit cloth of 1657, a double-sided swivel lectern, a polygonal font cover (with a modern volute crown) and panels of a pew reset in the NE angle of the nave. The mid 17th-century Communion rails are of unusual form. The wooden casement windows that light the gallery are 18th century although the present gallery dates from 1903. On the N wall of the nave hangs a panel of the Royal Arms of 1678. Two panels of medieval stained glass, one depicting St Nicholas and the other a Crucifixus, are now in a window on the N side of the nave.

There are two 13th or 14th-century grave slabs inscribed with floriate crosses; one housed in the tomb recess of *c*. 1500, the other loose in the chancel. Also in the chancel, against the S wall, is an early 17th-century tomb, to Edward Younge (+ 1607), combining both traditional and Classical motifs and including a brass effigy of the deceased and his family. Flanking the altar are two mid 18th-century monuments erected by a later Edward Younge. On the W wall of the chancel are two simple tablets commemorating servants of the Harris family.

307

308

307. Pulpit of 1619 with pulpit cloth of 1657.
308. Lectern.

DURRINGTON

ALL SAINTS   SU 157449   *Civil Parish of Durrington*

The exterior of the church, apart from the tower, now appears Victorian, but much of the earlier building survives or can be reconstructed from documentary evidence. The original nave was Romanesque and its former N doorway, of *c.* 1125, survives reset in the S aisle. The original S aisle was of the late 12th century, the chancel of the mid 13th century. The W tower was built *c.* 1500 but its topmost stage was altered two centuries later. In the early 17th century the nave was elaborately furnished with carved woodwork. In 1850–1 the whole building was restored by the architect J.W. Hugall: apart from the tower all the external walls were taken down; the chancel was rebuilt on the old foundations; the S aisle was widened; a N aisle was added; a new chancel arch was inserted; the 17th-century furnishings were much altered and rearranged. In 1973 a vestry was added S of the chancel to the designs of R. Townsend (information from incumbent).

The body of the church is of knapped flint rubble incorporating many fragments of earlier stonework. The tower is of regular flint chequerwork but the parapet and the stair tower are ashlar.

The chancel was rebuilt in 1851 re-using the original side windows and S doorway. The triple lancets of the E window were inserted by Hugall, supposedly on good evidence, in the place of a Perpendicular window. The double-drain piscina has a chamfered two-centred arch: an aumbry,

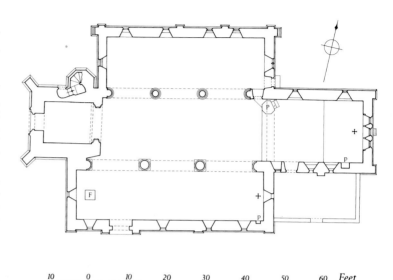

309

discovered in 1851, is set under the NE window.

The original 12th-century nave had a doorway in the N wall which in the later Middle Ages was blocked and concealed internally by a large wall painting of St Christopher. In 1851 the doorway was reset as a shallow porch to the new S door. The arch and the capitals, but not the shafts, are Romanesque. The capital on the W side is not

310. Exterior from SE showing Romanesque arch reset as S porch.

original to the doorway. The three-bay S arcade, cleaned but otherwise untouched in the 19th century, has comparatively short, round piers and responds on high plinths. The arches are round, the capitals, except for that of the first pier from the W, are moulded. The N and S aisles and the S porch are of 1851. The S aisle is much wider than the medieval aisle it replaced and preserves no features from it.

The W tower, of *c.* 1500, was inserted into the nave in such a way as to overlap the W bay of the S arcade. The jambs and soffit of the tall tower arch are panelled with tracery, as is the external splay of the W window. The W window is divided by a transom into two tiers of trefoil-headed lights. The parapet and pinnacles and the truncated upper part of the stair-tower date from the late 17th century: they may be replacements required after storm damage in 1693 (Jackson 1862, 357).

An octagonal late medieval font was replaced in 1851 by one of a neo-Romanesque design. The 17th-century wooden fittings, which included pulpit, pews and benches, have largely survived although cut up and rearranged. All the pieces incorporate panels of carved ornament and, on the pulpit and reading desk, figures as well. The furnishings also include a late medieval plank chest and a 17th-century table, probably of secular origin. The late 17th and the 18th-century memorials consist of black marble floor-slabs in the chancel to members of the Moore and Poore families who were successive lay rectors. There is also an early 17th-century inscribed brass plate, and a mid 17th-century decorated tablet to Hester Conham (+ 1647). The 19th-century tablets in the chancel are again to members of the Moore family.

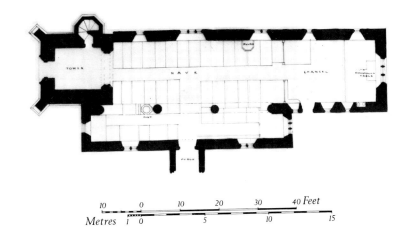

311. Plan from faculty, 1850.

312. Pulpit.

313. Exterior from NW before addition of N aisle, *Buckler* 1805.

137

EAST GRIMSTEAD   (Chapelry of West Dean)

HOLY TRINITY   SU 225273   *Civil Parish of Grimstead*

The church appears always to have been a dependent chapel of the parish church of West Dean although the settlement of East Grimstead was already quite distinct from West Dean at the time of Domesday (VCH 1955, 203–4). The church was never linked with that of West Grimstead. The present Victorian church, built in 1856 on the foundations of the former medieval church (a simple building with nave, chancel and N porch), is in Middle Pointed style. It was built to the designs of F.H. Pownall and paid for by the Glossop family (DRO Faculty 6/6). It consists of a nave, chancel, S porch, and vestry on the N side, with a bellcote on the gable over the chancel arch. It is built of coursed knapped flint with freestone dressings.

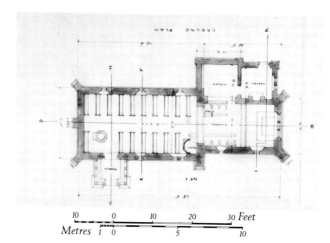

314.   Plan from faculty, 1856.

316.   Exterior from SW.

315.   Interior looking E.

FARLEY   (Former chapelry of Alderbury)

ALL SAINTS   SU 224296   *Civil Parish of Pitton and Farley*

The present late 17th-century building replaces a medieval chapel dependent on the parish church of Alderbury. It was built in 1688–90 at the expense of Sir Stephen Fox as part of his charitable foundations in the village which was his birth-place: it cost £2,014 (Dorset Rec. Off. Ilchester MSS). The architect has not been conclusively identified. Sir Christopher Wren, to whom the church is traditionally attributed, had no direct involvement with the building although he may have been consulted in general terms since he knew Fox well. In an undated list of the building costs a John Heysenbottle was paid for a model of the church (Dorset Rec. Off. Ilchester MSS), but the most likely attribution is to Alexander Fort, the master-joiner who had acted as surveyor when the nearby hospital was built in 1680–2 (Colvin 1978, 314).

The church, which is of brick laid English bond with ashlar dressings, comprises a nave, chancel, W tower and two projecting 'chapels' to either side of the nave, that on the S forming the main entrance vestibule and that on the N the Fox mausoleum. The plaster ceilings are steeply pitched.

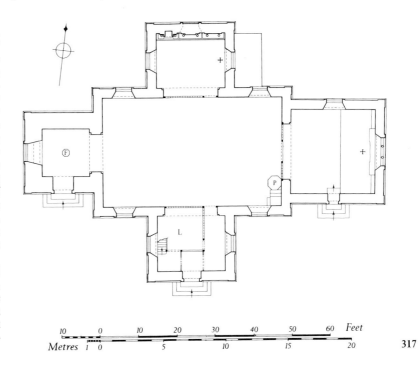

10 0 10 20 30 40 50 60 *Feet*

Metres 1 0   5   10   15   20   **317**

318.   Exterior from S.

319

320

321

The church was extensively repaired in 1790–1 (Dorset Rec. Off. Ilchester MSS; WRO 490/1001), and then restored by Ewan Christian in 1874 (DRO Faculty 22/7), when the furnishings were reduced in height and rearranged and a reredos of inlaid marble and mosaic, designed by W.F. Dixon and executed by Salviati, was erected against the E wall of the chancel. Most of the texts and other painted decoration applied to the walls in 1874 have been erased. In 1912 an organ and organ loft were erected in the S chapel over a vestry (*Salisbury Diocesan Gaz.* May 1912).

Original fittings include the polygonal font and its cover, the screens to the chancel and to the N chapel, and the pulpit and the benches (both of which have been severely reduced in height). The screen to the S chapel is of 1874. The three principal monuments in the N 'chapel' are to Sir Stephen Fox (+ 1716), to his first wife Elizabeth (+ 1696) and to his son Charles (+ 1713). That to the first Lady Fox includes a bust of the deceased; the others, of similar though not identical design, have no figurative sculpture beyond cherub heads. The iron railing in front of the monuments is contemporary with them. The other major monument in the church, that to the second Lord Ilchester (+ 1802) on the N wall of the nave, was designed by the younger Westmacott. There are four hatchments of the Fox-Strangways family.

319. Font and cover.
320. Pulpit (19th-century base).
321. Interior looking E.

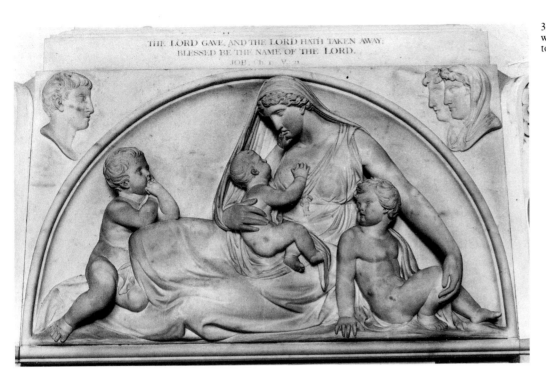

THE LORD GAVE, AND THE LORD HATH TAKEN AWAY:
BLESSED BE THE NAME OF THE LORD.
JOB. Ch. 1. V. 21.

322. Detail from monument on N wall nave by R. Westmacott junior, to 2nd Earl of Ilchester (+ 1802).

Cy Gist Le Très Honorable
et Le Très Ancien Chevalier
Sir STEPHEN FOX
Fondateur De Ceans
Qui Trespassa age de 90 Ans,
Le Vingt troisieme de Septembre
1716

Cy Gist La Très Honoree Dame
Chrisune Hope epouse en seconde Noces
Du Très Honorable Chevalier
ETIENNE FOX
Elle Trespassa agee de 39 Ans
Le dix septieme de Fevrier
1715
Dieu Aye Merci de Leurs Ames.

323. Monument in N chapel to Sir Stephen Fox (+ 1716).

324. Exterior from NW.

325

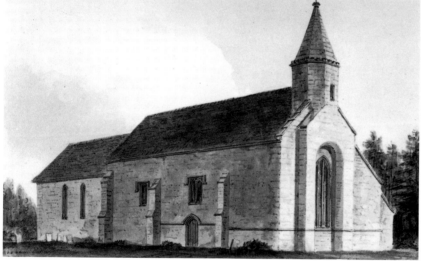

327

326

325. Exterior from NW before early 19th-century alterations, *Buckler* 1805.
326. Exterior from SE showing chancel before restoration, *Buckler* 1805.
327. Interior of chancel looking E.

FUGGLESTONE

St Peter   su 102314   *Civil Parish of Wilton*

The only evidence of a Romanesque church on the site is the detailing of the nave arcade which, although much altered, appears to be of 12th-century origin, suggesting that the plan of the nave and S aisle are of that period. The chancel was built in the mid 13th century. During the 15th century the nave and S aisle were extensively rebuilt and their windows renewed; a polygonal stone bellcote was erected on the W gable. About 1830 the openings in the N wall of the nave and the S aisle window were altered and a new chancel arch was inserted. In 1840 both nave and aisle, including the W gallery, were comprehensively refitted (WRO 930/15). The chancel was restored in 1861 when a vestry was added on the S side.

The nave and S aisle (much of it rendered) are built of rubble, roughly coursed and mixed with flint; the chancel and W front are of ashlar.

The chancel has original 13th-century openings. The triple lancet windows in the E wall are shafted both internally and externally. The piscina and aumbry are original. The roof is Victorian. The early 19th-century chancel arch replaces a round arch of uncertain date.

The nave has a three-light Perpendicular W window which had already lost its tracery by 1803; flanking its head internally are two splayed corbels which support the E face of the gable bellcote. Until *c.* 1830 there were two straight-headed Perpendicular windows set high in the N wall. There was a doorway below the window in the centre bay. The window in the S aisle was of the same type with a small dormer above, perhaps to light a gallery. The nave has a pointed, plaster, barrel roof, which could be of late medieval origin. The two-bay S arcade has square responds and pier with simple imposts carrying pointed, slightly chamfered arches. In the S face of the E respond are the remains of a rood stair. The brick S porch probably dates from *c.* 1800; it has late 19th-century alterations to the gable.

The baluster font is of the 18th-century. The 'Gothic' pews, pulpit, reading desk and gallery front were installed in 1840, but the panelling of the rear and sides of some of the pews incorporates fragments of 17th-century seating. The panel of the Royal Arms is of the reign of George III, before 1801. Lying *ex situ* S of the altar is a late 13th-century recumbent effigy of a gowned figure. On the N wall of the nave is a pedimented grey marble tablet of 1771.

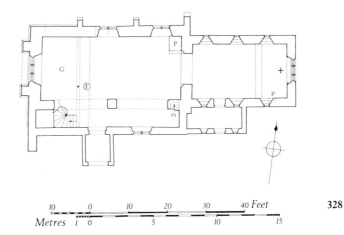

330.   13th-century effigy in chancel.
331.   Interior of nave looking NE.

10   0   10   20   30   40 *Feet*   **328**
Metres   1   0   5   10   15

329.   Interior of nave looking SW, showing furnishings of 1840 and baluster font.

HOMINGTON

ST MARY   SU 123260   *Civil Parish of Coombe Bissett*

The earliest parts of the present church, certain features of the chancel and probably the plan of the nave, are of *c.* 1250. The N arcade was added in the mid 14th century, the S arcade a century later, and *c.* 1500 the tower was erected over the E bay of the S aisle. There was an extensive restoration in 1794 which involved the removal of the main entrance from the N side to the W, and much repair and refitting (DRO Dean and Chapter Records 61, Court Records, non-contentious). Further restoration, by T.H. Wyatt, took place in 1860 when the chancel and the external walls of the N aisle were taken down and rebuilt and the interior, including the roofs, was stripped and refitted. The church is of coursed rubble flint chequered with freestone.

The chancel, although substantially of 1860, preserves the 13th-century plan and some 13th-century features. The heads of the lights of the triple-lancet window in the E wall are original; the piscina has a two-centred, chamfered arch and a square projecting drain. The roof is Victorian.

The early nave survives only in plan; the N aisle and chancel arch are of the mid 14th century, and the W window and the S aisle of the 15th century. The 15th-century roof was replaced in 1860 (the roof corbels, though much scraped, may be original) at which time the W window was raised several feet and its tracery renewed. The N arcade is of four bays with short octagonal piers carrying moulded capitals and double-chamfered arches. The S arcade has only three bays, the piers being taller and the arches of greater span than those of the N arcade. The capitals are moulded to a different profile from those of the N arcade and the arches are hollow-chamfered. In the E wall of the N aisle is a piscina, and in the W wall of the S aisle a blocked doorway; both are contemporary with their respective aisles. The raising of a tower over the E bay of the S aisle may represent a change of

plan, since there is no provision to support the extra weight beyond a thickening of the E and S walls of the bay. The arch across the aisle that now carries the W wall of the tower could originally have been intended to delimit a chapel. The head corbel at the S respond of the arch has been severely defaced. The two-light S window of the tower at ground level, with its round uncusped heads, may date from *c.* 1600. The upper openings of the tower and perhaps much of the fabric itself are also of the 17th century or later.

The font appears to be entirely Victorian though perhaps similar in design to its medieval predecessor. There is one late 18th-century tablet with a coloured marble frame; to Edmund Wyndham (+ 1723) and other members of the Wyndham family.

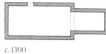

c. 1300

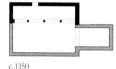

c. 1350

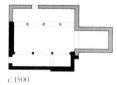

c. 1500

332. Development.

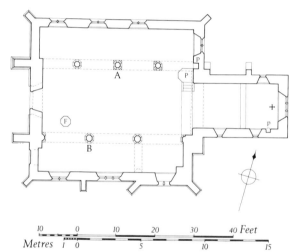

10   0   10   20   30   40 Feet
Metres 1   0   5   10   15

333

334. Interior looking E, showing base of tower on right.

IDMISTON

ALL SAINTS   SU 197373   *Civil Parish of Idmiston*

The lowest stage of the W tower, and perhaps the plan of the nave, are all that survive of the Romanesque church which once stood on the site. The chancel was built in the first part of the 13th century and in the latter part of the same century N and S aisles were added to the nave. Either then or during the Perpendicular refashioning of the church the aisles were prolonged to embrace the tower. During the 15th century the nave was almost entirely refenestrated, the nave walls were heightened to include a clearstorey, a two-storeyed porch was added and new roofs built; the wooden bosses in the roofs and the stone corbels carrying the wall posts were richly carved. In 1668 the medieval steeple was taken down (WRO Idmiston Churchwardens' Presentments). The church was extensively restored in 1865–7 by the architect J.L. Pearson; major alterations were the heightening of the W tower and its crowning by a shingled broach spire and the rebuilding of the chancel arch. He also replaced the S door of the nave with a window, altered the porch stair and rebuilt the N wall of the chancel. Nearly all the furnishings were renewed. The church was transferred to the Redundant Churches Fund in 1978.

The building is constructed of flint with stone dressings.

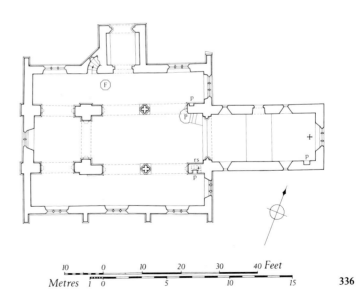

336

c. 1150

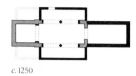

c. 1250

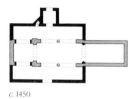

c. 1450

337. Development.

338. Exterior from NE photographed before 1866 restoration (*see* also 339).

The structure of the chancel is still essentially 13th century but it was thoroughly restored in 1866 and the N doorway, much of the N wall and the roof are entirely of that date. The piscina has a simple two-centred, chamfered arch.

The nave may have the plan of its Romanesque predecessor but probably preserves none of the fabric; a fragment of decorated Romanesque stonework was re-used in the base of the 13th-century arcade pier. The arcade piers consist of four clustered shafts with moulded capitals. The capitals for the responds are carried on figurative or stiff-leaf corbels partly restored. The chancel arch prior to 1867 was low, perhaps to accommodate the rood screen the stair of which is still visible on the S side. The position of the damaged late medieval recesses at the E end of both aisles suggests that they were originally piscinae. The traceried E window of the S aisle, with its two-centred head, is of *c.* 1400. The other windows are straight-headed and date from the later 15th century; the central window on the S side is a Victorian replacement of a former doorway. The clearstorey and the roofs to both nave and aisle are also of the 15th century. The arch-braced nave roof and the aisle roofs are carried on sculpted corbels of heads or half-length figures in contemporary costume and the bosses at the intersections of the roof members are similarly carved with faces or foliage. Before the Victorian restoration the roof was elaborately painted, but this may not have

been original. A late medieval wall painting of St Christopher on the S wall has disappeared (*see* Table 11).

The N porch is two storied and has the original roof. The window to the upper room was re-opened in 1867 and at the same time the roof of the stair turret was aligned with the aisle parapet and a stair window inserted. The tower is entirely of the 19th century above the first stage (the medieval steeple removed in 1668 had been replaced by a wooden belfry). The W window is a 19th-century replacement of a Perpendicular one similar to those in the nave.

The tower has the original strip buttresses not only on the W wall but also on the N and S walls, both now enclosed within the aisles. The arches that lead from the tower to the aisles and which are carried by sculpted corbels are of the 15th century; formerly the aisles may have enveloped the tower, without such communicating arches. The E arch into the nave is of the late 13th century but its head corbels (re-used) are Romanesque.

The 13th-century octagonal font has survived the Victorian restoration unscathed. No other noteworthy fittings remain. In the S aisle and formerly on the N side of the chancel arch is a Jacobean monument to Giles Rowbach (+ 1633) with a kneeling effigy. At the E end of the N aisle there is a large tablet of the later 17th century. The chancel contains a series of 17th and 18th-century tablets to members of the Bowle family.

339. Exterior from SE, showing spire added by J.L. Pearson.

340. Nave roof.
341. Interior looking E, showing former chancel arch and painting on nave roof, *Kemm* 1864.
342. Interior looking E.

340

341

342

343. View of church site from SW showing fragment of house before post-war remodelling.

344. View of church site from S.

IVYCHURCH   (Remains of the former priory church)

su 183276   *Civil Parish of Alderbury*

The former Augustinian priory of Ivychurch (or Ederose), dedicated to The Blessed Mary, was founded in the reign of King Stephen, possibly by the king himself (VCH 1956, 289). From the first year of Henry II's reign until the dissolution of the house in 1536 the priory received an annual grant from the royal treasury for saying the offices in the chapel of the nearby palace of Clarendon, and this may have been the purpose for which the priory was established (RS 99, 1896, 49). The priory appears to have been on the site of an earlier chapel, dependent, like Farley and Pitton, on Alderbury parish church. It possessed a relatively modest endowment and by the late 14th century had declined almost to extinction but experienced renewed prosperity in the 16th century.

345. Plan with conjectural reconstruction of pre-Dissolution layout of priory. (Recent (1986) soundings on the site suggest a 'double-nave' plan for the church rather than a conventionally aisled nave.)

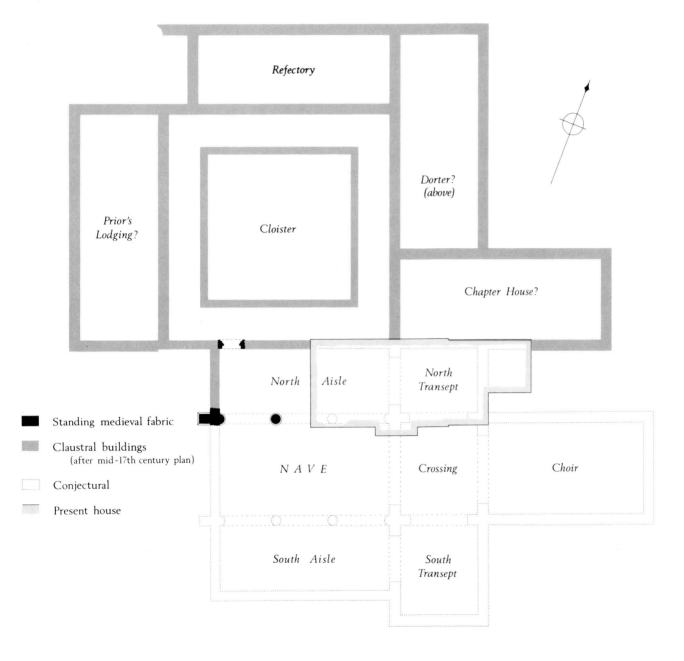

Refectory

Dorter? (above)

Prior's Lodging?

Cloister

Chapter House?

North Aisle

North Transept

■ Standing medieval fabric

▨ Claustral buildings
(after mid-17th century plan)

▢ Conjectural

▨ Present house

N A V E

Crossing

Choir

South Aisle

South Transept

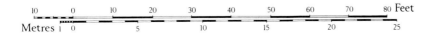

10   0   10   20   30   40   50   60   70   80 **Feet**

Metres ⌐ 0   5   10   15   20   25

After the Dissolution most of the church appears to have been demolished swiftly, but the N aisle, the cloister and the three ranges surrounding it were transformed with little alteration into a house. The W range was rebuilt in the late 17th century, extending across the former cloister; much of the medieval fabric survived, however, either *in situ* or as re-used material, until the final destruction of the house in 1889 (Nightingale 1891b, 352–5). At this time the W part of the N arcade of the nave of the priory church was exposed and left standing and a part of the S range of the later house, which covered the E parts of the N aisle, was retained as a farmhouse. The windows and ground-floor level of the house were altered in the 1950s.

The architectural history of the priory can be tentatively reconstructed since, in addition to the surviving architectural and sculptural fragments, there is a mid 17th-century plan showing all four sides of the cloister (Muniment Room Longford Castle, copy in Devizes Museum FF 89), and a further plan of the mid 18th century that includes some details of the medieval features in marginal drawings (BL Kings Libr. Topog. XLIII 42–4).

The priory was planned with the claustral buildings to the N of the church, perhaps because the drainage in that direction was more effective. Although the church has disappeared excepting the westernmost one-and-a-half bays of the N arcade of the nave, it is known from an account of the election of Richard Page as prior in 1493 that it had a S aisle in addition to a choir and high altar (VCH 1956, 294–5). By the end of the monastic period, there was 'a stepall of the parish', perhaps associated with the S aisle, since the aisle appears to have been the section of the church used parochially by the inhabitants of Whaddon (their original church, as part of the manor of Whaddon, was acquired by the priory in the 14th century but later abandoned: SC 12/33/27, 1 July 28 Henry VIII 1536). The identification, by Sir Harold Brakspear (1934, 437), of the S range of the post-Dissolution building as the nave of the church rather than its N aisle appears mistaken, given its width of 16 ft (4.88 m)–unusually narrow for the nave of a conventual church with a cloister 55 ft (16.76 m) square. The E parts of the church, to the E and SE of the present house, would have comprised a choir and probably a regular crossing with transepts (bones, perhaps from the monks' cemetery, have been found to the E of the house, between the possible sites of chancel and chapter house). The 17th-century plan shows the double

346. 17th-century plan of site, taken from transparency in the *Library of the Wiltshire Archaeological and Natural History Society* of original at Longford Castle.

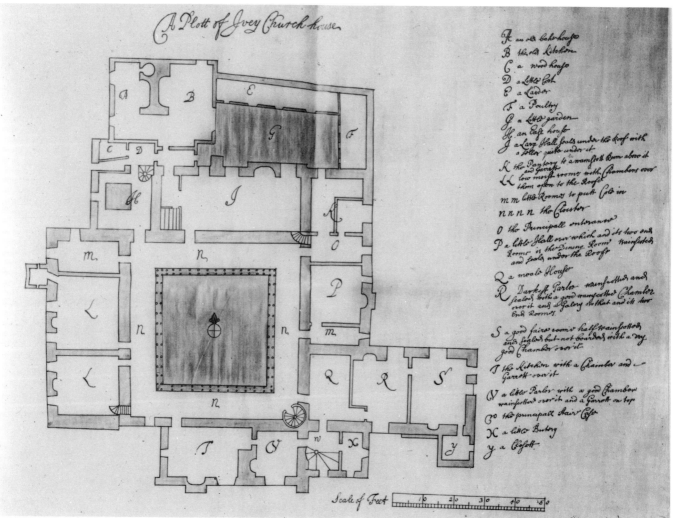

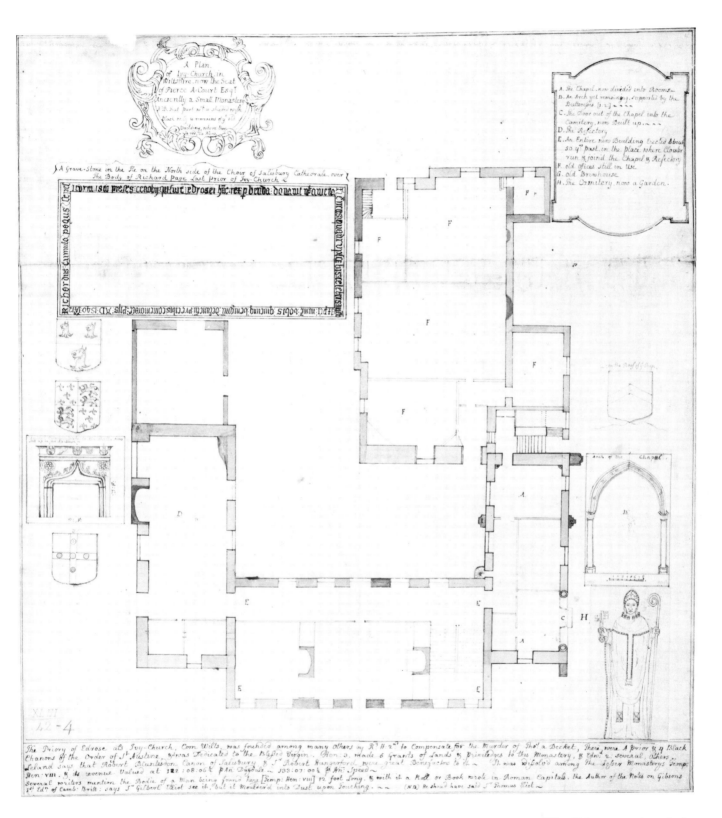

347. 18th-century plan of site, with marginal illustrations of medieval features then surviving. By kind permission of *The British Library* (*see* also 24).

348. Double capitals from former cloister re-used in Edwardian drinking fountain in Alderbury.

shafts of the cloister arcades and at least 13 bays to each side. About 30 double capitals survive in whole or part. The chapter house (termed 'Chapel' by Brakspear) was in the normal position adjoining the N side of the church and would have been an acceptable size for the prior and twelve canons reported as belonging to Ivychurch in the mid 14th century (VCH 1956, 292); there is no sign of the usual intervening slype. The wide staircase, just S of the chapter house on the plan, may have incorporated parts of the night stair. The dorter presumably ran along the E range of the cloister, which would explain why there was a suite of good rooms along the upper storey of this range in the post-Dissolution house. The refectory, in the N range, survived intact until 1889. The hall (for a general description before demolition *see* Nightingale 1891b, 354) dated from at least the late 13th century (a wall painting of the Last Supper on the E wall was of that date: *see* Table 11) but the building was refurbished in the later Middle Ages, probably at the end of the 15th century. The moulded roof beams were cut up and re-used over the organ chamber of Pewsey church *c.* 1890; a few bosses survive in Salisbury Museum. The roof, the two-light trefoil-headed window (the only surviving medieval window by 1889) and the richly decorated fireplace (moved in the 18th century to the Green Dragon Inn in the village and later taken to America) can be dated by the heraldry on the lintel, suggesting its insertion by Prior Thatcham *c.* 1485–90 (information from J.A. Reeves). The fireplace may have been set into an earlier pulpit, built into the N wall, thickened for the purpose. The service court shown N of the refectory on the 17th-century plan may also have been of monastic origin. The range W of the cloister probably constituted the prior's lodgings. As with the E range, the principal rooms appear to have been on the first floor.

The E parts of the church were probably built first; in the second quarter of the 12th century. The sculpture of the cloister capitals suggests that the building of the cloister followed in the third quarter of the century. The last part to be completed was the nave; the surviving pier and respond date from *c.* 1200. The W end of the N aisle finished short of the S range of the cloister, suggesting a slackening of interest or diminishing resources. The two-centred, continuously moulded doorway leading from cloister to N aisle and still *in situ* suggests a 13th-century date for this part of the church. Surprisingly few fragments of 13th-century work survive considering the amount of building activity of that period in Salisbury and at Clarendon Palace (Henry III, although a notable patron of ecclesiastical foundations and often at nearby Clarendon, was not generous in his gifts to Ivychurch). The lack of 13th-century evidence may, however, be misleading: in 1891 Nightingale recorded shafts of Purbeck and 'a very large quantity' of what he deemed to be 14th-century work, all of which has since disappeared (Nightingale 1891b, 353).

The revived fortunes of the priory in the late 15th century, after it had acquired the alien priory of Upavon, were apparent in its buildings. The commissioners of Henry VIII in 1536 were struck by the 'very good state' of the building 'with much new building of stone and brick' (SC 12/33/27). The church and the refectory were partly reconstructed. The 18th-century plan includes marginal drawings of a late 15th-century arch spanning the N aisle one bay E of the surviving pier, perhaps to delimit a chapel, and of contemporary shield bosses in the roof. Further sculptural fragments exist *ex situ* built into the W wall of the present house, notably four corbel heads, a three-centred moulded arch and a large traceried panel.

349. Female head stop built into W front of present house.

350

351

350. View to SE over site of cloister.

351. Site of church photographed during demolition of house, 1889.

352

353

352. Exterior from N.
353. Exterior from NW photographed before addition of organ chamber and vestry in 1882.

354

355

354. Interior looking E (*see* also 162).

355. Tablets in S chapel to Robert Eyre (+ 1762) and his wife Jane Simpson (+ 1775) (*see* p. 66).

LANDFORD

St Andrew   su 261202   *Civil Parish of Landford*

The present church was built in 1858 to the designs of William Butterfield and largely at the expense of Frances Elizabeth, Dowager Countess Nelson. The previous building, which was on the same site, consisted of a nave and chancel, a weather-boarded W belfry, a N chapel and a N porch and, to the S, a mortuary chapel for the Eyre family. From the old church survive the Romanesque N doorway and a sculpted stone panel. The doorway, of one order with volute capitals, dates from the first half of the 12th century. Although it was widened when re-erected in the present church the original detailing was respected. The stone panel, found in the foundations of the old chancel and reset above the rear arch of the N doorway, depicts two women, each under an arch, holding a cross between them. Cut into the surface are six square holes, perhaps to house relics. The subject is probably the Invention of the True Cross and the date *c.* 1125.

The new church originally comprised a chancel with a vestry on the N side, a nave and a S aisle and chapel. In 1882 Butterfield enlarged it by raising the vestry into a N 'transept' and adding a new vestry to the E (Landford Parish Book). Earlier a small heating chamber had been added in the angle between the S chapel and the S aisle, probably also by Butterfield. The W end has a bell turret supported by a buttress between the two W windows. The roofs are carried down low; there is no clearstorey and no windows in the S wall of the aisle. The exterior is of red brick, laid English bond, banded with Bath stone and with header courses of slightly vitrified, unglazed brick.

The church has contemporary floor tiles and stained glass, the latter all by Lavers, Barraud and Westlake. The reredos, by Butterfield, was not erected until 1879 and replaced an earlier design of two tin Commandment tables set in patterned tiling. The font and cover date from *c.* 1810.

The monuments from the old church are arranged in the present S chapel which stands on the foundations of the former mortuary chapel and so covers the old burial vault. Nearly all the tablets are to members or connections of the Eyre family. The earliest is that to Elizabeth Eyre (+ 1758) but most date from the late 18th and the early 19th century.

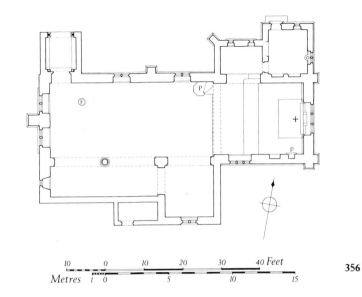

10 0 10 20 30 40 *Feet*
Metres 1 0   5   10   15

356

357. Exterior of former church from NW, *Buckler* 1806.

358. Exterior of former church from SE, *Buckler* 1804.

359. Interior looking E.

LAVERSTOCK

St Andrew   su 159309   *Civil Parish of Laverstock*

The present church was built in 1857–8 to the designs of T.H. Wyatt in Early Decorated style to replace a building occupying a different site to the SW but in the same churchyard. It is constructed of coursed knapped flint with random stone chequers and stone dressings. A low vestry, also of flint and stone, was added to the W in 1906 by Briggs and Gordon and was extended westwards in 1979 (information from incumbent).

The former building consisted of a chancel, probably Early English, a nave with W belfry and a prominent S porch entered through a two-centred 13th-century arch ornamented with saw-tooth chevron and carried on triple clustered shafts with moulded capitals. The arch, much restored, was re-erected in the same position in the Victorian church. The only other features transferred to the new church were the late medieval octagonal font bowl, a brass inscription plate of 1530 and five monuments of the 18th and the early 19th century.

Fittings original to the present church include a carved stone pulpit, now on the N side of the chancel arch but designed to stand S of it, and the stained glass of the E and S chancel windows, of the S chapel windows, of the nave clearstorey windows and of all but the westernmost of the S aisle windows. The windows were made up by Ward and Co. out of hundreds of fragments of differently patterned and coloured glass, few of which appear to be earlier than the 19th century. In the E window of the S chapel are three roundels

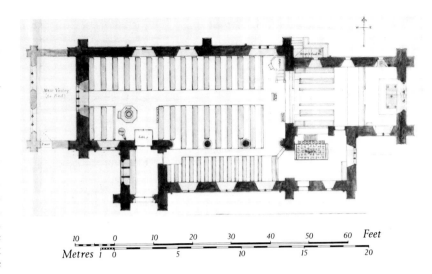

360.   Plan from faculty, 1906.

of gold and white glass, perhaps Flemish work of the 16th-century, depicting episcopal saints. Fragments of 13th-century grisaille glass, removed from Salisbury Cathedral in the late 18th century and rediscovered in 1933, were incorporated into the W window in 1939. At that time the chancel screen was erected; the heads of the lights include early 16th-century panels of complex tracery, perhaps of Welsh origin.

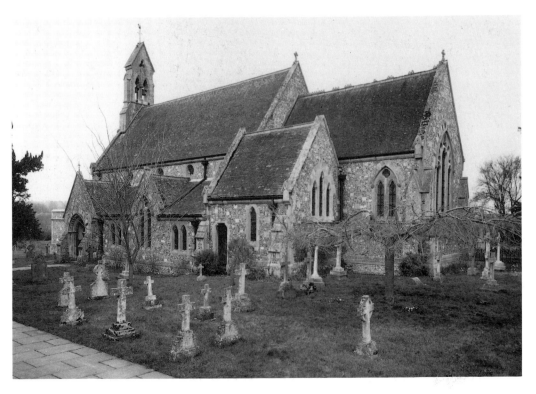

361.   Exterior from SE.

362. Exterior from NE before 19th-century restorations, *Buckler* 1801.

363. S arcade of nave, with former Communion rails in background.

MADDINGTON

St Mary   su 067438   *Civil Parish of Shrewton*

No part of the present church fabric is earlier than the 13th century, although the discovery *c.* 1900 of a Romanesque capital re-used in the chancel walling, and now set under the chancel piscina, is presumably evidence of an earlier building. The chancel, the tower and probably the nave are 13th century in origin although all have been rebuilt at later periods. The easternmost two bays of the S arcade, erected in the first part of the 14th century, opened into a short aisle or chapel. A century later the arcade was extended the full length of the nave and a narrow S aisle formed. During the 17th century the church was the subject of major alterations. About 1603 the nave was widened by some 18 in. (0.46 m) on the N, necessitating a new nave roof and N porch. The S aisle was rebuilt during the same period, perhaps as a result of the collapse and rebuilding of the S part of the tower, which can be dated to before 1637 (when a dated plaster panel was placed over the tower arch). In the mid 17th century a transverse aisle for a family pew was added at the E end of the S aisle; *c.* 1700 the chancel was rebuilt by the then patron Sir Stephen Fox, who had the E window blocked and elaborate plaster decoration inserted (WRO 1336/84). The nave was restored in 1846 by Wyatt and Brandon when a new chancel arch was inserted and a new font and pulpit installed (the roof had been repaired and in part renewed three years before). The chancel was restored in 1853. From 1896 to 1900 there was a further series of repairs, concentrated on the tower and S aisle (MS notes on church, probably by Rev. C. Goddard). The church was transferred to the Redundant Churches Fund in 1979.

The nave and chancel are constructed of flint and stone chequerwork; in the S aisle this is mixed with brickwork and fragments of medieval worked stone. In the tower the lower parts of the E, the N and the northern half of the W walls are of flint rubble; the remaining walls and the belfry stage are of ashlar.

The chancel retains much of its original 13th-century detailing, although the E window and the roof are entirely of 1853. The arch of the piscina, which is two centred and has three slender roll mouldings, is original but the bowl is 19th century. The Romanesque capital is *ex situ.* The strip buttress at the W end of the S wall owes its form to successive repairs and is not of Romanesque date.

The E and W walls of the nave may be of 13th-century origin. The S wall was reconstructed when the arcade was formed in the 14th and 15th centuries. The N wall was built on new foundations in the early 17th century: two late medieval windows were re-used and one contemporary straight-headed window was inserted. A window at the W end, which lit the former gallery, was blocked *c.* 1847. An inverted medieval base, perhaps for a cross, has been incorporated in the

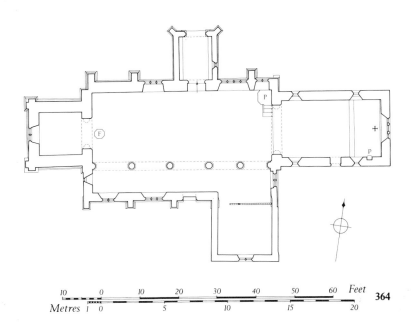

364

buttress to the E of the porch. The five bays of the S arcade are not uniform. The first two bays from the E are narrower than the others; they end to the W in what was formerly a respond and which, when the arcade was extended, was converted into a pier by the addition of a further respond to the W. The capitals of the later piers are more simply moulded than the earlier. The capital of the W respond appears to have been replaced when the tower was rebuilt in the 17th century. The S respond of the tower arch is of the same date although in imitation of the original 13th-century N respond. The nave roof can be dated to 1603 by an inscription on one of the corbels above the N door; it is essentially of the pointed barrel type but with decorative hammer-beam pendants. The curved principals were renewed in 1843. The N porch is entered through a moulded four-centred arch and has a decorated plaster ceiling, also of *c.* 1603.

The S transverse aisle must have been built up against the S aisle as its W wall incorporates one of the aisle buttresses; it may also incorporate the footings of an earlier aisle or chapel. Its S window was straight-headed and mullioned until altered in 1847. The S aisle, of 15th-century origin, was refenestrated and its roof lowered in the 17th century. The four-centred S doorway is original but was blocked in 1847 at which time the adjoining window was altered from 17th-century to neo-Gothic form. The window to the W was a new insertion of 1897. The lancet window in the W wall has a straight-headed rear arch, suggesting that it was reset in the 17th century. Fragments of moulded medieval stonework have been built into the external face of the S wall.

365. Development.

c. 1250

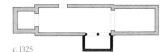

c. 1325

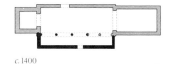

c. 1400

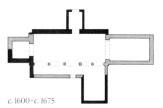

c. 1600 - *c.* 1675

The N half of the tower, which is of rubble, dates from the 13th century but the S part was rebuilt in solid masonry after a threatened or actual collapse in the early 17th century. The two-light W window with its freize of recessed panels above the lights is probably also of that date. Traces of an earlier opening exist above, at the level of the floor of the ringing chamber. The traceried belfry openings are of late medieval character but the belfry stage as a whole is probably early 17th century. It was formerly crowned by battlements and angle pinnacles upon which were set vanes bearing the arms of the Tooker family who were lords of the manor in the 16th and 17th centuries.

The 17th-century Communion rails, which have been incorporated in a screen, are the only pre-Victorian furnishing to survive. The stone pulpit and font are of 1846, the latter replacing a polygonal medieval font. The monuments include two 18th-century architectural tablets; one of marble, *c.* 1760, and the other of painted stone, 1783. A canvas of the Royal Arms, of 1816, has disappeared.

369

366

367

368

366. Maddington: tower from NW.

367. Maddington: former font, *Buckler c.* 1801.

368. Maddington: tablet in nave to Gilbert family, 1783 (*see* p. 64).

369. Maddington: tablet in nave to Richard Woodroffe (+ 1692), *c.* 1760 (*see* p. 64).

NETHERHAMPTON

ST KATHERINE   SU 108298   *Civil Parish of Netherhampton*

The main body of the church was built in 1876 by the architect William Butterfield. It replaces, largely on the same foundations, a medieval building of nave and chancel that had been altered in the 18th century by the insertion of a Venetian window at the E end of the chancel and by the addition of a brick W tower the coursed stone base of which may, however, be of medieval origin. In 1846 two 14th-century windows were inserted; these were from St Mary, Wilton, a church at that time being dismantled (Jackson Wilts. Coll. fol. 39). These windows and the tower were the only architectural features retained for the present building, which is of flint and stone chequerwork with stone dressings.

The new chancel was built to the same width as the old nave. The stones of the former chancel arch were re-used in the new chancel arch. The new nave was built to the same dimensions as the former nave but a S aisle was added. To the W tower were added a stair turret and a timber belfry; the tower openings were Gothicised. Of the two windows from Wilton, the three-light traceried window which had replaced the Venetian E window in the old church was again set in the E wall; the two-light window formerly inserted in the chancel N wall of the old church, was re-placed as the easternmost of the S aisle. An elaborate chimney built in the S aisle has since been dismantled above the roof line.

All the furnishings were designed by Butterfield including the font (which replaces the original Romanesque tub font), the reredos and the woodwork; the Minton floor-tiling is of contemporary date. There is one tablet of 1830 by Osmond above the N door; in the chancel is a tablet to the poet Sir Henry Newbolt (+ 1938). The stump of a late medieval cross survives in the churchyard.

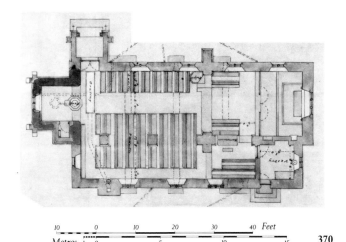

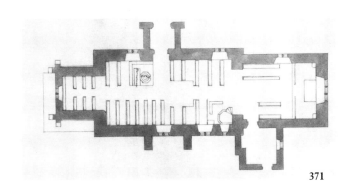

370. Plan from faculty, 1876.
371. Plan of church before enlargement, from faculty, 1876.

372. Exterior from NE before 1876 rebuilding, *Buckler c.* 1804.

373. Netherhampton: exterior from SE, showing E window formerly in Wilton St Mary.

374. Netherhampton: interior of chancel looking E.

375. Netherhampton: font by Butterfield.

NEWTON TONEY

St Andrew   su 218402   *Civil Parish of Newton Toney*

The present church was built to the designs of T.H. Wyatt and D. Brandon in 1843–4. It occupies approximately the same site as its medieval predecessor which consisted of chancel and nave with S porch and W belfry. A N chapel had been added *c.* 1800 to house the pew and vault of the Malet family (Colt Hoare 1826, 104).

The new church consists of a chancel, nave and SW tower-porch. It is constructed of uncoursed knapped flint with stone dressings in plain Early Decorated style. In the later 19th century a small vestry was added in the angle between the N wall of the chancel and the nave.

The wooden furnishings are of 1844 but the stained glass was mostly installed in the late 19th century. The Romanesque font, the William III carved Royal Arms and the memorial tablets were brought from the old church. The chest of 17th-century style was made up from old woodwork in 1853. The monuments include the following: two plain 17th-century tablets, the later of which is to the family of Nathaniel Fiennes (+ 1669) including the writer Celia Fiennes; an 18th-century brass plate, formerly silvered, to the family of William Benson (builder of Wilbury House); two tablets of *c.* 1800 to two generations of the Earle family; a simple early 19th-century Gothic tablet. The remaining fifteen tablets in the nave are all to members of the Malet family of Wilbury House. The earliest is of 1817 and was designed for the Malet chapel in the old church by John Bacon for Sir Charles Malet (+ 1815) who bought the property. The sequence, which includes some elaborate neo-Jacobean designs and a late 19th-century portrait bust, continues well into the 20th century. A late medieval brass indent and fragments of 14th or 15th-century stonework, all of which were recorded by Kemm in 1867 (watercolour now in Salisbury Museum) are now lost.

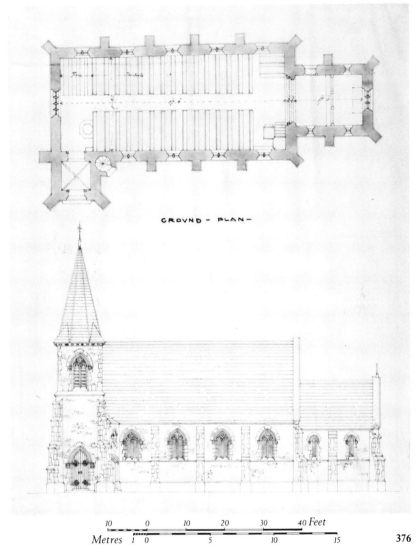

GROUND · PLAN

10   0   10   20   30   40 *Feet*

Metres   1   0   5   10   15   376

377

376. Plan and S elevation from faculty, 1843.
377. Exterior of former church from SW, *Buckler* 1805.

378

379

380

381

378. Newton Toney: Royal Arms of William III.

379. Newton Toney: font brought from former church, *Kemm* 1867.

380. Newton Toney: exterior from W.

381. Newton Toney: interior looking E.

NUNTON (Former chapelry of Downton)

St Andrew   su 159261   *Civil Parish of Odstock*

The church was extensively rebuilt and extended in the 19th and 20th centuries but preserves the major elements of its medieval form. The carved imposts of the chancel arch are of *c.* 1125, reset in a later, wider arch. A chapel of one bay was added on the S side of the chancel later in the 12th century. In the 13th century the chancel was lengthened, the nave rebuilt and a S aisle added. Probably at this time a low tower was built at the W end of the nave. In the mid 14th century new windows were inserted in the S walls of both chancel and nave aisles; a century later, the chancel chapel was reroofed and given a new E window. About 1840 the chancel chapel was extended to the E by one bay. In 1854–5 the rest of the church was reconstructed to the designs of T.H. Wyatt: the nave and the chancel, except for the E wall, were rebuilt from the foundations; the nave was extended to the W over the site of the former W tower; and a new three-stage tower built at the W end of the S aisle. In 1933 a N aisle (comprising vestry and organ chamber) was added to the chancel and the S chancel chapel refitted, both to the designs of W.H. Randoll Blacking (DRO Faculties).

The church is constructed mainly of flint and stone chequerwork but the chancel N aisle and the medieval S chapel are of flint rubble. The eastward extension of the S chapel has alternate courses of flint and brick.

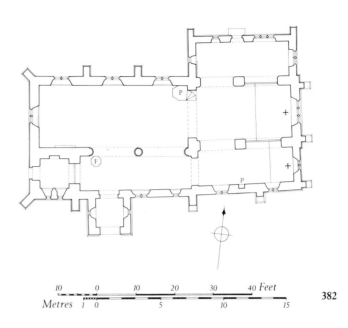

382

c. 1125

c. 1175

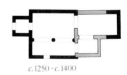
c. 1250 - *c.* 1400

383. Development.

384. Exterior from S.

Excepting the lower course of the E wall and the simple responds of the W bay of the S arcade, which are Romanesque (the pointed arch is probably an alteration), the chancel is largely 19th century. The E bay of the S arcade is a 19th-century replica of the W bay. The original eastern limit of the S chapel can be seen externally at the break between the medieval flint rubble and the 19th-century brick and flint bands, and internally at about the line of the round-headed piscina in the S wall. The head of the 14th-century two-light window in the S wall is cut out of a 13th-century grave slab incised with a cross (Montgomerie 1944, 194). The medieval E window of the chapel was similar to the present one but had three lights, not two. The late medieval wagon roof was lengthened to cover the 19th-century extension of the chapel and a boss bearing the arms of the Batt-Buckley family was added at the centre. The chancel arch, apart from the 12th-century impost blocks, appears to be completely Victorian.

The date of the original nave is uncertain. It was not aligned with the Romanesque chancel, so it may have been later, although it must antedate the S arcade. The two-bay S arcade was taken down and re-erected in 1854–5 in its original form. It has round responds and pier, and moulded capitals. All the other features of the nave and tower are of the 19th century except for the War Memorial Calvary of 1920, by W.D. Caroe, on the exterior of the S wall of the nave (DRO Faculties).

The plain polygonal font is probably a 17th-century version of a late medieval type. The Communion table now in the S chapel is also of the 17th-century but the coffin stool is dated 1736. The stained glass in the E windows of both chancel and S chapel is by Christopher Webb.

The oldest monument is a plain mid 17th-century tablet to Charles Hartshorne (+ 1644), steward to Lord Gorges of Longford Castle. The other monuments are mostly to the successive 18th or 19th-century owners of New Hall, Bodenham. The most noteworthy is that to John Thomas Batt (+ 1831) by the younger Westmacott and formerly on the N wall of the chancel but now at the W end. It includes a tall panel with almost life-size figures in high relief of Faith and Hope.

385. Grave slab re-used as head to window in S wall of chapel.

386. Monument, now at W end nave by R. Westmacott junior, to John Thomas Batt (+ 1831).

387. Interior looking E.

388. Exterior from SE before 19th-century alterations, *Buckler* 1805 (*see* also 384).

389. Exterior from SE.
390. Exterior from NW, showing stair turret, *Buckler 1805*.

ODSTOCK

St Mary   su 152261   *Civil Parish of Odstock*

Only three features of the former, Romanesque, church survive, all *ex situ*: a round-headed window and two grotesque corbels. The 13th-century chancel was rebuilt in 1871. The nave, which dates from *c.* 1250, is intact. The building sequence of the W end, tower and tower stair turret is difficult to interpret precisely. The most likely reconstruction is that in the mid to late 15th century it was decided to rebuild the church from the W end. The lower stages of the tower were built (possibly upon the foundations of a relatively small earlier tower) with angle buttresses not only on the W side but on the E side extending to ground level as if the tower were intended to be free-standing. The W wall of the nave had to be canted at each end to accommodate the buttresses. The stair turret was begun at the same time, as a large polygonal structure. About 1500 there was a change of plan and a wider tower-arch was built, possibly in order not to obscure a new three-light window in the W wall of the tower. When the tower had reached the apex of the nave roof and the stair turret the eaves of the roof, building was abandoned. In the early 17th century, perhaps *c.* 1607 (*see* below), the work was made good; the tower was completed by the addition of a low belfry stage and the stair turret roofed as it stood but with two thirds of its internal space infilled with rubble and a wooden staircase installed in the remaining third, giving access both to the upper stages of the tower and to a gallery under the tower arch. In 1869–71 the church was restored by the architect J. Fowler: the walls of the chancel were rebuilt, the S wall being realigned parallel to the N (WRO Bishop's Mortgages 189); the church was almost entirely stripped of its furnishings, including the chancel screen. The tower was restored in the early 20th century and the Victorian decorations removed in 1946 (WRO 784/7).

The tower, the chancel and the nave buttresses are constructed of flint and stone chequerwork. The nave is of flint rubble.

The chancel, though mostly of the 19th century, retains two earlier windows: the Romanesque window now in the N wall, which was discovered in the former S wall, and the 13th-century three-light E window, reset in its former position in the E wall. The nave, including the chancel arch, is mid 13th century; both N and S walls have the same elevation of a continuously moulded doorway towards the W end and two lancet windows to the E. The piscina at the E end of the S wall is also original. Only the buttresses are additions. The roof may be contemporary with the fabric but it was much renewed when the plastering was removed in the 19th century. The tie beams are insertions. A masonry porch formerly sheltered the S doorway which was, until the mid 19th century, the principal entry to the church. The present wooden N porch, *c.* 1871, incorporates as corner-stones two large Romanesque corbels carved in the form of grotesque animals.

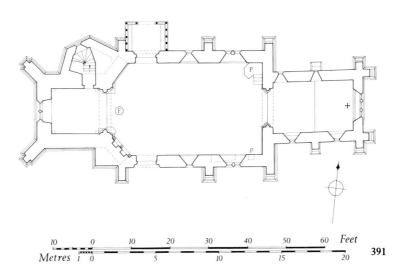

The Perpendicular rebuilding of the W end extends to within 2 ft (0.61 m) of the nave doorways, so a free-standing tower could never have co-existed with the Early English nave, but the mouldings of the internal plinth of the W wall of the nave are the same as those of the external plinth of the tower and its buttresses, suggesting that the base of the whole tower is of one build. The flint chequering and the unusual design of the western buttresses are part of the late medieval, not the 17th-century, work; the date of the latter is suggested by a stone in the NW buttress inscribed 1607. The tower archway, which has polygonal responds and hollow chamfers of Perpendicular type, must be an insertion since it breaks through the internal plinth. The present two-light W window is of *c.* 1910; until at least the early 19th century the W window had three lights and panel tracery. The 17th-century internal doorway in the N wall at the level of the W window was for a gallery whose occupants left many contemporary graffiti on the tower walls. Similar four-centred arched doorways open into the other two stages of the tower.

The round font is of 13th-century origin but it was retooled *c.* 1871 at which time the 14th-century monument in the S wall of the nave was revealed; within the cinquefoiled recess lies a slab incised with a gowned figure and a fragmentary inscription. The Classical monument now at the W end of the nave and formerly at the SW end of the chancel is Elizabethan, although the deaths commemorated upon it are of the 18th century. The carved wooden pulpit is also Elizabethan except for the loyal inscription dated 1580, which is a Victorian replacement. The sounding-board has been destroyed.

392. Exterior from NW.
393. N doorway, now within N vestry.

394. Exterior from SE (*see* also 56).

ORCHESTON ST GEORGE

St George   su 060449   *Civil Parish of Orcheston*

The proportions and thick walling of the nave and chancel of the present church suggest a 12th-century origin, although the two surviving Romanesque features, the N doorway and a carved male head, are not *in situ*. There is documentary reference to a church at Orcheston St George in the late 12th century. Early 14th-century work occurs in the chancel arch and in windows in the chancel, and formerly existed in the SW part of the nave. Thus, with the exception of the W tower, the comprehensive Perpendicular refashioning of the church *c.* 1500 involved the adaptation of earlier building, not the construction of new: the chancel and nave were embattled and straight-headed windows were inserted in the E wall of the chancel and in the nave; the W tower was built and the chancel arch was heightened and the W wall was pierced to allow a tower arch. Major post-medieval alterations to the fabric took place in 1833 when the roofs were reconstructed, the windows on the S side of the nave were rearranged to form a symmetrical composition and a brick N porch was replaced by a vestry built of flint. In 1858 the church was redecorated and stained glass inserted in the windows. In 1883 the church was repaired and refitted. It was transferred to the Redundant Churches Fund in 1985.

The church is built of knapped flint mixed at random with freestone, the tower is of ashlar.

The chancel, though possibly 12th-century in plan, is substantially of *c.* 1500. The plain three-light E window and the single-light windows at the E ends of the N and S walls are of this date, as is the piscina in the sill of the S window. The two lancet windows with trefoiled heads, at the W end of the N and S walls, are of *c.* 1300. The roof was reconstructed in 1833 but the Perpendicular battlements have survived.

The jambs of the chancel arch have broad single chamfers and pyramid stops; perhaps they originally formed part of a continuously moulded arch. In the Perpendicular remodelling the springing of the arch was raised and reworked in order to heighten the opening. A late medieval screen with four trefoil-headed lights on each side of a central opening was removed in 1883.

The doorway in the N wall of the nave, which now leads into the vestry, is of uncertain date. Internally the doorhead is four-centred; externally it is straight-headed. Set on the face of the wall around it is a Romanesque doorway of one order with a plain unchamfered arch supported by shafts with cushion capitals; that it is not *in situ* is shown by the poor fit of the arch on the capitals and the relation of the doorway to the present door-opening. The 12th-century carved head, seemingly hooded and with protruding eyes, set above the window to the W of the door is also *ex situ*. The form of the nave windows dates largely from the Perpendicular remodelling. Exceptions are the two-light, transomed window at the E end of the N

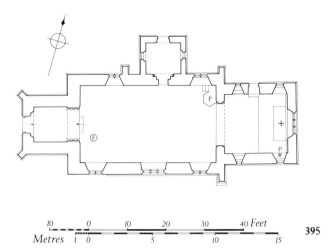

395

wall, which is 19th century, and the westernmost window in the S wall, which in 1833 replaced a single trefoil-headed lancet (the present window is a copy of the easternmost S window). In 1833 the easternmost S window was given a hood-mould similar to that of the central window and the stonework of both these windows was renewed. At this same date a small two-light window, high up towards the W end and perhaps lighting a gallery, was suppressed. When the nave roof was reconstructed in 1833, the battlements crowning the walls were removed and the walls heightened by a brick corbel table. A pitched roof was then erected, the apex reaching almost the height of the tower and concealing the E belfry opening.

396.   Interior looking E.

397

The W tower is of two stages. The W doorway and window both open into the lower stage which in turn opens into the nave through an archway with jambs and soffit decorated with tracery panelling. There is decorative foliage carving in the spandrels of the W doorway and the stops to the hood-mould of the W window are carved in the form of grotesque heads.

The panel of the Royal Arms of Charles I is dated 1636. The Communion table is also of 17th-century origin though altered in the 19th century. Most of the stained glass is of *c.* 1858 excepting a 17th or 18th-century roundel depicting a symbol of the Trinity. The church still has its 19th-century light fittings. In the nave there is one late 17th-century tablet with a painted inscription and one early 18th-century double tablet with oval inscription panels and sunflowers carved in the spandrels. On the S wall of the chancel is a tablet of *c.* 1830 by Reeves of Bath to the Rev. Chambre Brabazon Ponsonby Lowther, whose hatchment is preserved in the nave. On the S wall of the nave is a large Gothic monument of *c.* 1861 by Osmond to Stephen Mills.

398

399

397. Orcheston St George: tower arch with tracery panelling.
398. Orcheston St George: Communion table.
399. Orcheston St George: NW window of nave (*see* p. 35).

ORCHESTON ST MARY

St Mary   SU 059457   *Civil Parish of Orcheston*

The earliest parts of the church are the nave and the S aisle. The aisle dates from the mid 13th century but the nave could be earlier if it survives from a previous stage when the nave was unaisled. The tower, to the W of the aisle but not integrated with it, was added *c.* 1300. About 1400 new windows were inserted in the S aisle and a stair was added in the E wall of the tower. The chancel appears to have been rebuilt in the 16th century. A major restoration took place in 1832–3: a new chancel was erected on the old foundations and the N wall of the nave and the E and S walls of the S aisle were largely reconstructed; the former timber-framed S porch was replaced by a masonry structure in the same style as the chancel; new roofs and fittings were installed. In 1860–5 there were plans for further restoration and refitting but little was executed apart from the blocking of the upper part of the stair tower and the tiling of the church floor. Major repairs were carried out in the 1950s.

The E and S walls of the church and the tower are constructed of flint and stone chequers; the less conspicuous N and W walls are of flint rubble.

The chancel was completely rebuilt in 1832 upon the foundations of its predecessor thus perpetuating a different alignment from the nave. The style chosen was a mixture of Perpendicular elements, such as straight-headed windows with hood moulds, and Early English, such as the

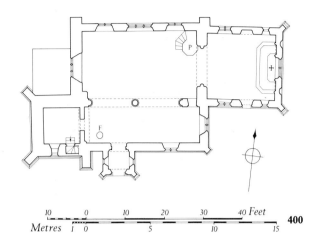

pinnacled buttresses. The chancel arch is contemporary with the chancel.

The W and S walls of the nave are medieval, but the N wall and its windows are of 1833. The 16th-century straight-headed W window, of three lights, is set high in the wall because of the external ground level and is deeply splayed internally to allow maximum light. The present roof, of 1833, replaces a medieval one reputedly having traces of painting (Colt Hoare 1825, 41). The two-bay S arcade consists of two tall two-centred arches

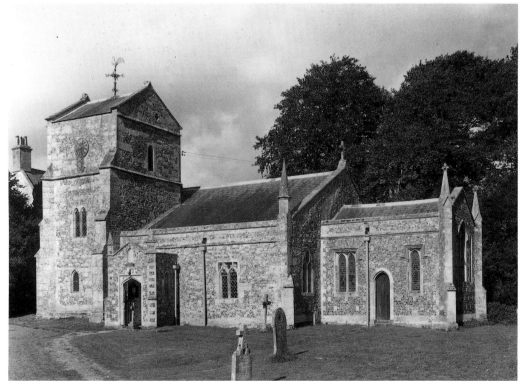

401.   Exterior from SE.

402

supported by a round pier and responds with moulded capitals. The S doorway is of the same mid to late 13th-century date. The E and S windows of the aisle both have tracery of *c.* 1400: the latter window is straight headed. In the 1833 restoration the windows were replaced in their former positions but a pinnacle was added to the exterior SE angle of the aisle.

About 1400 a stair was inserted into the E wall of the tower. To accommodate it the wall was widened eastwards, thus intruding into both the W end of the S aisle and the SW angle of the nave, and was supported on a low and crudely formed arch. The S window in the lowest stage of the tower is of 1833 but the other openings in the tower, including the quatrefoil in the E gable of the saddleback roof, are medieval.

The only fitting to survive from before the 19th century is a 17th-century chest of three panels. The font and the stone altar, which has a panelled tracery front, date from 1833. Other furnishings are Victorian.

403

404 **405**

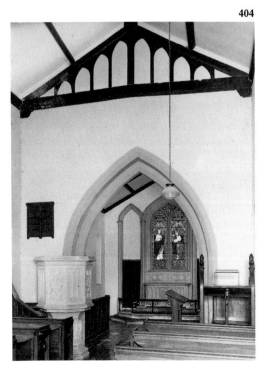

PITTON   (Former chapelry of Alderbury)

St Peter   su 213316   *Civil Parish of Pitton and Farley*

The medieval building is still largely intact in spite of a drastic restoration in 1880 by Ewan Christian. The earliest identifiable features are the Romanesque volute capital, now *ex situ* above the pulpit, and the S doorway of the nave, possibly also reset; the basic plan of the nave and chancel may also be of 12th-century origin. The fabric of the present building, with the exception of the 19th-century N aisle and vestry, is of the 13th century although only the tower-porch preserves openings of that date. In the first half of the 14th century new E and W windows of similar design were inserted; straight-headed windows were inserted in the S wall of the church *c.* 1500. A transverse N aisle with a gallery was built in the early 19th century. In the 1880 restoration the transverse aisle was demolished and replaced by a vestry, partly on the same site, and by a conventional N aisle to the nave. The tower was heightened and the nave windows altered.

The chancel retains its straight-headed single-light side windows but the E window has lost its original tracery which was of the same form as that of the W window. The alteration may have been carried out in 1886 when the stained glass, by Kempe, was inserted. The tripartite chancel screen, in existence in the early 19th century, has disappeared. The chancel arch was replaced in 1880 and the nave refenestrated except for the W window. The S doorway of the nave is of the late 12th century but the depressed four-centred rear arch suggests that it has been reset. Only the lowest stage of the S tower-porch is of medieval origin; its original S doorway has a tall shouldered

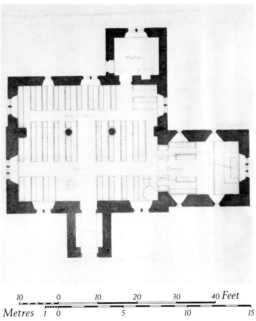

406.   Plan from faculty, 1879.

10   0   10   20   30   40 *Feet*
Metres   1   0   5   10   15

arch, moulded with one deep hollow chamfer.

The font is of the 13th century; the bowl is decorated with a cable moulding. The 17th-century 'crown' font cover has been lost but the Communion table, of the 17th or early 18th-century, survives in the vestry. The late 18th-century organ case is a recent introduction from a Nonconformist chapel near Westbury. There is one brass inscription plate of 1580 now without the coat-of-arms which formerly surmounted it.

407.   Exterior from SE before restoration of 1880, photographed in 1853 (*see* also 411).

408. Plan of church before restoration, from faculty, 1879.

409. Interior of nave looking SW.

410. Interior looking E before restoration, *Kemm* 1865.

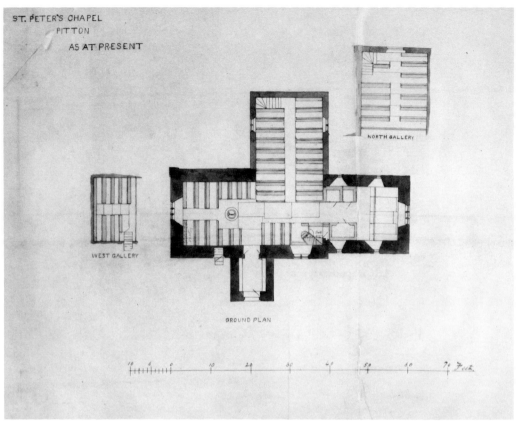

408

409

410

411. Exterior from SE (*see* also 407).

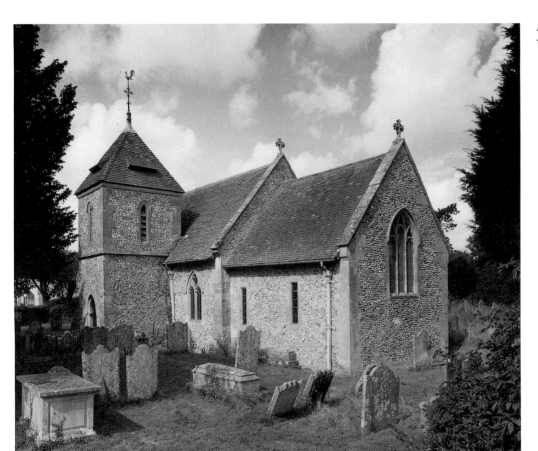

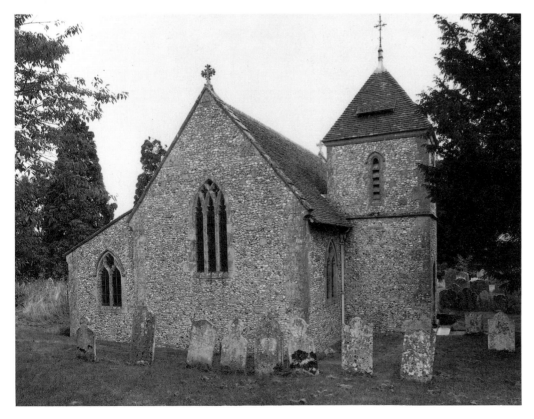

412. Exterior from W.

PORTON

413. Exterior from SE.
414. Interior looking E, before alterations in 1973.
415. Interior of former chapel looking E, *Kemm* 1865.

413

414

415

PORTON   (Former chapelry of Idmiston)

St Nicholas   su 190365   *Civil Parish of Idmiston*

The present building replaces a medieval chapel which stood about 200 yards to the NW and consisted of a chancel, nave with bellcote on the roof, and S porch. From that church are the 15th-century polygonal font, now lacking its 17th or 18th-century crown cover, and a pair of 17th-century coffin stools. The new church was built in 1876–7 to designs by J.L. Pearson in Decorated style. It consists of a chancel, nave, N vestry and S porch. In 1973 the church was restored and the design of the roof altered internally by Brandt, Potter. It has now become the parish church, in place of Idmiston. Two 17th-century oak arm-chairs, one of which has been brought from Idmiston church, are preserved in the church; that original to the church has renewed feet.

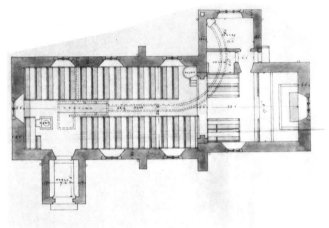

416

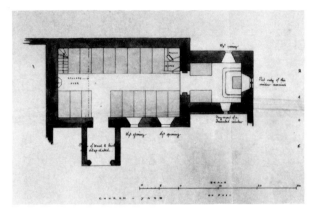

417

416. Plan from faculty, 1876.
417. Plan of former chapel, from faculty, 1876.
418. Exterior of former chapel, *Buckler c.* 1805.

REDLYNCH

St Birinus, Morgan's Vale   su 198211   *Civil Parish of Redlynch*

The church was erected in 1894–6 to serve as a chapel of Downton church and in 1915 was assigned an ecclesiastical district. It was built to the designs of C.E. Ponting in a free Gothic style and consists of an unaisled nave and chancel, under a continuous roof, with a W belfry and porches. The body of the church is of red brick with stone dressings to the windows and purple brick panels below the nave windows. The belfry and porches include elements of timber framing.

The original fittings survive, except for the chancel screen.

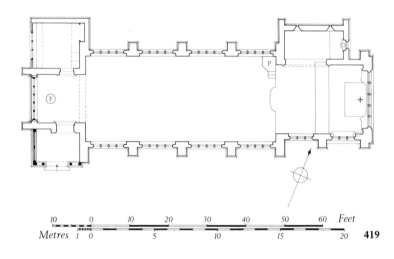

420. Interior looking E before removal of chancel screen, *A. Needham Wilson c.* 1920 (?).

419

421.   Exterior from S.

REDLYNCH

St Mary   su 211202   *Civil Parish of Redlynch*

The church was built in 1837 to serve the eastern part of the large ancient parish of Downton, at the instigation of the vicar, Archdeacon Liscombe Clarke. In 1841 an ecclesiastical district was assigned to it. The church consists of an unaisled nave, a separate chancel, a S porch and an ogee-capped bell turret on the W gable. The architect was probably James Dean (*see* p. 68). The style chosen was, except for the bell turret, of a late medieval character. It is constructed of grey stock brick with sparse stone dressings.

The only original fittings to survive are the stone, tracery-panelled altar and the font. The church was restored and refitted in 1902–3 and the W gallery was almost entirely removed in 1951.

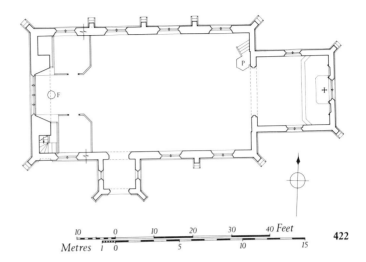

422

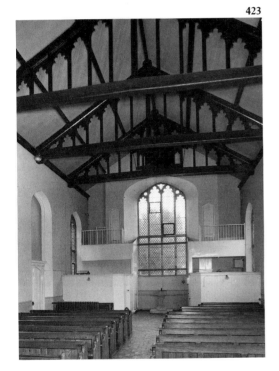

423

424

423. Interior looking W.
424. Exterior from SW.
425. Exterior from SE, print 1837.

425

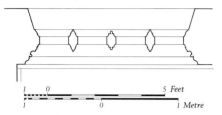

426. Section of N (above) and S (below) windows of nave (*see* also 72–73).

427. Interior looking E.
428. Exterior from SW, before alteration of S doorway, *Buckler* 1805.

ROLLESTONE

St Andrew   SU 074431   *Civil Parish of Shrewton*

The church, although small, served an independent parish until recent times. Both nave and chancel were built in the 13th century. The nave was perhaps the earlier; of the first quarter of the century. During the later Middle Ages two large windows were inserted in the nave. The church was restored in the 1840s when a bellcote was erected on the W gable, the chancel and the chancel arch largely rebuilt, the S doorway altered, a S porch added and hoodmoulds were placed over every window. The building is constructed of flint and stone chequerwork.

In the chancel the form of the original windows is preserved although much of the detail is of the 19th century. The chancel arch, with head corbels, is also Victorian. The original openings of the nave have all been altered. The S doorway formerly had a decorated lintel and a plain pointed tympanum but these features were lost when the opening was heightened in the 19th century. Only the jambs are original. The N doorway is blocked. The window on the N side has three lights and panel tracery within a two-centred head and dates from *c.* 1400. The window on the S, of *c.* 1500, has four lights and a four-centred head with small tracery

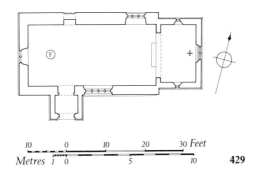

10   0   10   20   30 *Feet*
Metres 1 0   5   10   **429**

mouchettes above the main lights. The cambered tie-beam roof is of the 15th or 16th century.

The font is of the early 13th century and appears to have the original stem and base. The 'crown' font cover is of the 17th century as are the Communion rails and Communion table. The carved panel between the front legs of the table is a Victorian addition. The 17th-century decorated bench ends were introduced in 1981 from the church of St Catherine at Haydon, near Sherborne in Dorset.

430.   Exterior from NE.

431. Exterior from SE.

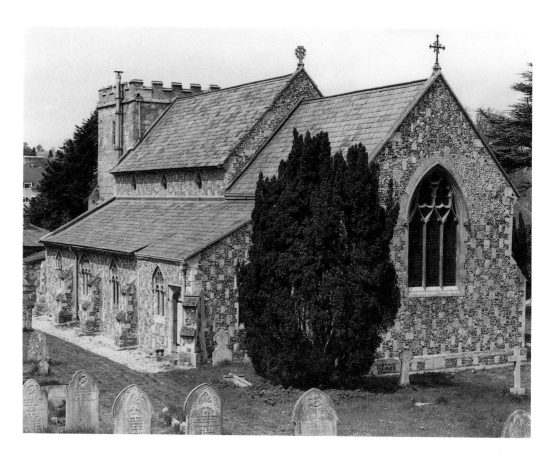

432. Exterior from NW before 1854 rebuilding, *Buckler* 1805.

SHREWTON

St Mary   su 070444   *Civil Parish of Shrewton*

The church was extensively altered by T.H. Wyatt in 1854 but preserves many earlier features. Before alteration the nave was Romanesque, the chancel Early English and the W tower Perpendicular; there was also, apparently, post-Reformation work, for example a porch at the W end of the S aisle. In the 19th-century rebuilding the W tower was retained but the nave was lengthened to the E by one bay. The chancel thus had to be rebuilt on new foundations, although the early 13th-century responds of the former chancel arch were re-used. The aisles were completely reconstructed and a N doorway and porch added. Nearly all the furnishings, including the font bowl, were replaced. A spire was intended for the W tower but never erected. The body of the church is built of flint and stone chequerwork, the medieval W tower is of ashlar.

The chancel has no medieval features except for the 13th-century piscina with carved stops and the contemporary window reset above it. The responds of the chancel arch date from *c.* 1200. They each consist of three shafts carrying capitals decorated with crocket and foliage motifs. The arches and the two E piers of the nave arcade are entirely of the 19th century (the faculty plan of 1854 marks the SE pier as medieval and the SW pier as new; however, such a complicated re-arrangement seems unlikely). Much of the detailing, even on the medieval W piers and responds also, seems Victorian. The W tower is of *c.* 1500 although hood-moulds were added to the W doorway and W window in 1854.

The present neo-Romanesque bowl of the font replaces a plain 12th-century font of similar shape: the stem is medieval. There are some *ex situ* fragments of medieval carved stone, notably the volute capital of an angle shaft, perhaps from a Romanesque doorway, and a late medieval cross-head found in a nearby cottage wall in the 19th century (Devizes Mus., Parish Notes for Rev. J. Wilkinson). The head of a wooden arcaded screen of the early 17th century from the old church has been re-used behind the benches on the N side of the chancel. The Communion table is a Victorian reworking of a Jacobean original and was formerly in the church of Fittleton and then Maddington (WRO 1336/84). The monuments are mostly to members of the Goldisborough and Wansborough families. There are some plain 17th-century tablets and three decorated 18th-century tablets. There is another such tablet on the external face of the E wall of the N aisle. The churchyard railings are of 1832 (WRO 1336/37, Churchwardens' Accounts).

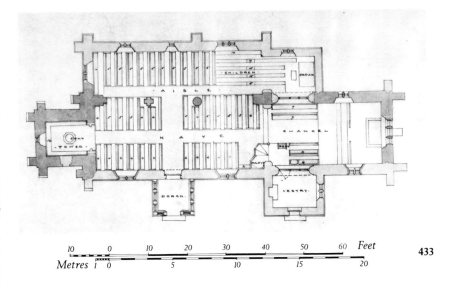

10   0   10   20   30   40   50   60   *Feet*   **433**
Metres 1 0   5   10   15   20

434. W elevation with proposed spire on W tower, from faculty, 1854.

436

438

435. Shrewton: interior looking SE with original NW pier and neo-Romanesque font of 1854 in foreground.

437

436. Shrewton: Romanesque volute capital of angle shaft, *ex situ*.

437. Shrewton: churchyard railings, 1832.

438. Shrewton: late medieval cross-head, *ex-situ*.

SOUTH NEWTON

ST ANDREW   SU 088343   *Civil Parish of South Newton*

The church was extensively rebuilt by T.H. Wyatt in 1861–2 but its general form was little altered. The medieval building consisted of a chancel, apparently of the 13th century, a nave with a N aisle, and a W tower. In the early 19th century a vestry/schoolroom was built S of the chancel but it was soon removed (Colt Hoare 1825, 53). Wyatt added a new vestry to the S and an organ chamber to the N of the chancel. The external walls of the N aisle were rebuilt, the S porch replaced and the openings of the W tower altered. The narrow 13th-century chancel arch was moved to serve as the tower arch. The furnishings were completely renewed and the walls painted with texts; both furnishings and decoration survive unchanged. The corbels for the roof principals and for the Victorian responds have elaborate naturalistic carving. The church is built of flint and stone chequerwork.

The original E and N walls of the chancel survive, at least in the lower courses, and the windows, although largely renewed, retain the old design. The plan of the nave is probably Romanesque, but the Romanesque arch, *c.* 1150, set as the S doorway, may not be *in situ*. The carved tympanum and outer frieze of the arch seem original; other elements are Victorian. The E respond and pier of the three-bay N arcade date from *c.* 1200 but the profile of the central arch of

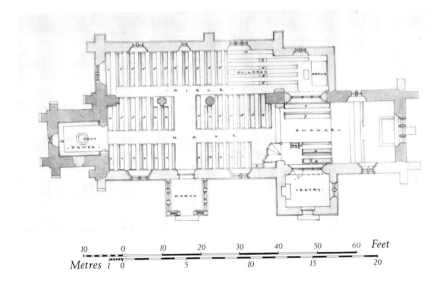

the arcade changes abruptly and the remainder of the arcade to the W dates from the 14th century. The pier of *c.* 1200 is round and has a single-moulded capital; that of the 14th century has a complex section of four conjoined octagonal shafts. The two-light 14th-century window in the N aisle and the two straight-headed 15th-century windows in the S wall of the nave have been reset

439.   Plan from faculty, 1861.

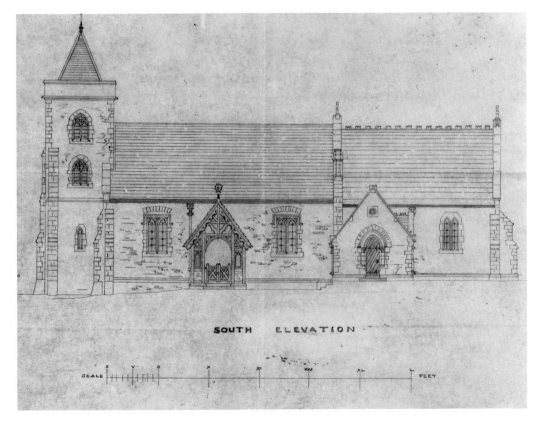

SOUTH ELEVATION

440.   S elevation (vestry not as built) from faculty, 1861.

approximately in their original positions. The roofs of chancel, nave and aisle are all Victorian. The two-centred tower arch, formerly the chancel arch, has moulded round capitals; the abaci, however, project in three lobes to carry the orders of the arch. The marble shafts to the capitals are Victorian. Before 1861 the tower apparently contained Romanesque features, but these are no longer visible (Colt Hoare 1825, 53). The general appearance of the tower was not altered although the fabric itself appears to have been almost entirely rebuilt.

The bowl of the font seems entirely Victorian but the shaft may retain its original form. The plain wooden chest is dated 1703. There are three tablets of the mid 19th century, two by Mitcherd and one by Osmond.

441. Romanesque arch and tympanum of S doorway.

442. Exterior from N.

443. Exterior from NE before 1861 restoration, *Buckler* 1804 (*see* also 442).

444

445

444. Tower (formerly chancel) arch.
445. Interior of chancel looking E.

446. Nave arcade, looking W.

447. Exterior from SE.

448. Interior looking E with, in foreground, tomb on N wall by Osmond, to 2nd Earl Nelson (+ 1835).

STANDLYNCH   (Chapelry of Downton)

ST MARY   SU 183235   *Civil Parish of Downton*

The chapel was founded *c.* 1147, as a dependency of Downton church (VCH 1980, 71). It exercised certain parochial functions but remained closely associated with the lords of the manor of Standlynch, and by the mid 19th century it had become annexed to Standlynch House (renamed Trafalgar House) as a private chapel. The original building of nave and chancel dates from *c.* 1400 although it incorporates a few Romanesque fragments and may follow the Romanesque plan. It was substantially rebuilt in 1677 by Maurice and Joan Buckland when mullioned and transomed windows and a central doorway were inserted in the S wall of the nave. The chapel was restored by the 3rd Earl Nelson in 1846 when windows of Gothic form were reinserted, and again in 1859–66 under William Butterfield, who added the S porch. In 1914, when the 4th Earl Nelson converted it into a Roman Catholic place of worship (with a rededication to Mary Queen of Heaven and St Michael and All Angels), the building was refitted and enlarged by the addition of a N vestry. Since the sale of the Trafalgar estate by the Nelson family in 1948 the chapel has remained disused. It is built of flint and stone chequerwork.

The chancel has a three-light panel-traceried E window of 1846 and original straight-headed side windows with cusped lights. The modern ceiled roof may reproduce a late medieval or 17th-century original. The Perpendicular chancel arch has two orders of shafts with a deep hollow between them. It is flanked by two tabernacled niches enclosing miniature lierne vaults. The nave appears to have been substantially rebuilt in 1677. The W wall retains a two-light traceried window of *c.* 1400 and two stones decorated with Romanesque blind arcading; it also incorporates below the W window sill a date-stone of 1677 with roman numerals and, in the gable, another date-stone with arabic numerals and the arms of Buckland above. The present openings in the S wall are all Victorian. The former roof, of the late 17th

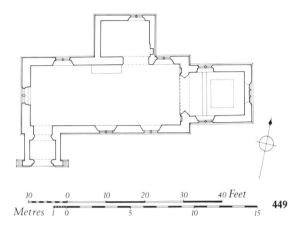

449

century, incorporated a bellcote under a dormer on the S slope. The apexes of the gables were surmounted by crosses, as now, and the kneelers of the gables by 'flaming torch' finials. The plaster coving of the eaves on the N side may also be of the 17th century. The 19th-century S porch shelters *ex situ* fragments of medieval stone sculpture: on the internal face of the S wall is a Romanesque male head and opposite, above the S door, are three late medieval panels, two with figurative religious subjects and a third ornamental.

The only fittings to survive are the plain polygonal font, probably of 1677 (now in a nearby garden), stained glass of the 19th and early 20th century and the panelling of 1914. On the S wall of the nave is a marble decorated tablet to Joan Buckland (+ 1689) and, above the S door, a plain commemorative tablet to the 1st Earl Nelson (+ 1835). Opposite, on the N wall, is the large Gothic monument by Osmond to the 2nd Earl Nelson (+ 1835). In the floor, a polychrome inlaid cross slab, perhaps designed by Butterfield, covers a burial vault.

450.   Exterior from SE after 17th-century and before 19th-century alterations, *Buckler* 1805.

451. Exterior from S.

452. Exterior from N, showing upper part of tower rebuilt in 1674.

STAPLEFORD

St Mary   su 071374   *Civil Parish of Stapleford*

The earliest parts of the church are the nave and the S aisle. The aisle dates from the later 12th century but the nave is possibly a survival from an earlier, unaisled, stage in the development of the building. In the mid 13th century the present chancel was erected and a chapel added on the N side of the nave. About 1300 the lower stage of the tower was built to the W of the chapel. In the first part of the 14th century the chancel was refurbished and a S chapel formed. A century later the exterior, particularly on the S side, was altered by the lowering of the nave roof, the creation of a clearstorey and the addition of a two-storeyed S porch. The upper part of the tower was raised in 1674. The church less the chancel was restored in 1861 by William Slater; the chancel was restored eight years later by Ewan Christian. Nearly all the old fittings were removed including a painted tympanum in the chancel arch.

The church is largely of flint mixed with freestone, but the tower, the nave clearstorey and the S face of the porch are ashlar.

The original 13th-century features of the chancel are the S doorway and the W window in the N wall. The easternmost windows of both N and S walls are 14th century; the W window in the S wall is a 15th-century insertion. The tracery of the E window is mostly Victorian. The sedilia date from the 14th century although the upper parts are largely a Victorian restoration. Below the window in the external face of the E wall is a wide trefoil-headed recess; above it, in the gable, is a 14th or 15th-century panel of the Rood. The chancel arch appears to be late medieval although similar in form to the N chapel arch.

The nave was partly rebuilt in 1861. The W wall was re-erected from the ground, the W window

reset at a higher level and its tracery altered. At this time the Perpendicular wall parapets and roof were removed and a steeply pitched roof substituted. The 13th-century arch to the N chapel consists of three chamfered orders the central one of which is carried on short shafts terminating in head corbels. The chapel itself dates from the 15th century, but the existence of the 13th-century arch shows there had been an earlier building on the site. There are 19th-century alterations to the fenestration and to the E wall parapet. A 15th-century corbel head depicting a bishop is built into the N wall.

The tower is of three stages of which the lower and middle are *c.* 1300; the upper can be dated to 1674 by an inscription on the S face. The N doorway is an insertion of the 19th century. The tower arch is carried on sculpted imposts and there are two further corbel heads built into the internal walls of the lower stage.

The S chapel was formed in the 14th century by dividing off the E bay of the Romanesque aisle and extending it to the S. The S window has reticulated tracery; the tomb recess below the window and the piscina have corresponding moulded ogee arches. The roof, which was lowered in the 15th century to allow for the nave clearstorey, is the only one in the church which was not replaced in the 19th century. The Romanesque arcade is richly ornamented both in its scalloped capitals and in the chevron and dogtooth of its arches. The piers have alternating courses of greensand and ironstone; early 13th-century foliage painting survives in the soffits of the easternmost arches. The S doorway is of the same date and design as the arcade except that its E capital and shaft were replaced in the 13th century. The S porch was

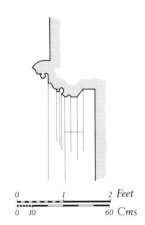

454. Section of arch of sedilia, chancel (*see also* 43, 457).

455. Development.

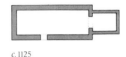

c. 1125

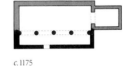

c. 1175

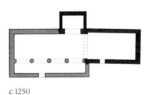

c. 1250

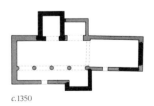

c. 1350

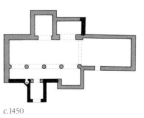

c. 1450

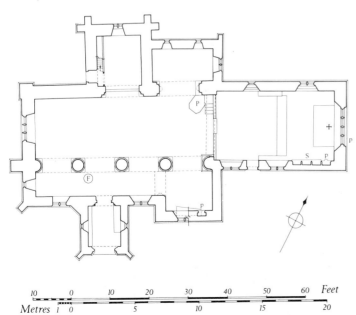

| Feet | 10 | 0 | 10 | 20 | 30 | 40 | 50 | 60 |
| Metres | 1 | 0 | | 5 | | 10 | | 15 | 20 |

453

originally two-storeyed but the floor has been removed and the stair in the NW angle blocked. The tomb chest within it, moved from the N chapel in the 19th century, has a slab incised with a floriate cross, perhaps of the 13th century. The Romanesque font has feather-like fluting round the upper part of the bowl. Around the base of the font are set much-worn tiles of *c*. 1300. From the 17th century survive a chest, coffin stools and a Communion table. On the N side of the chancel is a low tomb chest of the early 18th century with two inscription panels in moulded frames. The principal Victorian fitting, of 1861, is the stone pulpit inlaid with marble.

456. Stapleford: exterior from SE.

457. Stapleford: interior of chancel looking SE.

STRATFORD TONY

St Mary and St Lawrence   su 092264   *Civil Parish of Stratford Toney*

The present church dates essentially from the 14th century. The surviving features of the earlier church are all *ex situ*: an early 13th-century round arch of greensand now forming the entrance to the 18th-century brick S porch; the early 13th-century font; and the Purbeck piscina of half a century later. The chancel was built in the first part of the 14th century and the reconstruction of the church proceeded slowly westwards. The S doorway of the nave and the tower arch in the W wall date from *c.* 1500, the tower is early 16th century. Grave structural problems caused by the siting of the church on a steep riverside slope have made successive alterations necessary to both wall fabric and buttresses. The S wall of the nave was rebuilt or recased in the mid 18th century and the N wall was similarly treated later in the same century. A major repair and re-ordering took place in 1881–3 (WRO 576/8, Churchwardens' Accounts). The church was transferred to the Redundant Churches Fund in 1986.

The chancel and tower of the church are of flint mixed with freestone and with freestone dressings: the N and S walls of the nave have alternating bands of flint and brick, the flint of the N wall being cement rendered.

ˑThe chancel is entirely 14th century in design with no later alterations to plinth, buttresses or windows. The E window has reticulated tracery and the square-headed side windows have a similar design, adapted to their shape. There is a small

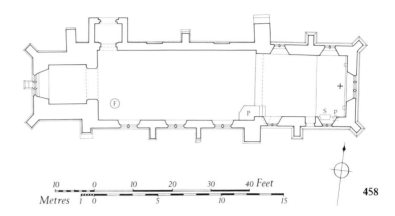

458

low-side window under the westernmost window on the S side. On the S wall near the altar (which incorporates a medieval slab with five consecration crosses) is the mid 13th-century piscina with finely moulded trefoiled head and projecting bowl carved with two fishes; a sedile is inserted below the sill. Two image brackets are set in the E wall on either side of the altar. Both chancel and nave roofs are ceiled. The chancel arch is contemporary with the chancel. The massive buttresses to N and S of the arch are 17th or 18th century, probably replacing medieval buttresses.

The nave, greatly rebuilt in the 17th and 18th centuries, has medieval foundations (and perhaps

459. Exterior from N.

much medieval fabric in the walls behind the recasing). The S wall has windows of two lights, each with a pointed arch and keystone, the segmental-headed windows of the N wall are blind. The difference in type of window and the different treatment of the brick and flint banding suggest that the N wall was rebuilt about 50 years after the S, but the bricks are of the same size and laid in the same English bond. The Perpendicular N doorway has continuously moulded jambs and a four-centred arch.

The tower arch is tall with a stilted head. The upper stage of the two-stage tower may be of a later date than the lower since it is constructed of coarser masonry and the W bell-opening is not in line with the W window. The gargoyles at the angles of the parapets seem to be authentically late medieval.

The bowl font, with roll mouldings under the rim and at the base, is of *c.* 1200; the stem and its base are 19th century. On the bowl is the fragment of a later medieval inscription in Latin. Parts of the 17th and 18th-century seating have been re-used as screens and panelling and more woodwork has been added in the same style. The early 17th-century pulpit has been reduced in height. The mid 17th-century Communion rails consist of turned balusters, with turned finials against the wall and flanking the centre gate. The stained glass, by Kempe, in the E window is of 1884. On the W wall of the nave is a small early 18th-century tablet with flanking Ionic pilaster and cherub heads below.

462

463

460. Stratford Tony: interior looking E.
462. Stratford Tony: interior of chancel looking SE, with 17th-century Communion rail in foreground.
463. Stratford Tony: chancel side window (*see* also 48).

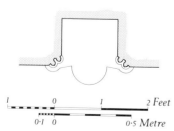

461. Stratford Tony: detail of piscina, chancel (*see* also 28, 462).

TILSHEAD

St Thomas à Becket   su 035480   *Civil Parish of Tilshead*

The earliest parts of the present church, the nave arcades and the responds of the crossing arches, appear to date from *c.* 1100; but the plan-type and the importance of Tilshead in the 11th century as a borough and royal manor raises the possibility that the building replaces a Saxon church of similar plan. The chancel is of the mid 13th century. Later medieval work is confined to the S side of the S aisle, where a new doorway was inserted and hood-moulds added above the late 13th-century windows. Extensive repairs took place in the 17th and 18th centuries, including new roofs to chancel and tower. In 1845–6 the church was considerably rebuilt and refitted by Wyatt and Brandon: the N aisle was widened and the W wall of the nave and S aisle completely reconstructed; a vestry was added in the angle between the N aisle and the tower; the nave was reroofed and the clearstorey refenestrated with windows of quatrefoil form. The church was again restored in 1904 by Medlicott and the furnishings re-ordered in 1967 by Potter and Hare.

The church is built of flint and stone laid chequerwise, treated with less regularity in the chancel than in the rest of the church.

The chancel is lit by original lancet windows in the N and S walls; at the far W end of each wall is a low-side window with a shutter. The E window of three lights with ogee trefoiled heads is an insertion of *c.* 1350. The roof is 17th century and the buttresses additions of 1846. The arches of the tower have plain responds of *c.* 1100 but later, two-centred, heads. The N and S windows of the lowest stage are 17th century; the N window was at some time blocked and given Gothic detailing when re-opened in 1846. The upper parts of the tower, including the domical roof, are probably 17th century or may even date to the 18th century

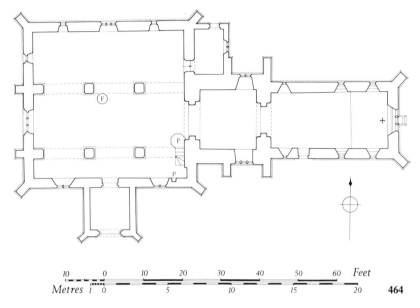

Metres							

10   0   10   20   30   40   50   60   *Feet*

Metres 1 0   5   10   15   20   **464**

when the present ring of bells was hung. The parapet on the S side is a Victorian replacement of medieval battlements.

The nave has a three-bay arcade of *c.* 1100 but the clearstorey was rebuilt in the 19th century. The W wall was completely reconstructed on the old foundations in 1846. The 'Perpendicular' W window, also of that date, may replace a late medieval window of the same design. The N aisle and the vestry to its E are additions of 1846. The S aisle was only repaired in 1846 and retains its original narrow dimensions; the windows,

465. Exterior from S.

466. Tilshead: low-side window with shutter in S wall chancel.

although replacements, reproduce the original form which was of two lights with plate tracery of late 13th-century type surmounted by a later hood mould. At the E end of the S wall is an ogee-headed piscina of the same form as the chancel E window. The 15th-century S doorway has a shallow contemporary niche above. The S porch appears to be substantially of 1846 although preserving the general form of its predecessor, including the two-centred entrance arch.

The font could be *c.* 1100, i.e. contemporary with the nave arcades. It has bands of zigzag carving below the lip and also, partly erased, round the base of the bowl; there is broad fluting between. It was removed from the church in 1846 but put back in 1888. There is a carved stone fragment of the 12th century and a stone cross of the 18th century, perhaps from a gable. The 17th-century fittings comprise turned baluster Communion rails and a Communion table the top of which has been renewed. The large canvas of the Royal Arms is of 1805. The stone pulpit, the pews in the N aisle and some of the stained glass (reset, in the nave) survive from the fittings installed in 1846. In the chancel is a pair of late 18th-century pedimented tablets and in the tower a more elaborate neo-Classical tablet of *c.* 1800. In the churchyard to the S of the church are two carved chest tombs of the early 19th century.

467. Tilshead: exterior from S before 1846 restoration, print 1846 (*see* also 465).

WEST DEAN

ST MARY   SU 257272   *Civil Parish of West Dean*

The present parish church was built in 1865–6 by
Pownall and Young about 300 yards to the S of its
predeccessor (*see* below). It consists of a nave and
apsed chancel under a continuous roof, an organ
chamber to the N, and a S porch. The W belfry
has a wooden tile-hung flèche. It was designed in a
free First Pointed style and was constructed in flint
with bands of red brick, with Bath stone dressings
to the openings. It incorporates some fittings from
the earlier church. The Romanesque font bowl is
now set on a 19th-century base of polychrome
marble. The lectern is made up of a shaft and two
waterleaf capitals of *c.* 1200, once used to support
the wall above the sedilia in the former chancel.
The 13th-century piscina and aumbry, which were
originally arranged with the arched aumbry standing on top of the straight-headed piscina, have
been reset separately with their functions reversed;
within them have been placed some tiles of *c.* 1300
from the old sanctuary. Other figurative tiles have
been lost. Seventeenth-century furnishings re-used
include three oak benches with moulded ends and
open backs. The carved reredos of the church was
erected in 1875 and was supplied, and possibly
designed, by Earp.

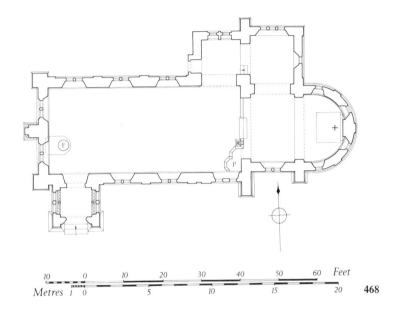

10	0	10	20	30	40	50	60	*Feet*
Metres 1	0		5		10		15	20

468

469.   Exterior from SE.

470.   Romanesque font bowl set
on base of 1865–6.

471. Upper part of former 'double decker' piscina, with medieval tiles reset within (*see* also 45).

472. Interior of present parish church looking E, showing carved reredos by Earp.

WEST DEAN

EVELYN CHAPEL   SU 257275   *Civil Parish of West Dean*
(Formerly the parish church of St Mary)

The medieval church was largely demolished in 1868 having been replaced by a new church of the same dedication but on a different site (*see* above). Only the former S aisle remains (in recent years termed the de Borbach chantry but properly called the Evelyn chapel, since the main purpose of its retention and refurbishment, paid for by George Evelyn, was to house the Evelyn monuments). The church can be reconstructed from the evidence of surviving fragments (*see* p. 80 n.90) and from notes and drawings made prior to demolition. It consisted of a chancel, nave, S aisle and S porch. A timber W belfry was carried by posts within the nave. The chancel appears to have been Early English with lancet side windows, including a low-side window; the chancel arch and nave were of a later date. In 1333 a chantry was founded in the church by Robert de Borbach and it seems that the S aisle was built to house it. The aisle was divided from the nave by a three-bay arcade the piers of which were later encased in brick. Part of the face of the easternmost arch and the medieval masonry outlining of the wall above it have been revealed by recent work. The aisle windows have two lights with quatrefoil tracery above. Similar

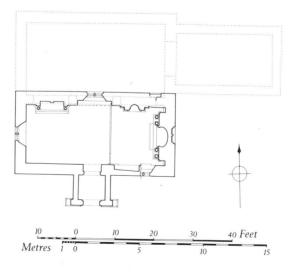

473. Plan with demolished parts shown by dotted outline.

windows, but with hood moulds, were inserted at the same period in the E and S walls of the chancel and in the N wall of the nave. That in the chancel S wall was transferred in 1868 to what had become the N wall of the surviving chapel. At the same

200

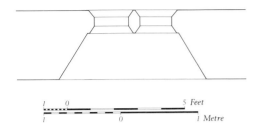

idiosyncratic inscriptions on both. The bust of the deceased is set within a recess in the side of a sarcophagus and was protected by iron doors recently removed. The monument is surmounted by allegorical figures reclining on the pediment and by a central pyramid bearing an achievement-of-arms. The latter two monuments were screened off from the rest of the chapel by a late 17th-century iron railing.

475. Monument, now on N wall, formerly in chancel, to John Evelyn I (+ 1627) and wife.

date the present S porch was built to incorporate a bell in its gable, since the building was to serve as a mortuary chapel as well as a repository of the Evelyn monuments. The chapel was transferred to the Redundant Churches Fund in 1973.

Some of the medieval fittings, such as the font and the piscina, were transferred to the new church (*see* above); others, such as the 17th-century pulpit, pews and Royal Arms, were destroyed. There survives in the present chapel an ogee cinquefoil-headed tomb-niche in the S wall, possibly the tomb of de Borbach, the 14th-century S door and a late medieval bench-end. The stone coffin comes from the site of the former church of All Saints (SU 253268), once the centre of the small Hampshire parish of West Dean. The parish belonged to the diocese of Winchester until it was united with St Mary's in 1473 and thus absorbed into the county of Wiltshire and diocese of Salisbury.

The major monuments in the chapel are all to members of the Evelyn family. The earliest was erected to John Evelyn I (+ 1627) and his wife Elizabeth, by their eldest son George. It can be attributed to the workshop of Nicholas Stone. It consists of a double-pedimented recess framing kneeling effigies of the deceased, with a relief of their children (also kneeling) below. Originally on the N side of the chancel, it was moved in 1868 to fill the westernmost arch of the arcade. On the S wall of the chapel and formerly on the S wall of the chancel is a monument, again perhaps from the workshop of Nicholas Stone, to Elizabeth Tyrell (the daughter of George Evelyn I) who died in childbirth in 1629. She is commemorated by a white marble bust within a recess with fictive curtains held back behind columns. The inscribed brass effigy now set vertically in the S wall of the chapel but formerly on the floor of the chancel, is of George Evelyn II (grandson of George Evelyn I and son of Sir John Evelyn II) who died aged six in 1641. The large monument, by John Bushnell, covering the E wall of the chapel, is *in situ*. It commemorates Robert Pierrepont (+ 1669), husband to Elizabeth the daughter and heiress of Sir John Evelyn II, and consists of a central niche, flanked by wings and closed by doors, which contains a life-size representation of the deceased rising at the Last Judgement. The latest monument, which blocked the E bay of the arcade of the former church, is to Sir John Evelyn II (+ 1685), and was, like the Pierrepont memorial, erected by Elizabeth Pierrepont who probably composed the

476. West Dean, Evelyn Chapel: monument on N wall to John Evelyn II (+ 1685) before removal of doors *c*. 1972 and restoration of chapel (*see* also 128).

WEST GRIMSTEAD

St John   SU 212266   *Civil Parish of Grimstead*

The proportions of the nave and chancel suggest that the church was probably in existence by *c.* 1150 but the only surviving Romanesque features are the font and a grotesque beast's head, perhaps a label stop, set *ex situ*. The N aisle was added to the nave in the early 13th century and at approximately the same time a chapel was built N of the chancel. Its width is unknown but it was possibly wider than the N aisle. A chapel was added to the S of the nave towards the end of the 13th century. In the 14th century the chancel was widened to the N and a new chancel arch formed and new roofs framed for the chancel, nave and N aisle. The N wall of the N chapel was aligned with that of the N aisle thus allowing a continuous roof over the whole. Also in the 14th century a new E window was inserted with three trefoil-headed lights and a cinquefoiled rear arch. During the 17th and 18th centuries the church was often the subject of repairs, as evidenced by the brickwork visible externally, but the major addition was in the late 18th century when the plain brick W tower replaced a timber belfry. In 1834–5 the church was restored (Colt Hoare 1837, 204): the N and S doors were blocked and made into windows with wooden Y-tracery; the E window of the S aisle was similarly treated; internally, whitewash was stripped from the nave arcade and new seating installed with cast-iron Gothic ornament of which fragments survive. There was a further restoration *c.* 1885 (information in church register).

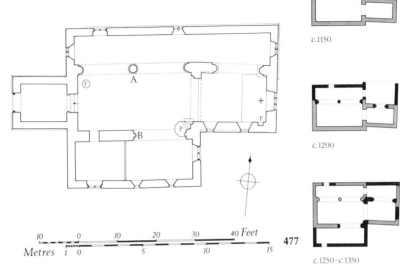

477

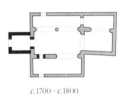

The church is built of flint rubble with freestone dressings; there is some use of greensand and brown heathstone, particularly in the nave arcade. The tower is of brick, laid in English bond.

The chancel lies on a different axis to the nave, but in the 19th century the S wall was refaced up to eaves level to make it parallel to the nave. The chancel E window is of the 14th century. The two round-headed windows in the S wall date from *c.* 1875 replacing two unevenly-spaced lancets the westernmost of which appears to have been

*c.*1150

*c.*1200

*c.*1250 - *c.*1350

*c.*1700 - *c.*1800

478.   Development.

479.   Exterior from SE.

rafters of the chancel roof, like those of the nave and the N aisle, are cut back into shallow curves either side of the purlin.

The two-bay N arcade of the nave has a round pier and responds on high plinths, carrying double-chamfered, pointed arches. The eastern arch to the S aisle is also pointed and double-chamfered, but both the arch and the responds with moulded capitals are of much greater height. The low, western arch to the S aisle is featureless and probably post-medieval. The windows at the W end of each aisle, the former doorways of *c.* 1300, have two-centred heads and hood-moulds now almost erased. The rear-arches are depressed. The only two unaltered windows in the church, apart from the E window, are those in the N and W walls of the N aisle which have two lights with trefoiled heads and sunk spandrels of 15th-century type. The E window of the S aisle is of 1835. The nave roof incorporates three arch braces; one at each end of the nave and one in the centre. The arch braces may be additions of *c.* 1500. The roof was formerly ceiled at purlin level.

The W tower is hard to date. It was in existence by 1805, but lacks any decorative features beyond a simple plinth and a pyramid roof capped by a vane dated 1867. Both E and W doorways have a plain pointed-arched head, that to the W doorway is a replacement.

The font has a plain circular bowl of the 12th century and a moulded stem of the 19th century. A medieval stone coffin within the church may have been covered by the cross slab now in the churchyard of the church. A 15th-century brass indent to Alicia Mompesson survives in the nave. The 17th-century fittings include a polygonal pulpit with foliage carving in its panels, a Communion table with an original frame but renewed top, and re-used panelling in the S aisle. The 18th-century lectern, which has a swivel desk top, is not original to the church. The panel of the Royal Arms has the arms and motto of Queen Anne after 1707. On the W wall of the N aisle is a mid 18th-century, shaped, tablet with a floral border in sunk relief and on the N wall, there is another tablet of *c.* 1800 with a double inscription.

lowered, perhaps to incorporate a low-side window. The piscina is contemporary with the E window. It was re-placed in the chancel in the late 19th century, having been moved to the S aisle in the 1835 restoration; the hood-mould is mostly a restoration. The arch to the N was rebuilt when the chancel was widened. The responds of *c.* 1200 were retained but set further apart and the arch made to spring from the N edge of the imposts rather than their centre. The chancel arch is continuously moulded and dates from the 14th century. The roof has two principal rafters and a central tie beam supported by curved wall posts to give the impression of an arch brace. The principal

480. West Grimstead: interior looking E.
481. West Grimstead: Royal Arms of Queen Anne.

WHITEPARISH

ALL SAINTS   SU 246236   *Civil Parish of Whiteparish*

The chancel, nave and aisles may be one build of *c.* 1200 although the detailing of the N arcade capitals suggests a slightly earlier date. There is no evidence of an earlier church except for some fragments of carved stone, possibly Romanesque, re-used in the W front. Such a sizable church may not have been needed until *c.* 1200 when the settlement of Frustfield, later called Whiteparish, established its pre-eminence over other settlements in the area, such as Whelpley, for example, which had its own, single-cell, chapel (Taylor: 1967, 88; 1968, 41–2). In the mid 14th century the W part of the S aisle was rebuilt, probably for structural reasons, and the W front was given a new door and window. During the 15th or early 16th century the chancel was extensively remodelled. In the early 17th century the S aisle was rebuilt or recased and new windows inserted. The N aisle was similarly treated a century later. The nave and aisles were restored by William Butterfield in 1869–70 when the aisles were rebuilt to a new design, a N porch was added and the W belfry was replaced but in approximately its original form; the church was almost completely refitted. A polygonal vestry, designed by A. Stocken, was added S of the chancel in 1969.

The exterior of the church is largely 19th-century work of flint, chequered with heathstone and Chilmark. The medieval chancel is of roughly rendered flint with brown, heathstone dressings.

The chancel walls are of early 13th-century origin but all the openings and the roof are Perpendicular except for the plain round-headed S door which might be of original fabric or a 17th-century rebuild. Both sidewalls have been much rebuilt, evidence of this is visible on the external face of the N wall and the internal face of the S wall. The tracery of the E window, with its transom and sparse cusping, may date from the early 17th century. The wagon roof, unceiled in the late 19th century, is late medieval. The chancel arch is built of alternating white and brown stone; Butterfield rebuilt the responds leaving the crooked form of the arch unaltered.

The four-bay nave arcades are early 13th century except the westernmost pier and respond on the S side, which are 14th century, and the E responds, which are Victorian. The grotesque head-corbel supporting the NW respond is original and *in situ*. The columns, of greensand, have round moulded or scalloped capitals and carry pointed arches of two unchamfered orders. The 14th-century replacements have octagonal, not round, shafts and more complex, moulded capitals. The Victorian roof replaces a late medieval one that was partly ceiled but had moulded feet to its principals. The W front formerly had only one, central, window the tracery design of which was repeated in the Butterfield restoration. At that time new windows were inserted in the W walls of the aisles. The W doorway appears to be medieval.

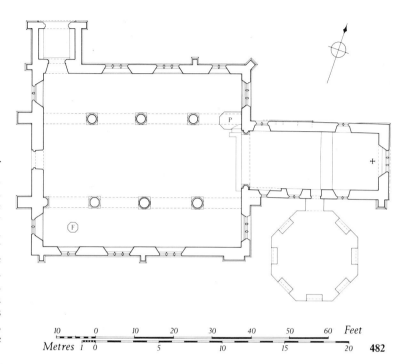

Metres					

482

483.   Exterior from SW (*see also* 129).

The only significant fittings, apart from the late
18th-century painting by J.F. Rigaud depicting St
Peter denying Christ, are the font and pulpit,
designed by Butterfield. The 17th and 18th-
century woodwork and hatchments (recorded in
drawings of before 1870) have disappeared but a
number of monuments of the same period survive.
In the chancel, flanking the altar, is a pair of late
17th-century tablets, to Edward St Barbe (+ 1671)
and his wife (+ 1692), which have carved
achievements-of-arms above and skulls and bones
below. Other memorials are chiefly to the Eyre and
Younge families. On the nave W wall is a tablet to
Gyles Eyre (+ 1655) framed with a gadrooned
base; a second tablet to Henry and Harriot Eyre
(+ 1799), is carved with foliage and neo-Classical
motifs. Above the S face of the S arcade are four
tablets of the late 17th or early 18th century, and
on the S wall of the S aisle is a further series,
mostly of the early 19th century. The late 16th-
century Eyre funeral helm has been stolen.

484. Whiteparish: interior looking W before restoration, watercolour 1869.

WILSFORD

St Michael   SU 135398   *Civil Parish of Wilsford cum Lake*

The present church was built in 1857 to the
designs of T.H. Wyatt and on the foundations of
the earlier church. The mid 12th-century tower
was preserved, but in the Victorian restoration the
bell openings were renewed and the S window and
the parapet stage were altered. The tower has a W
doorway with one order of shafts carrying scalloped capitals, and the tower arch has simple
responds with ball-like ornament on the underside
of the imposts. Other fragments of carved
Romanesque stonework, perhaps from another
doorway, are built into the 19th-century fabric.
The medieval chancel and nave were built in the
13th century. A timber-framed S porch was added,
probably in the 16th century. In 1628 a pulpit was
installed and, possibly at about the same date, the
chancel screen, which had balusters framing the
lights and a carved panel of the Hanoverian Royal
Arms before 1801 over the central opening. The
Ionic reredos was of c. 1700. None of the fittings

485. Wilsford: plan from faculty, 1856.

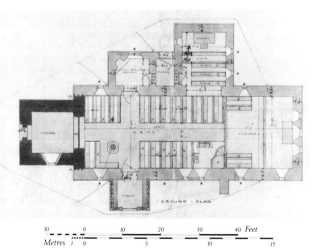

was retained for the new church except the Royal Arms and the late medieval polygonal font.

The present church has a continuous nave and chancel separated internally by a timber arch. On the N side are a vestry and an organ chamber with a vestibule between; on the S side is a timber-framed porch. The body of the church is constructed, like the tower, of knapped flint with stone dressings. Some fragments of medieval stonework were incorporated in the external walling. Most of the windows are positioned as they were in the 13th century and incorporate some original stonework; exceptions are those in the organ chamber, and the SE (lancet) window of the nave. The latter replaces a two-light Perpendicular window which was re-sited in the N wall of the vestry. The cusped and shafted rear arches of the E window are Victorian. The medieval piscina was discarded. All the principal furnishings are by Wyatt but many additional items, such as the small panel of late medieval glass in the S chancel window and the 18th-century brass wall sconces, are more recent additions.

Within the church are two neo-Classical tablets by Earlsman and two Gothic monuments, of the later 19th century, by Osmond. The most notable of the 20th-century memorials is the tablet to Wynlayne Lodge (+ 1922) by Eric Gill who also designed her tomb which stands in the churchyard to the S of the nave. At the W end of the churchyard is a headstone, to Pamela, Lady Grey (+ 1928), designed by Rex Whistler.

487.   Wilsford: exterior from SE.

488.   Wilsford: interior looking E.

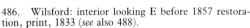

486.   Wilsford: interior looking E before 1857 restoration, print, 1833 (see also 488).

489. Exterior of chapel and alms-houses from SE.

490. Exterior of chapel and for-mer hall range from NE.

489

491. Exterior of chapel and alms-houses from SE, *Buckler c.* 1805 (*see* also 489).

492. Exterior of chapel and for-mer hall range from N, *Buckler c.* 1805 (*see* also 490).

491

492

490

WILTON

St John's Hospital   su 094314   *Civil Parish of Wilton*

St John's Hospital, which was in existence by 1195, stands just outside the former west gate of Wilton. It consists of a single-cell chapel, four contiguous but distinct ranges (one of which was recently demolished) and a detached pair of almshouses. The buildings are constructed chiefly of ashlar, greensand and flint, but brick has been extensively used for alterations and repairs.

The fabric has been so adapted and altered that any history of its development must be tentative. Of medieval date is the hall range, which may embody part of the original 12th-century aisled infirmary hall of the hospital, and the chapel which extends E from it. Possibly, by analogy with other contemporary hospitals, a chapel originally lay on axis with the hall, in this case to the S of it. In the 14th century, perhaps *c.* 1388 when there was an Indulgence in favour of repairs to the hospital, the present chapel was built (or an earlier one substantially rebuilt) and the N wall of the hall range was modified or rebuilt with new windows. The S part of the hall range was truncated; at the same time or subsequently (in the 15th century) the present three-bay arch-braced roof was erected, and later, in the 17th century, a two-storey building was added, possibly for the four poor brethren and sisters maintained by the hospital. During the early 16th century an E–W range was built to the W of the hall, perhaps as a residence for the warden, and in the early 17th century it was extended westward. This extension was later absorbed in a N–S cross wing. During the late 18th and the early 19th century the other hospital buildings, including the medieval hall, were subdivided into small dwellings; by 1821 the chapel was disused. Victorian reorganisation included the building in 1851 of a detached pair of almshouses to the S of the chapel and the restoration of the chapel itself in 1868 and again in 1902. With the exception of the N–S cross wing (now demolished) the main complex of buildings was stripped and refurbished in 1980–2 and certain minor accretions removed (*see* plan).

The chapel in its present form is of the mid or late 14th century but possibly the foundations and some of the walling are of an earlier building. The E window, the eastern windows in the N and S walls and the piscina are all of the 14th century but the NW window and the SW doorway date from the 1868 restoration when the entrance was shifted from the N to the S side. At that time the roof was renewed and a W gable formed, crowned by a bellcote. The blocked opening in the W wall giving access from the hall range is possibly of 13th-century origin (*see* below). The plain Romanesque font (now sold) may have come from one of the four parish churches in Wilton the rectories of which were acquired by St John's in 1435.

493. Plan RCHM, 1982.

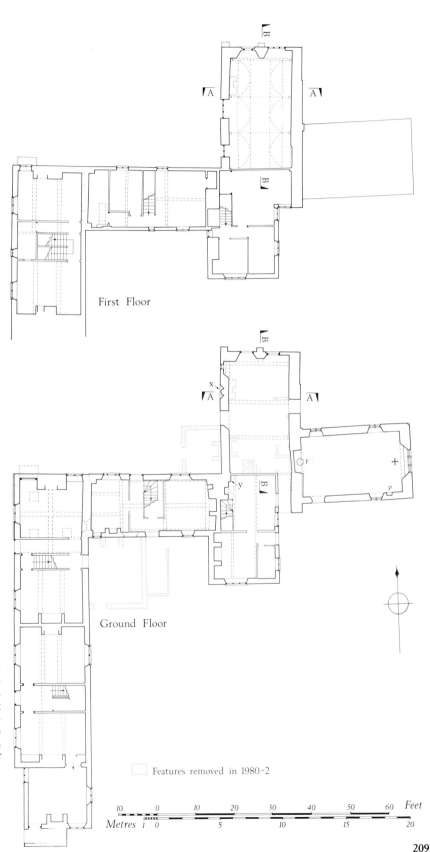

First Floor

Ground Floor

Features removed in 1980-2

Feet

Metres

494. Longitudinal and transverse sections of former hall range.

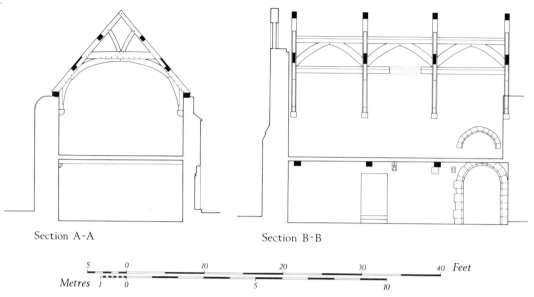

Section A-A   Section B-B

5   0   10   20   30   40 *Feet*

Metres 1 0   5   10

495. Detail of plasterwork in ceiling of ground-floor room at N end of N–S range, now demolished.
496. Roof truss over E–W range.

495

The hall range (NW of the chapel) may preserve part of the plan and other elements of a 12th-century building. Embedded in the W wall is a circular pier with scalloped capital, apparently *in situ* (x on plan), suggesting the former presence of an aisle. In the N wall is a straight-headed window with cusped tracery in the upper corners, perhaps inserted as part of the work of *c.* 1388; it was probably balanced by a second, identified, window to the E but, if so, this had been removed before 1805. In the gable of this wall is a pair of lancet windows, probably reset in the 15th century when the present roof was built and the building apparently heightened; the earlier eaves-line is marked by a weathered offset in the side walls. The three-bay arch-braced roof has double purlins and windbraces. The original roof corbels are plain; the two carved head corbels in the E wall were re-used in the post-medieval period to support the inserted floor (a third carved corbel has recently been set in the N wall). The roof originally covered an open hall. It lacks any evidence of smoke blackening, which suggests that, if the room was heated, it had a side-stack, possibly where the wall thickens on the site of the present E doorway. Two blocked greensand arches, one above the other, survive in the S part of the E wall; neither is moulded and the upper does not appear to be a relieving arch. They are the remains of former archways to the chapel, the lower probably constructed when the floor was inserted in the hall.

The thick walling continues S of the hall range on the E side but the hall roof does not appear to have extended further S than at present. The purlins proper stop at the southernmost truss, but on the E side the purlin projects through the truss as a long tenon (on the W side the comparable tenon has been sawn off flush) which was probably once embedded, or intended to be embedded, in a stone gable. The polygonal masonry at the S end of the W wall (y on plan) has been interpreted as a pier, but is more likely to be the dressed stub of a

former cross wall or the E respond of an arch in such a wall. The W wall of the southward continuation of the hall range probably survived at least until the erection of the cross wing to the W, since the latter is built up to its line, but was then gradually demolished to make way for two chimney stacks and a staircase. The present two-cell, two-storey building which extends S from the hall range is probably not earlier than the 17th century but may utilise earlier foundations and walling. It has simple chamfered beams and in 1805 still preserved a three-light mullioned window in the E wall. It was substantially remodelled and heightened after this date, perhaps as late as 1868 when the chapel was restored. In the SW ground-floor room are a fireplace and cupboard of early 19th-century date.

The cross range is two-storeyed. The difference in wall thickness between the lower and upper storeys and the change in masonry from chequered flint and rubble to brick above suggests that the upper floor was originally timber framed. There are, however, no surviving posts or other timbering. The ground floor of the range is divided into a relatively large room with heavily moulded beams and, at the W end, a half-bay room with two plain parallel beams. A moulded doorway with four-centred head, in the S wall, formerly gave access to the major room. There is no evidence of the original position of the stairs. The roof is of 16th-century date and comprises three bays. Each truss has an arched collar with raking struts from

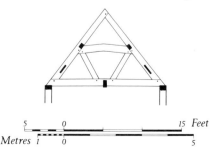

5   0   15 *Feet*

Metres 1 0   5   **496**

tie to collar and one pair of continuous purlins; intermediate collars have been added. The purlins formerly projected beyond the E truss and have been sawn off, but it is unlikely that the roof extended further in this direction as the wall plate does not continue. A one-cell extension slightly wider than the cross range was added to its W end in the early 17th century. That it was two-storeyed is shown externally by the height of the greensand masonry of the N wall. The ground-floor room had chamfered cross beams, originally exposed, plaster decoration in each section, in the form of a lion in a square panel, and a fireplace with moulded stone jambs.

Subsequently this addition was absorbed into a new three-storied range (recently demolished) which extended S from it and was of the same narrow width. The fenestration, the use of white brick, and the internal fittings suggest that the range was of early 19th-century date but may have incorporated elements of an earlier (? early 18th-century) wing. The date 1827 on the N gable of the range presumably recorded when it was built or substantially rebuilt. The wing was arranged into two roughly symmetrical but by no means identical houses with two rooms upon each floor and a central staircase. Each room had two cased beams. The ground-floor rooms contained early 19th-century panelling and fittings. The staircases had moulded circular newel posts and banisters of square section. The northernmost first-floor room, over the room with the ornamental plaster ceiling, had wide 18th-century floor boards.♪

A pair of symmetrical almshouses were built, perhaps to the design of T.H. Wyatt, to the S of the chapel, probably in 1851. In the N gable is a shield bearing the arms of C.B. Pearson, warden from 1831 to 1881.

497. Interior of chapel looking W, before restoration in 1983, showing font, now removed.

498. W elevation of N–S range, now demolished.

499. Exterior from SW, *Buckler* 1803 (*see* also 500).

500. W front of present church (former chancel) seen from NW across site of former nave.

499

501. Former Communion rails, made up as reading desk in Wylye church.

502. Model of church *c.* 1845.

501   502

500

WILTON

ST MARY   SU 097312   *Civil Parish of Wilton*

The church was the only surviving of eight churches recorded in medieval Wilton, but after its replacement in 1845 by the new church of St Mary and St Nicholas it was largely demolished. It had N and S aisles of four bays dating from the late 14th or the 15th century and a shallow chancel in the body of the building that was extended E by a single bay in 1751 to serve as a mortuary chapel for the earls of Pembroke. The arcades may not have been built at the same time; the remaining arches are of similar section but the capitals on the S side are moulded and those on the N sculpted with angels or beasts. The former E window of the S aisle, now in Netherhampton church, has Decorated tracery but the other windows appear to have been straight-headed, of a late Perpendicular type. In the second half of the 16th century the W tower was added, the aisles rebuilt and perhaps enlarged, and the S porch erected.

The church had many good furnishings, some of which survive: the richly carved pulpit and sounding-board of 1628, parts of the 17th-century Communion rails and the brass candelabra of 1814 are now in the church at Wylye; the major monuments, the iron chest and the mayoral insignia-rest are at St Mary and St Nicholas. The octagonal Perpendicular font with carved panels has not survived.

In 1845 only the two chancel bays were kept roofed: the arcades and a pastiche of the W front, without the tower, were made into a picturesque ruin. The chapel was restored in 1872 and again in 1938–9 at which time the ruins were consolidated and made into a public garden. It was transferred to the Redundant Churches Fund in 1977.

The E bay, the Pembroke chancel, has an E window of three-lights with slightly pointed heads, and a plaster cross-vault with decoration along the ribs. The W bay, the rector's chancel, has no openings except in the 19th-century W wall, which appears to be made up of re-used material. The Romanesque tub font, introduced in 1980, comes from the church of Farrington, near Iwerne Courtney in Dorset. The chapel also houses a wooden model of the former church showing it in general, but not always precise, detail both inside and out. The walls of the E bay are lined with memorial tablets, dating from the early 17th to the early 19th century, amongst which the most notable are those to Thomas Mell (+ 1625), sometime servant to the 3rd Lord Pembroke, Edmund Philips (+ 1677–8), 'Farer to the Earl of Penbruck', Walter Dyer (+ 1706), founder of Wilton Free School, the Rev. Henry Pitt (+ 1733) and John Thomas (+ 1798), a local clothier and philanthropist.

503. Plan with reconstructed outline of pre–1845 church in stipple.
504. Interior looking E into Pembroke chancel.

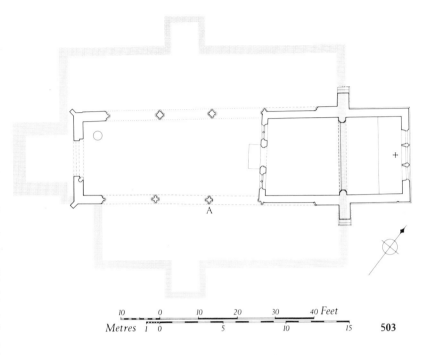

503

505. 'W' front from N.

WILTON

St Mary and St Nicholas   su 095313   *Civil Parish of Wilton*

The church was built in 1841–5, possibly on the site of the medieval church of St Nicholas. The architect of the church was T.H. Wyatt but the inspiration for the design as well as the funds for its execution came from the Hon. Sidney Herbert (later Lord Herbert of Lea) and his mother Catherine Woronzow, Dowager Countess of Pembroke.

The church (*described below according to its liturgical orientation*) is constructed of brick with Bath stone facing, and planned as an aisled basilica with a one-bay sanctuary: each aisle is terminated to the E by an apse. Standing to the NW but joined to the main building by a short cloister is a bell tower 109 ft (33.22 m) high. The style of building is Italian Romanesque, and derives specifically from the two churches of S. Pietro and S. Maria Maggiore in Tuscania (formerly Toscanella), near Viterbo. The church, which incorporates a great number of fittings from both English and Continental sources, remains substantially as built except that the porch/vestry on the N side of the sanctuary was extended E by one bay in 1906. The

only other important alterations are re-arrangement of the seating (1866), the replacement (from 1908) of painted decoration by mosaic, first in the main apse and later in the S apse, to the designs of Sir Charles Nicholson, and the creation of a Lady Chapel in the S apse by the Herbert family (1946).

The church has a richly decorated W front including three recessed portals and a large wheel window surrounded by the Evangelist symbols. The central portal opens to a vestibule flanked by small apsidal-ended 'chapels', the side portals open to rectangular lobbies from which spiral staircases give access to the W gallery, originally allocated to children. The gallery front is in the form of a stone screen supported by marble columns and surmounted by an elaborate parapet carved with a text. The five-bay nave is 57 ft (17.37 m) high. It has a false triforium and two-light clearstorey windows. The arcade columns have richly ornamented capitals with figures above carved by William Osmond junior. The open timber roof of the nave and aisles is of the medieval Italian type

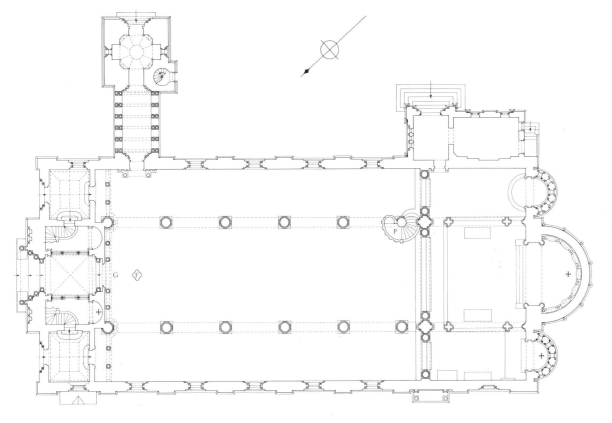

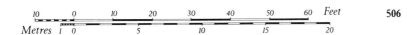

506

507. 'E' front from SW showing entrance to crypt below main apse.

508. Interior looking towards 'E' end.

509. Interior looking towards 'W' end.

508

509

found, for example, at Monreale Cathedral, Sicily.

The raised E end lies above a burial vault (*see* below) and is entered through three arches, each incorporating black-veined marble shafts. Those of the two flanking arches are antique columns from Porto Venere in Liguria. The chancel is divided from the side aisles by triple arcades and from the E apse by a further tall arch; it is covered by a polychrome painted vault. The lowest stage of the main apse is articulated by an order of twisted marble columns with volute capitals of various types either of genuine medieval origin or in imitation. Above, the original painted decoration has been replaced by mosaic in Byzantine style, depicting angels and Christ with St Mary and St Nicholas. In 1874 the N apse became the organ chamber and, in 1946, the S apse a Lady Chapel. The N apse has the original painted decoration but the S apse is now adorned with mosaic, depicting the Cross.

The fittings in general consist of, or incorporate, earlier features. An exception is the Communion table, of *c.* 1850, which has twisted legs and inlaid panels echoing the decoration of the apse wall. An important source for several of the fittings was the Cosmatesque 'Shrine of Capocci': erected in S. Maria Maggiore, Rome in 1256; dismantled in the 18th century; the parts were re-used by Horace Walpole at Strawberry Hill, Twickenham, and finally sold at the 1842 Strawberry Hill sale. Probably from the shrine are two inlaid panels in the surround to the NW door, two pairs of similar panels in the N and S walls of the main apse and ten small panels under the apse colonnettes although some parts of them may be modifications of the 18th or 19th century. Also from the shrine: the pair of twisted and inlaid columns with acanthus capitals, flanking the NE (vestry) door; the pair of freestanding twisted columns with capitals and the twisted angle shaft with capital, in the S apse; and the four twisted colonnettes with capitals incorporated in the upper part of the pulpit. The pair of larger free-standing twisted columns with foliage capitals, in the main apse and now supporting candelabra, are not from the shrine although of similar type and date (Gardiner 1970). The columns and the pink marble sanctuary steps were given by the then Speaker of the House of Commons, Evelyn Denison. The inlaid floor in the centre of the W portal is said to be medieval Italian work, but the similar, larger, floor beside the pulpit was made in Rome for the church.

Much of the carved wood of the doors and furnishings is 17th or 18th century, from northern France and the Low Countries. The NW door incorporates two sets of 17th-century Flemish panels depicting scenes from the Birth of Christ. The central W doors have four 17th-century Flemish panels of female allegorical figures. The flanking doors had a pair of similar panels (one showing St Jerome) and a pair with larger reliefs, perhaps German, showing the Martyrdoms of St Peter and St Paul; in 1979 three of these four panels were stolen. The reading desk incorporates three 18th-century panels from the southern Netherlands or northern France. The central

510. Doorway to vestry in 'N' wall of 'N' apse, with Cosmatesque shafts and painting in tympanum by Willement.

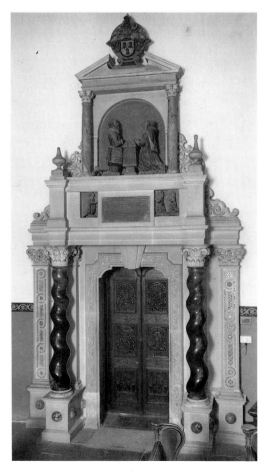

511. Internal face of doorway at 'W' end of 'N' aisle incorporating monument (from St Mary's) to William Sharpe (+ 1626).

217

512. 18th-century wooden panel depicting the Faithful Centurion, now part of reading desk.

panel, roughly signed and dated 1761, depicts the Four Evangelists and their symbols; the side panels depict St John the Baptist and the Faithful Centurion and appear to have been doors of a cupboard, perhaps in a sacristy. The door to the vestry incorporates eight pierced panels of confronting tailed monsters, probably English work of c. 1600.

The windows all contain stained glass, much of which, though greatly restored on installation, is of medieval English and Continental origin (see Appendix 3 for detailed account).

The original decorative painting in the church, which survives in the chancel, N apse, the vestry door and in the texts over the arcade arches, is by William Willement.

The elaborate pulpit is of a design inspired by the 13th-century examples at Pisa and Pistoia. Besides the Cosmatesque colonnettes (see above) it incorporates, in the lower part, two groups of marble shafts and capitals of late Classical style but probably 19th century. The lectern is in the form of a gilded plaster eagle, perhaps of the 18th century, set on a 19th-century base. The font bowl, probably 16th-century northern Italian, is of red and white veined marble carved with foliage. It is of quadrilobe form and at the tip of each lobe is a grotesque head with bronze teeth which once held a bronze ring. The scrolled black marble base may also be Italian (17th-century) but the stem, with sgraffito decoration, is of 1845. In the N aisle is a late medieval iron chest from northern Italy or southern Germany, cross-banded with rosettes at each intersection. The wrought-iron stand for the mayoral insignia, fixed to the Corporation pew in front of the pulpit, is from the former parish church. It is dated 1677.

Several monuments are from the former church: over the NW doorway, parts of the early 17th-century tomb of William Sharpe (+ 1626) and his family, with kneeling effigies; on the wall to the E of the NW doorway a late 16th-century brass with stone frame, to John Coffer (+ 1585) and his wife, also depicted kneeling. In or near the S apse are

the following monuments: to the 9th 'architect' Earl of Pembroke (+ 1749), a high base of different marbles, surmounted by a bust of the deceased, designed and executed by Roubiliac; in the nave and formerly lying across the chord of the S apse, to the 10th Earl (+ 1794), a white marble sarcophagus (now lacking its lion feet) designed by James Wyatt and executed by the elder Westmacott; to the 11th Earl (+ 1827) a tablet incorporating a bust of the deceased in a roundel and a large relief of a rustic family, by the younger Westmacott; to Elizabeth, first wife of the 11th Earl (+ 1793) and two of their sons, a tablet with an allegorical scene in low relief, by Rossi.

On the S wall is a late 18th-century hatchment to the 10th Earl and opposite, on the N wall, two mid 19th-century hatchments to the 11th and the 13th Earls. A stone inscription from above the S porch door of the former church and placed above the door of the new tower in 1845 is now in the nave on the S wall; the text records the birth and christening in 1580 of William Lord Herbert, son of the 2nd Earl and his third wife, Mary Sidney. In the chancel are the tombs of the two founders, Sidney Herbert and his mother. They are of similar type, each having a recumbent effigy supported by angels and lying on an arcaded tomb chest, but that to Sidney Herbert is larger and has spandrels carved in low relief with scenes illustrating his career. Both were designed by T.H. Wyatt and carved by J.B. Philip.

Against the S exterior wall of the church is a raised and canopied sarcophagus (of medieval Italian type and incorporating a stone cross of 12th-century origin) in which human bones found at the time of building were re-interred.

The crypt, built as a burial-vault for the earls of Pembroke, is divided into three compartments by two three-bay arcades; it is reached by an outer barrel-vaulted vestibule lit by two cruciform windows. The walls of the crypt are decorated with five figurative white marble reliefs of the 16th and 17th century surrounded by marble framing and bosses.

513. Interior of crypt.

514. Font.

515. Stand for mayoral insignia, 1677, formerly in St Mary's.

516. View across central portal of 'W' front showing stair to gallery.

517. Two reliefs depicting scenes from the Crimean War on W end of tomb of Lord Herbert of Lea, including (R) Florence Nightingale (see also 170).

219

WINTERBOURNE DAUNTSEY

St Edward, The former church of   su 175349   *Civil Parish of Winterbourne*

The church was demolished in 1867 when the new church of Winterbourne Earls (su 175345) was built in its stead (*see* p. 221). It had been restored in 1858 and was well recorded before destruction. It consisted of a continuous nave and chancel and a three-stage S tower-porch; all apparently of one 13th-century build and with many contemporary fittings. The chancel had twin lancet windows in the E wall, each containing a contemporary roundel of stained glass, and two lancets in both the N and the S wall; the single-framed roof was probably contemporary. The nave had lancets at the W end of the N and S walls, the other windows were Perpendicular; the roof (of lower pitch to that of the chancel) was late medieval or 17th century.

The 15th-century rood screen was of four bays, each with five trefoil-headed lights, and two central doors, each of two lights; there was running ornament on the beam above. There were apparently three piscinae in the church, one in the chancel with a cinquefoiled head and two of simpler form flanking the screen. There was a stoup by the S doorway. The polygonal font, probably 15th century, had a 17th-century crown cover. In the floor of the porch was a heart-burial slab of *c.* 1400.

The only fabric or fittings to survive (now in Winterbourne Earls church) are some of the windows, the stained-glass roundels and the heart-burial slab. Demolition revealed a virtually complete set of late 13th-century wall paintings which were recorded in photographs and tracings; the latter (formerly in Salisbury Mus.) are now lost (*see* p. 25 and Table 11).

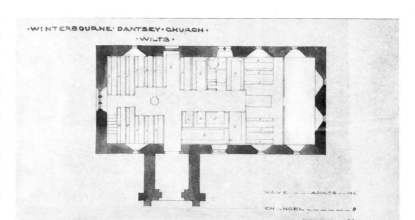

518

519

518. Plan from faculty, 1867.
519. S doorway, piscinae and other features recorded before demolition, *Kemm c.* 1863.

520. Exterior from SE, photograph *c.* 1866.

WINTERBOURNE EARLS

ST MICHAEL   SU 175345   *Civil Parish of Winterbourne*

The present church of St Michael was built to replace the medieval churches of Winterbourne Earls (of the same dedication, *see* below) and Winterbourne Dauntsey, both of which were demolished. The church was built in 1867–8, on a new site, to the designs of T.H. Wyatt. It has a wide chancel with a N vestry, a nave with a S aisle, and a tower at the SW angle. It is built of coursed knapped flint with stone banding.

The E and W windows in the S wall of the aisle are from the S wall of the nave of the former church of St Michael. The straight-headed two-light windows in the N wall are from the naves of the former churches of Winterbourne Earls and Winterbourne Dauntsey; the easternmost window was once the W window of Winterbourne Dauntsey. The lancet windows in the N and E walls of the chancel are from the chancel of Winterbourne Dauntsey, those in the S wall are Victorian. The single-framed chancel roof is of the same type and dimensions as that formerly over the chancel at Winterbourne Dauntsey and may incorporate some of the original timbers.

Fittings from the former church of St Michael include the late medieval polygonal font (less its original cover), a 13th-century cross slab, a 15th-century brass indent in a traceried frame, now on the E wall of the tower porch; also the 17th and 18th-century monuments of the Nicholas and Elliot families which include an inscribed brass and a pedimented wall monument of *c.* 1661 to the Nicholas family and a late 18th-century tablet to Nicholas Elliot (+ 1776). The only wall monument from Winterbourne Dauntsey is the early 19th-century tablet to Susanna Skinner (+ 1805) by King, of Bath. The 17th-century Communion table is probably from Winterbourne Dauntsey but the contemporary pulpit is from Imber church, Wilts., and was set up in the 1950s. The two 13th-century roundels of stained glass in the easternmost window on the N side of the nave were formerly in the E windows at Winterbourne Dauntsey; from the same church is the heart-burial slab of *c.* 1400 now on the N wall of the chancel. The medieval fragments of glass assembled in the quatrefoil in the W gable come from the former church of St Michael and from Winterbourne Dauntsey.

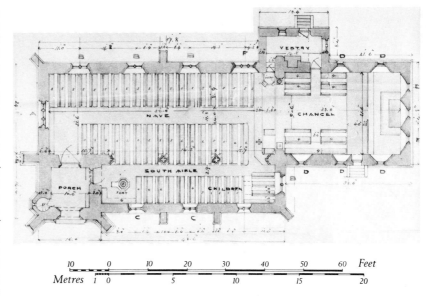

10   0   10   20   30   40   50   60   *Feet*
Metres 1 0   5   10   15   20

521.   Plan from faculty, 1867.

522.   Exterior from SE.

523. Interior looking E.

The former church of St Michael (SU 173345) can be reconstructed with the aid of drawings and photographs and from materials re-used in the present church. It consisted of a nave and chancel on markedly different axes and a S tower-porch with timber belfry. The chancel windows were of the first part of the 14th century; the nave had a Romanesque S doorway and Perpendicular windows, perhaps of *c.* 1553. The S tower-porch was of the mid 13th century. The nave windows were re-used in the new church but the doorways and the chancel windows were destroyed.

Various fittings and monuments were transferred to the new church (*see* above) but the font cover, the pierced splat Communion rails and the pulpit were discarded. Late medieval wall paintings were discovered during demolition (*see* Table 11).

524. S doorway to tower (L) and to nave (R), former church, *Kemm* 1863.

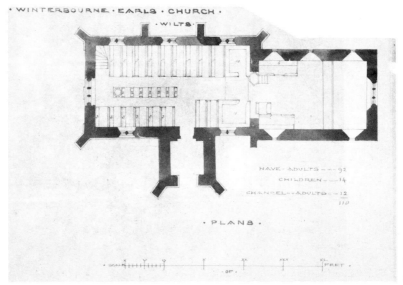

525. Plan of former church from faculty, 1867.

527. Late medieval font from former church, transferred to present building in 1868.

526. Exterior of former church from SE, *Buckler c. 1805.*

528. Interior of former church looking E into chancel, photographed *c.* 1867.

529. Exterior from SE.

530. Interior looking E, showing blocked S arcade.

WINTERBOURNE GUNNER

St Mary   SU 181353   *Civil Parish of Winterbourne*

The nave is Romanesque in plan, and the W tower, although not built at the same time as the nave, may include some 12th-century fabric. A small Romanesque window head is set *ex situ* in the rebuilt external face of the N wall of the nave. A S aisle was added *c*. 1200 but was later dismantled. The tower arch and W window were altered in the early 16th century. Inscriptions record that the E wall of the chancel was rebuilt in 1687 and the N wall in 1810. The church was closed in 1876 but re-opened ten years later after repair. The seating was re-ordered in the 1950s.

The church is built of rubble flint and stone, with stone dressings; the tower is rendered.

The chancel is essentially of the 13th century, although the N and E walls have been rebuilt. The only medieval window is the single-light window with an ogee head cusped into a trefoil, at the E end of the S wall. The E window is of 1886, replacing a two-light mullioned window, and the SW window is of 1810. The roof is ceiled. The chancel arch is of the late 13th century although the imposts and parts of the responds may be of 12th-century origin. The window in the N wall of the nave is of 1886 but the blocked N doorway, not visible externally, is late medieval. The nave roof, also late medieval, is of the ceiled wagon type although now stripped of its plaster. The tie beams are probably 17th-century insertions. The two-bay S arcade, now closed on its S side by the S wall of the church, has simple responds and a central polygonal shaft carrying a square capital with bold angle spurs. The unusual combination of forms may indicate that a Romanesque arcade has been reconstructed. The window is of 1886 but the two-centred doorway is presumably medieval work reset. The S porch is a late 19th-century replacement of a 17th or 18th-century structure. The plan and proportions of the tower suggest a 12th-century origin but the tower arch, the blocked N doorway, the W window and the W belfry openings are all of the early 16th century.

The font is Romanesque and has one simple moulding round the stem; the cover is 17th century. Some worn 14th-century tiles are set in the floor of the tower. On the E wall of the nave, and formerly on the N wall also, are fragmentary painted texts of the 16th or 17th century, probably covering late medieval painting. Two panels of the Commandment tables, dated to 1787, survive in the tower. In the chancel there is one carved bench of *c*. 1650 incorporated into 20th-century seating of the same style, and plain re-used panelling on the E wall. The most prominent monument is the mid 18th-century draped tablet to Elizabeth Powell (+ 1753), on the N wall of the chancel.

532. Tablet on N wall chancel to Elizabeth Powell (+ 1753).

531

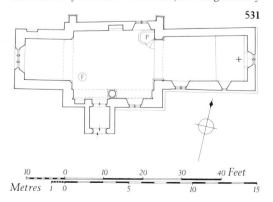

| 10 | 0 | 10 | 20 | 30 | 40 *Feet* |

Metres 1   0   5   10   15

533. Exterior from SE.
534. Interior looking E.
535. Plan of crossing with arch profile.

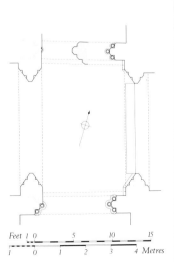

Feet 1 0   5   10   15

1   0   1   2   3   4 Metres

WINTERBOURNE STOKE

St Peter   su 077406   *Civil Parish of Winterbourne Stoke*

A church at Winterbourne Stoke was mentioned in Domesday; since it had belonged to a royal manor, and had recently been given to the abbey of Jumièges, it may have been relatively large. Inconsistencies in the plan of the present crossing may be attributable to this early church, but the earliest clearly identifiable part of the existing fabric is the nave, built *c.* 1150. The crossing, transepts and chancel were added a century later. In the 14th century there was a major reconstruction of the crossing whereby the E and W arches were widened and the W arch was moved eastwards, concealing the W responds of the transept arches. A traceried window was inserted in the S transept. The tower was completed in the 15th century. The nave was reconstructed *c.* 1500 when traceried windows were inserted in the N, S and W walls, and a four-centred doorway inserted under the W window. At some time between 1600 and 1800 the N transept was removed. In 1838–9 the church was rebuilt: the chancel was taken down and rebuilt in stock brick on the old foundations; the following year the nave was reroofed, the N and S windows altered and a further pair of identical windows were inserted further to the W; a N porch was added. In 1880 the N transept was re-erected as a vestry, the porch was altered and the interior rearranged.

Except for the brick chancel the church is built of flint rubble mixed with stone, with stone dressings.

The chancel has the dimensions of its medieval predecessor; the lowest courses of the walls may also be medieval. The lancets in the N and S walls were replaced in 1838–9 by windows of a Perpendicular type, but the triple lancets of the E window are original in form if not in detail. The 13th-century piscina and aumbry were also kept. The

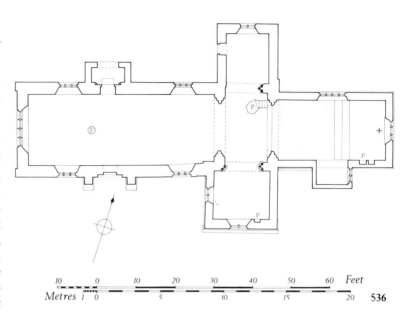

organ chamber on the S side is an addition of 1881. The 14th-century E and W arches of the crossing have three continuously chamfered orders. The S arch, perhaps of the second quarter of the 13th century, has triple-shafted responds with undercut moulded capitals set against a central octagonal shaft. The N arch is similar but its E respond (the W one is mostly concealed) has less distinct shafts and more generalised capitals and may therefore be later. Visible externally in the S wall of the S transept and presumably reset are the heads of two lancet windows, but the S window has 14th-century tracery consisting of a quatrefoil over two ogee trefoil-headed lights. The piscina also has a depressed trefoil head. All elements of the original

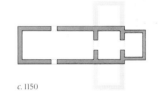

c. 1150

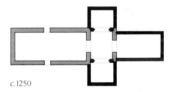

c. 1250

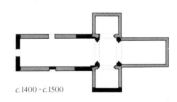

c. 1400 - *c.* 1500

537. Development.

538. Exterior from NW, after removal of N transept and before alteration of nave windows, *Buckler c.* 1805.

N transept have gone except for a short length of the E wall, retained to buttress the crossing. A small fragment of Romanesque work has been built into the W wall. The rainwater head nearby, with grotesque medievalising carving, appears bogus. The present tower was raised in the late 14th or early 15th century on the oblong plan of the reconstructed crossing and has no earlier features. The belfry windows have simple tracery and the string-course below the parapet is pierced at intervals by gargoyles.

The nave walls retain much of the 12th-century fabric. The N doorway has one order of chevron carried on shafts with carved capitals and an inner order carried on imposts; the outer border of the main order is also decorated. There is no tympanum. The detailing has been extensively but faithfully renewed. The blocked S doorway is less well-preserved than the N doorway (having lost both shafts and bases) and it is plainer, the main order being moulded, not ornamented. The buttresses flanking the doorway are of 1839.

The W window, of four lights with panel

tracery, is unaltered but the panel tracery in the N and S windows E of the doors was replaced in 1839 with Y-tracery. Windows of the new form were inserted W of the doors. The W doorway, now blocked, has a sill 2 ft (0.61 m) below the present level of the nave which was raised and levelled in the restorations of 1839 and 1880. The floor formerly followed the slope of the hill against which the church lies. The roof is 19th century but the wall plate may be late medieval.

The font, of the later 12th century, has a plain bowl set directly on the roll-mouldings of the base around which have been set a number of 14th-century tiles. Furnishings of 17th-century date include the font cover, with volutes rising to a central finial, and a polygonal pulpit carved with floral motifs, set on a Victorian base. The Communion rails are of the baluster type, but only the four larger balusters against the wall and framing the central gate survive. The benches are 18th century but were cut down in 1880. The stained glass in two windows in the nave was inserted by local glaziers in 1839.

539. Winterbourne Stoke: W window and doorway (*see* also 61).

540. Winterbourne Stoke: stained glass of 1835, nave S window.

WINTERSLOW

ALL SAINTS SU 228324 *Civil Parish of Winterslow*

The eastern part of the S arcade and the plain tub font are of the late 11th century. The eastern part of the N arcade and the chancel were constructed in the early 13th century; a S tower-porch was added later in the same century. New windows were inserted in the 14th and 15th centuries. In 1849–50 the church was much altered by Wyatt and Brandon: the nave was doubled in length, each arcade keeping its original form, arches were pierced in both E responds, and the N aisle was prolonged eastwards; all the roofs and furnishings were renewed. The timber belfry on the tower was replaced in masonry a few years later. In 1975 the chancel was re-ordered by Keith Leaman.

The church is built of coursed knapped flint with stone dressings.

The chancel retains few medieval features. The E window and the buttresses are of 1850. The splays of blocked side-windows on the N side had medieval painted masonry outlining until their demolition in 1849. The Romanesque part of the S arcade consists of two bays with simple square responds carrying unchamfered round arches. The N arcade has round shafts with moulded capitals supporting chamfered pointed arches. The chancel arch is similar in design. The W wall formerly stood immediately to the W of the S tower-porch. It had a panel-traceried Perpendicular window to the nave, a traceried Decorated window to the N aisle and a straight-headed Perpendicular window to the S aisle; in the present W wall the arrangement is the same.

Two fragments of 15th-century stone sculpture survive within the church; a corbel head and, beneath a tabernacle, a carved panel of a bearded male head. The late medieval Doom painting over the W face of the chancel arch was destroyed during the 19th-century restoration. The polygon-

al carved pulpit, formerly on the S side of the chancel arch, appears to be Victorian though of a 17th-century style and possibly incorporating a few details of that date. The majority of the 17th and 18th-century monuments are to members of the Thistlethwayte family. There are five from the mid 17th century (four with inscribed tablets and one incorporating a late 16th-century brass inscription plate) set in stone frames surmounted by coats-of-arms. There are also two early 18th-century tablets to Peregrine (+ 1694) and Dorothea (+ 1715) Thistlethwayte carved in white marble with drapes and cherubs.

In the eastern part of the village (SU 247326) is a small dependent chapel built in 1860 and dedicated to St John.

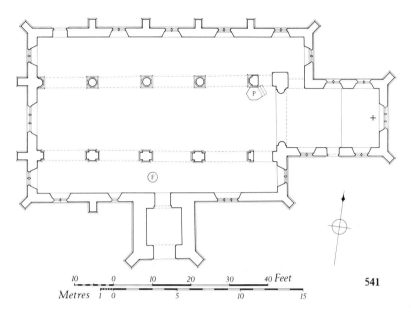

10 0 10 20 30 40 *Feet*
Metres 1 0 5 10 15

541

542. Church under reconstruction, *J. Luard* 1849.

543. Winterslow: exterior from SW (*see* also 7).

544. Winterslow: interior looking E.

WOODFORD

ALL SAINTS   su 120361   *Civil Parish of Woodford*

The S doorway and possibly also the plan of the nave survive from the Romanesque church on the site. A Romanesque window in the N wall of the nave was destroyed in 1845. The chancel of the former church was built in the 13th century. The rest of the church was altered and enlarged in the 15th century: the nave was rebuilt, a two-bay S aisle added and a tower erected at the W end of the nave. In 1845 the entire building, except the tower, was reconstructed from the foundations by Wyatt and Brandon. The detailing of the original building was respected although a N aisle was added to the nave and a vestry to the chancel.

The present church is built of ashlar except for the lower stages of the tower, which are of flint and stone chequers.

When the fabric was renewed in 1845 most of the 13th-century features of the chancel were kept including all the lancet windows, the N doorway and the piscina. The low-side window in the S wall was blocked in 1845 and the triple lancets of the E window were replaced by a traceried window in the early 20th century. The roof and the chancel arch are of 1845. The S doorway of the nave is of the late 12th century, reset in the 15th century. It has one order of shafts with scalloped capitals carrying an arch of beaded saw-tooth chevron. In 1845 the opening was heightened by lengthening the shafts and cutting the head of the doorway into the blind tympanum. The S aisle, of which the N

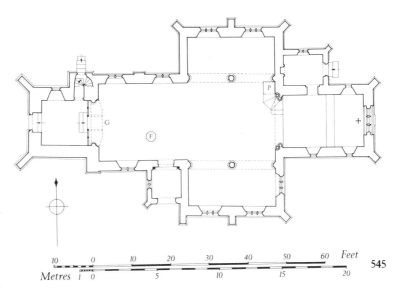

545

aisle is a direct copy, is divided from the nave by a two bay arcade with moulded capitals and polygonal responds and pier each face of which is cut to form concave fluting. There is a shallow ogee-headed niche in the shaft and, in the S wall, a piscina with a trefoiled head. The S porch dates from 1845 and replaces a timber-framed structure

546.   Exterior from NE.

231

of the 16th or 17th century. The W gallery was reconstructed in the early 20th century, incorporating 16th and 17th-century woodwork in the screen below. The tower arch has two hollow-chamfered orders of which the inner has round shafts with octagonal moulded capitals. The three-light W window has panel tracery but, like the W doorway, lacks a hood-mould. A N window, inserted in 1838 to light a gallery, has been blocked. The three-stage tower has no set-backs but has a single chamfered string-course below the belfry. The belfry stage, including the lean-to roof of the stair turret, may be a 17th-century rebuilding.

The Perpendicular font is octagonal. It is deeply carved: on the sides of the bowl with foiled quatrefoils and on the stem with chamfered ribs. The 17th-century furnishings include a five-panel chest, not original to the church, and a gate-leg table in the nave. A similar table in the sanctuary is a Victorian assembly of 17th-century elements. The Royal Arms, on canvas, are those of George III before 1801. The early 20th-century stained glass in the E window and in two windows in the N aisle is by Ninian Comper. In the S aisle is a late 16th-century inscribed brass, to Gerard Errington (+ 1596), which is set in a stone frame decorated with strapwork, and a mid 18th-century tablet of veined marble. There is a Gothic monument in the chancel by Osmond; other memorials are plain, early 19th-century tablets.

547. Woodford: interior looking E.

APPENDIX 1

AMESBURY PRIORY AND ITS RELATIONSHIP TO THE PRESENT CHURCH

During the Middle Ages one of the major religious foundations in south-east Wiltshire was the nunnery at Amesbury, established first as a Benedictine abbey and then, after the refoundation by Henry II in 1177, as a priory of the Order of Fontevrault (VCH 1956, 244). Nothing is known of the buildings or even of the site of the Benedictine abbey. It is possible they were undistinguished, as they were replaced by Henry II with new conventual buildings, including a church, at the considerable expense of £881 (Colvin 1963, 88–90).[1] The priory continued to enjoy royal favour, especially in the late 13th and the early 14th century. The mother of Edward I, Queen Eleanor, chose to live out her last days and to be buried there, and the king's daughter, Mary, was a nun there all her life. Some account of the number and size of the conventual buildings at the time of the Dissolution has been preserved in the Seymour papers which now form part of the archives at

Longleat House. The principal documents are the royal grant or, rather, exchange of lands which brought Amesbury Priory to Edward Seymour, the future Protector and Duke of Somerset, and the reports of Seymour's agents concerning the demolition of the buildings (Longleat: MSS 6524–6529; Seymour Papers ix fol. 227). The church and the cloister, with their associated buildings, were condemned and their lead roofs stripped, but some other parts, in particular the prioress's lodging, were retained to form a house, which survived until the mid 17th century (Talbot 1901, 22–3) when it was replaced by a new mansion built to the design of John Webb but substantially reconstructed by Hopper in 1834–40.

No trace of the medieval buildings survives above ground around the present house although some walling remained in the park to the W of house until the early 19th century. In the winter of 1859/60 extensive medieval foundations and re-

548. Amesbury: map reconstructing layout of priory buildings and parish church before the Dissolution. *Crown copyright reserved.*

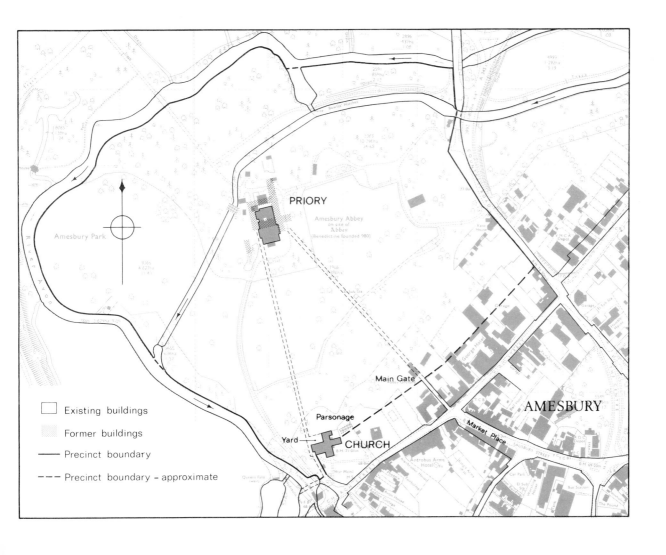

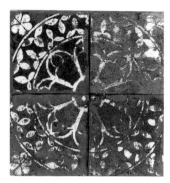

549. Amesbury: pattern of four tiles, found on site of priory (*see* pp. 26–7).

550. Amesbury: respond attached to NW corner of parish church (*see* also 5).

mains were revealed immediately N of the present house, including those of a rectangular room with a stone bench around the walls and a richly tiled floor (Kite 1901, 439–45).[2]

At about this time the idea developed that the present church, which lies over 300 yards SSE of the house, had been the church of the priory.[3] In the late 19th century this theory was discussed in great detail, the arguments on both sides being drawn from the documents of the time of the Dissolution as much as from the church itself.

The argument in favour of the identification of the parish church as the priory church rests principally on the close correspondence of the main dimensions of the priory church, as given in a survey of 1540, with those of the existing parish church, except that the nave of the priory was twice as long as that of the parish. The discrepancy is not due to a later shortening of the parish church nave. The W wall of the nave, though rebuilt in Butterfield's restoration of 1853, was not moved; neither do the trusses of the 15th-century nave roof appear to have been curtailed.[4] Attached to the NW angle of the nave there remains *in situ* the respond of a doorway with recessed orders of *c.* 1200.[5] There are other details recorded of the priory church, besides the length of the nave, which do not accord with the present church. The roofs were described as 'steep', whereas all the roofs of the parish church had been rebuilt to a shallow pitch *c.* 1500 (Longleat MS 6524). There is also mention of a 'mid wall' to the choir, presumably the stone pulpitum usual in a major monastic church, quite different from the late medieval wooden rood screen still surviving in the parish church.[6]

There are other general objections to the identification of the two churches as the same building. First, it would be unusual for a major monastic church to be separated by a distance of well over 300 yards (274.32 m) from its conventual build-ings (whose site was confirmed by the 1860 excavations). Secondly, there is no record of the Seymours granting to the parish either the whole priory church, or even a part of it (assuming that the parish could have had rights to a part of the church), even after the lead had been stripped in 1542. On the contrary, in the original exchange of lands with the King, Seymour was charged with paying the £8 stipend of the local priest; and in 1541 Seymour allocated priory lead to the chancel of the parish church, surely to repair a building in use, not to replace lead on one which had just been stripped (Longleat MS 6526).[7] Indeed the detailed record that survives of the scale and thoroughness of the stripping of the priory church in 1541–2, which included the sale of paving and glass, timber and lead, and the demolition by gunpowder of the spire over the crossing, makes it clear that the church was so wrecked as to have been unusable without restoration on a scale certain to leave some evidence.[8] Moreover, in 1542 a certain Nicholas Chamber of Amesbury directed in his will that his body was to be buried before the rood of the parish church and that certain vestments were to be given to the church and lights instituted in it, which again implies the continuing existence of a separate parish church since it would have been an absurd bequest to the derelict priory church (Ruddle 1900, 30–1).[9] A third objection is the difficulty of matching the history of the priory with the architectural history of the present church. The nave is of the early 12th century, a period when the Benedictine abbey appears to have been already in decline, but there is no work of the late 12th century, the period of the refoundation, except for the respond outside the NW corner of the nave. The crossing, transepts and chancel are one build of the mid 13th century, with only two Decorated windows to mark the climax in the priory's fortunes in the 14th century. No trace has been found of the tomb of Queen Eleanor, buried at Amesbury in 1291,[10] or of the other important burials recorded in the priory church.[11]

It is possible that the existing building has always been simply the parish church.[12] The generous proportions of the Romanesque nave could then be explained as due to the secular importance of Amesbury as a royal manor from Saxon times until the 13th century,[13] and the equally generous scale of the eastern parts of the church to the interest of the priory, as patron, although the other churches in the area held by the priory, such as Maddington or Durrington, display no comparable architectural achievement.[14]

The present church is, however, markedly different from all the other parish churches of the area. Even if abundant evidence disproves its identification with the priory church, the transeptual chapels of which the survivor, at least, is rib-vaulted, and the evidence for substantial buildings to the N of both nave and chancel all point to a special status.

The most acceptable hypothesis, which was first advanced by C.H. Talbot in 1899, is that the nave always belonged to the parish, but that the crossing and chancel were rebuilt by the priory in the 13th century to accommodate the male canons, introduced according to the custom of the Order of Fontevrault, in order to form a joint community. Their presence at Amesbury by 1246 and their possession of a separate church are attested by Henry III's gift of lead to 'the church of the brethren' in that year (Cal. Lib. Rolls 1245–51, 63: 29 June 1246). The explanation of the almost identical dimensions of the choir and transepts in both the present church and the priory church would thus be that this part of the church of the brethren was copied directly from that of the nuns.[15] The position of the church astride the southern boundary of the priory could serve both the canons, living to the N of the chancel (perhaps on the site of the later vicarage, within the priory precinct but at a distance from the nuns), and the Amesbury townspeople to the S.[16] The latter would have had access to the church only through the S doorway of the nave (or, later, the aisle); the present entrance in the S transept appears to have been formed in 1721. At the W end of the church the respond at the NW angle and the lack of any opening in the W wall save for a high window, indicate that there was a subsidiary entrance to the priory at this point (the principal entrance lay some 200 yards (182.88 m) to the E, opposite the Salisbury road). If this entrance was for the male canons, the pentice, the roof crease of which is visible on the N wall of the nave, would have given them covered access to their own part of the church, bypassing the parochial nave and entering by the door in the W wall of the transept.[17]

By the 15th century the institution of canons in the Order seems to have lapsed and the place of the canons to have been taken by chaplains, who could have continued to live in the same lodgings N of the parish church and to serve both priory and parish. By c. 1500 a chaplain is recorded as the parish priest, but his status as an appointee of the priory rather than as a proper incumbent of the living is shown by the absence of his name or that of any other Amesbury parish priest from the diocesan registers, and also by the way that Seymour, when he acquired the property, had personally to make provision for the priest (Ruddle 1901, 32; Longleat, Seymour Papers ix fol. 227). The minister of Amesbury church continued to be a poorly endowed perpetual curate until well into the 19th century.

1. There is no mention in the royal accounts of temporary accommodation for the Fontevraultine nuns while building was in progress, so possibly they continued to use the former abbey buildings.

2. W.C. Kemm, who saw the excavations, considered the room to be part of the Infirmary, but it seems, from its size and its quality, more likely to be part of the principal buildings of the convent, perhaps even the chapter house: C.H. Talbot, 'Amesbury Church. Reasons for thinking it was not the Church of the Priory', WAM 31 (1901) 23.

3. Early 19th-century writers such as Colt Hoare or Glynne seem not to have been aware of the possibility.

4. The dimensions of the nave given in R. Colt Hoare, Modern History of South Wilts. 2 pt 2 (1826), 73, are the same as those today.

5. Butterfield stated categorically that he consolidated, rather than moved, the respond. It was drawn in its present state and site in 1820 by G. Engelheart. It seems unlikely to have been moved to its present position in the course of the 18th-century landscaping of the area, since the W front of the church although on axis with the S front of the house was screened from view by trees. The boundary between the park and the churchyard was at the SW, not the NW, angle of the church.

6. The chancel screen which must be contemporary with the roofs, was removed in 1852 but replaced in 1907. A similar parclose screen to the S transept disappeared completely in the restoration of 1852–3.

7. Lead was also allocated to the 'new convent kitchen', apparently that of the prioress, which was also to be retained, while the kitchen of the convent proper was to be demolished.

8. In the late 19th century it was claimed that the crossing tower still bore the scars caused by the blowing up of the steeple in 1541 and that the Perpendicular chancel roof, removed in 1852, was a poor post-Reformation replacement: E. Kite 'Notes on Amesbury Monastery . . .', Wilts. Notes Queries 3 (1901) 300 n. 1.

9. There are other wills of the 1540s which refer to the parish church in a similar way.

10. The queen's heart was buried elsewhere: H. Colvin, ed. History of the King's Works, 1 (1963) 486. A stone coffin containing the body of a richly dressed lady, possibly Queen Eleanor, was discovered in the priory ruins in the early 17th century: Kite 1901, 358–9 and 365.

11. The carved female head, possibly from an effigy, in the recess by the SW doorway of the nave was discovered in situ in the 19th century.

12. A less likely hypothesis is that the church is that of the original Benedictine abbey and that it was retained in 1177 for the use of the parish, the Fontevraultine buildings being erected on a new site.

13. A late Saxon minster church may have existed at Amesbury (see p. 11) and the plan of the Romanesque nave of the present church may well reflect its dimensions.

14. Amesbury church formed part of Henry II's refoundation grant to the priory. At the Dissolution the patronage passed to Lord Hertford but was exchanged by him with the Dean and Chapter of St George's Chapel, Windsor in 1547.

15. The present crossing and transepts are each one square in proportion and the chancel two squares. They are on a completely different axis from the nave.

16. The S boundary of the priory site, which remained unchanged until the 19th century, met the W end of the church at the SW corner of the S aisle, and the E end at the NE corner of the chancel. The slant in the side walls of the former SW porch and the way in which the S aisle is correspondingly stepped back from the W wall of the nave confirms the oblique line of the boundary at this point.

17. The way that the crease on the W wall of the N transept does not show a return of the roof but only the slope of the roof pitch indicates that the roof belonged not to any form of cloister but to a pentice running parallel to the nave.

APPENDIX 2

The Origins of the Cholderton Roof

The history of the ten-bay late medieval roof now covering the 19th-century church of St Nicholas at Cholderton is in part obscure and certain facts are few: it was sold on 22 May 1840 at an auction in Ipswich (*Ipswich J.* 16 May 1840), acquired by the Reverend Thomas Mozley, rector of Cholderton, then dismantled, transported to Wiltshire, repaired and re-erected over his new church (Mozley 1882, 163–4). It formerly roofed an Ipswich malt house in Pleasant Row, off Star Lane, near the church of St Mary at Key. The malt-house may not have been built as such: though devoid of decorative features, it had stone walls about 2 ft (0.61 m) thick and 20 ft (6.10 m) high. There is no evidence that it had been 'a municipal building belonging to the corporation' (Mozley 1882, 163).[1]

The roof was illustrated covering the malt-house in *Picturesque Antiquities of Ipswich*, by Russel and Hagreen (1845). The proof of the engraving is dated 11 November 1842, so the original drawing by Hagreen (now lost) was probably made at the time of the sale and dismantling of the roof in 1840–1.[2] The roof now differs in several ways from the engraving, which shows the principals and the braces unmoulded, the hammer beams raked (not, as now, vertical) and tie beams (known to have been removed by Mozley).

There is little doubt that the roof was not original to the malt-house. Both Mozley and Wodderspoon (who wrote the text to the illustration by Russel and Hagreen) agree that the roof had covered another building also 80 ft (24.38 m) in length but at least a foot wider than the 19½ ft (5.94 m) of the malt-house. Mozley claimed the roof was from a 'house of Cistercian monks' (*Br. Crit.* 1841, 465) but no monastery of the order existed in the vicinity. There is no proof that the roof is of ecclesiastical origin (all the religious emblems in the spandrels were added by Mozley), but its size and proportions, with ten relatively short bays, are not typical of secular halls. The shears in the spandrels, which are original, could indicate a Guild or Cloth Hall but the history of such institutions in Ipswich is obscure and does not suggest the existence of a building the scale of the roof.[3] The three friaries of the town are possible sources, particularly the Blackfriars, taken over by the Corporation at the Dissolution for public uses such as the grammar school. The frater, the building which had the most appropriate proportions, was demolished after sale by the Corporation in 1763 (Gilyard-Beer 1977) but is shown by a plan of 1748 by Kirby to have measured only 65 ft by 22½ ft (19.81 m by

551. Cholderton: roof as re-erected over present church.

552. Roof, now over Cholderton church, in its former state over malt-house in Ipswich. From *Picturesque Antiquities of Ipswich* 1845 (after contemporary drawing by Hagreen). Photographed by kind permission of *Suffolk Record Office, Ipswich*.

6.86 m). The roof over the E, dorter, range was different in appearance and dimensions and continued to cover the grammar school till 1842. The most likely origin of the roof is one of the buildings of the Augustinian priory of St Peter and St Paul, a few hundred yards to the W of the malt-house. The priory was the major monastic establishment in Ipswich; dissolved and the fabric re-used by Wolsey for his new college in Ipswich, it was then demolished and its site covered by malt-houses. At the time of its first dissolution in 1528, one roof was bought by a Dame Elizabeth Gelgit and bequeathed to the church of St Mary at Key to cover an aisle.[4]

Also uncertain is the degree to which the present roof preserves the form and timbers of the original. In 1841 Mozley published (anonymously) a sketch of the roof in its present form and measured sections of the various timbers (*Br. Crit.* 1841, 466–7). However, these do not accord entirely with the Ipswich engraving of the roof (*see* above) and it is known that Mozley brought from Suffolk a team of carpenters to repair the roof, acquiring a 'great baulk' of New Forest oak to provide the timber (*Br. Crit.* 1841, 451). Furthermore, open roofs had ecclesiological importance to an early

Tractarian like Mozley: he removed the tie beams as impious objects, claiming them (probably rightly) to be additions; 'We must have no tie-beams, and we must have spandrels as good as the old ones' (Mozley 1882, 164). In spite of these reservations, comparison with other Suffolk roofs such as those of St Mary at Stoke, Ipswich or Westerfield shows that the essential framework of the roof is authentic, whatever the date of individual timbers.[5]

1. Possibly the building had been acquired by the Corporation along with the nearby common quay but there is no mention of this in the auction particulars.
2. The proof is preserved in Woolnough Collections (Suffolk Illustrations vol. 2) housed in Suffolk County Record Office, Ipswich.
3. The titling of the print of the roof in Russel and Hagreen as The Old Cloth Hall seems to have had no authority, but *c.f.* M. Clegg, 'Roof Wanderings in Ipswich', *Suffolk Rev.* **4** no. 6 (1974) 138.
4. Norfolk Record Office, Norwich Consistory Court, Palgrave 295d.
5. For a detailed account of the building of Cholderton church, *see* R.G. Gibbon, 'Cholderton Church and its Builder', *WAM* **70/71** (1975/6) 104–8.

APPENDIX 3

LIST OF STAINED GLASS, MEDIEVAL AND NINETEENTH-CENTURY, IN THE CHURCH OF ST MARY AND ST NICHOLAS, WILTON

Window lights are ordered to accord with the system used by the *Corpus Vitrearum Medii Aevi* (*see* sketch of I, below), i.e. from left to right (alphabetically) and from bottom to top (numerically). The window numbering system (*see* plan) is also that adopted by the *Corpus*.

Only the principal panels in each window are described here. The backgrounds and borders of those windows incorporating earlier glass are mostly 19th-century but include some medieval fragments. Many of the medieval panels have been extensively altered to adapt them to their present positions (e.g. windows sII: panels 1.e.; 2.b. and 2.e.—all three were originally cusped tracery lights). All the glass earlier than the 19th century was given by Sidney Herbert and a few of his close relations. Several of the items when still in Sidney Herbert's private collection were seen by Charles Winston and illustrated in his book, *An Inquiry into Ancient Glass Painting* (*see* below).

Principal sources consulted for the identification of the glass are the following: E. Dorling, 'The Heraldry of Wilton Church', *WAM* **35** (1908) 453–9; L. Grodecki, *Les Vitreux de Saint-Denis. Étude sur le Vitrail au XIIᵉ Siècle*, 2 vols (1976); C. Winston, *An Inquiry into the Differences of Style Observable in Ancient Glass Painting*, 2 vols (1st edn 1847, 2nd edn 1867) and *Memoirs Illustrative of the Art of Glass Painting* (1865).

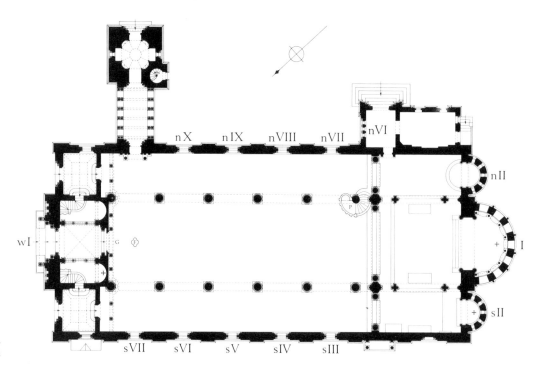

553. Plan and sketch (p. 239) indicating CVMA designation of each window.

I (window of seven lights)

1.a. Angel: Ile-de-France/Champagne, *c.* 1250.
  b. Bishop celebrating Mass (fragmentary): Ile-de-France/Champagne, *c.* 1225.
  c. Flight into Egypt: St-Denis, Infancy of Christ cycle, *c.* 1150.
  d. Cleansing of the Temple: Rouen Cathedral nave, Life of Christ cycle, *c.* 1230.
  e. Christ with two apostles and holy woman: Rouen Cathedral nave, Life of Christ cycle, *c.* 1230.
  f. Bishops celebrating Mass: Ile-de-France/Champagne, *c.* 1225.
  g. Deacon, saint and martyr: Ile-de-France/Champagne, *c.* 1200–25.

2.a. St Catherine visited in prison by the Empress: Ile-de-France/Champagne, *c.* 1200–50.
  b. Part of the Adoration of the Magi: St-Denis, Infancy of Christ cycle, *c.* 1150.
  c. Moses striking the Egyptian: Ste-Chapelle, Paris, Exodus cycle, *c.* 1250.
  d. Bust of unbearded saint: ?Chenu (Sarthe), *c.* 1180–1200.
  e. King and canonised monk: ?St-Germain-des-Prés, Paris, *c.* 1250.
  f. Wedding at Cana: Rouen Cathedral nave, Life of Christ cycle, *c.* 1230.
  g. Execution of St Catherine: Ile-de-France/Champagne, *c.* 1200–50.

3.a. Return of the Prodigal Son: northern French, *c.* 1220.
  b. King and canonised monk: ?St Germain-des-Prés, Paris, *c.* 1250.
  c. Two cherubim: ?Ste-Chapelle, Paris, *c.* 1250.
  d. Prodigal Son receiving his inheritance: northern French, *c.* 1220.
  e. Christ with book: Rouen Cathedral nave, Life of Christ cycle, *c.* 1230.
  f. Prophet (?Balaam) from Tree of Jesse: St-Denis, *c.* 1150.
  g. Prodigal Son menaced by a demon: northern French, *c.* 1220.

554. Bust of unbearded saint, I 2d.
555. Return of Prodigal Son, I 3a.

554

555

556   557   558   559   560

556–560. Glass in the five lights
of N apse, n II.

nII (window of five lights)
1.a. Censing angel: ?English, *c.* 1325.
  b. Two youths: German, 16th-century.
  c. Three male figures and one female: St-Denis (?Infancy of Christ cycle), *c.* 1150.
  d. Heads of youths: German, 16th-century.
  e. Martyr saint (?St Felix) holding head in hands: ?Swiss, 16th-century.

2.a. Censing angel: ?English, *c.* 1325.
  b. Canonised nun: German, 16th-century (canopy, English *c.* 1375; roundel of pelican in apex, German).
  c. Prophet (Osee) from Tree of Jesse: St-Denis, *c.* 1150.
  d. Episcopal saint: German, 16th-century (canopy, English, *c.* 1375; roundel of pelican in apex, German).
  e. Martyr saint holding head in hands: ?Swiss, 16th-century.

3.c. Male and female in architectural setting, perhaps from Presentation in the Temple: St-Denis (?Infancy of Christ cycle), *c.* 1150.

nVI (medallions set in window of three lights)
2.a. ?Triumph of Constancy: Flemish, early 16th-century.
  b. Arms of the Herbert family: English, *c.* 1700.
  c. Vision of the Risen Christ with the symbols of the Evangelists: Flemish, early 16th-century.

3.b. ?Triumph of Death: Flemish, early 16th-century.

nVII (the medieval panels, heavily corroded, are possibly Austrian of *c.* 1400, the 19th-century panels were supplied by Ward & Co.)
1. *Left*—Presentation: 19th-century. *Right*—Christ amongst the Doctors: 19th-century.
2. Scene of Baptism or Consecration: medieval.
3. *Left*—Adoration of Shepherds: medieval. *Right*—Nativity: 19th-century.
4. Pentecost: medieval.
5. *Left*—Ascension: 19th-century. *Right*—Christ in Judgement: medieval.

nVIII
1. Healing of Jairus's Daughter
2. Raising of the Widow's Son   }   1853, by M. and A. O'Connor (initialled)
3. Raising of Lazarus

nIX
1. Sermon on the Mount
2. Giving of the Law   }   *c.* 1853, by M. and A. O'Connor
3. Expulsion of Adam and Eve from Paradise

nX
1. Pietà: ?Flemish, early 16th-century.
2. God the Father (altered to St Nicholas) and architectural frame: both Flemish, early 16th-century, from a window by Arnold of Nijmegen and formerly in the church of St Jacques at Malines/Mechlin (the remaining panels now form the E window of St George's, Hanover Square, London).
3. Angel with IHS medallion: mostly 19th-century, probably by Ward & Co.

561. Early 16th-century glass, n x.

562. Virgin saint, s II 1a.

sII (window of five lights)
1.a. Virgin saint: English, 15th-century.
  b. Virgin saint (composite figure): English, 15th-century.
  c. Female martyr (?St Cecilia) holding head: Swiss, 16th-century.
  d. Kneeling youth (probably a composite figure): French or Flemish, late medieval.
  e. Female saint with hood: English, 15th-century.

2.a. Canonised, vested monk: English, 15th-century.
  b. Cherubim (composite figure): English, 15th-century with 19th-century elements.
  c. Christ as King: Swiss, 16th-century.
  d. Canonised, vested monk (?pair to light 2.a.): English, 15th-century.
  e. Cherubim: English, 15th-century.

sIII
1. Christ receiving the Children
2. Resurrection   1847, by Wm. Wailes (initialled)
3. Ascension

sIV
1. Job feeding the Needy
2. Feeding of the Five Thousand   1883, by Clayton and Bell
3. Caleb's description of Canaan

sV
1. Good Samaritan
2. Christ receiving the Blessed   c. 1861, by O'Connor
3. Solomon building the Temple

sVI
1. Noli Me Tangere
2. The Resurrection   c. 1882, by Gibbs and Howard (initialled)
3. The Three Marys at the Tomb

sVII (glass brought from Wilton House)
1. Arms of the 1st Earl of Pembroke: English, 16th-century.
2. First Earl of Pembroke with his two sons: English, 16th-century.
3. Arms of King Philip II of Spain: English, 16th-century.
4. Ann, 1st Countess of Pembroke with her daughter: English, 16th-century.
5. Arms of 2nd Earl of Pembroke: English, 16th-century.

WI (rose window with twelve lights and central oculus, the radiating lights described clockwise starting from top)
1. Two music-making angels: English or Flemish, 15th-century.
2. Heraldic glass in Renaissance border: ?German, c. 1600.
3. Two panels of heraldic glass: German, c. 1550.
4. Trinity: Flemish, 16th-century.
5. Arms of Hans Graf zu Mountfort Vogt zu Veldkirck: German, 1526.
6. Allegorical panels: ?German, 16th or 17th-century.
7. High Priest with censer: German or Flemish, c. 1500.
8. Arms of a dauphin: ?French, date uncertain.
9. Shield-of-arms: ?English, ?late 13th-century.
10. Virgin and Child (very faded).
11. Donor figures and shield-of-arms: ?German, c. 1500.
12. Arms of a bishop incorporating the shield-of-arms of the von Bernstatt, von Toggenburg and von Hahn families: ?eastern German, c. 1500.
Oculus. Arms of Queen Victoria: English, 1854.

563.   1st Earl of Pembroke with his two sons, s VII 2.

564.   Arms of 1st Earl of Pembroke, s VII 1.

565.   Ann, 1st Countess of Pembroke, with her daughter, s VII 4.

566.   Arms of 2nd Earl of Pembroke, s VII 5.

554–66.   Courtesy of the *Parochial Church Council of St Mary and St Nicholas Wilton.*

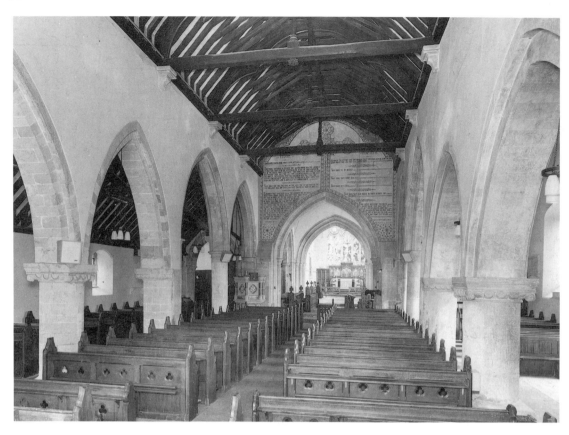

567. Downton: interior looking E.

568. Downton: exterior from SW.

569.   Coombe Bissett: exterior from NE, showing former low spire, *Buckler* 1805.

570.   West Dean, Evelyn Chapel: exterior from SE before demolitions of 1868, *Buckler* 1805.

571. Durnford: Romanesque features including font and N and S doorways, *Buckler* 1805.

572. Cholderton: Royal Arms in ante-chapel floor, depicted in Minton tiles.

573. West Dean, Evelyn Chapel: interior of former nave and chancel, looking E, *Kemm* 1862.

ABBREVIATIONS

BL   British Library
DRO   Diocesan Record Office
ICBS   Incorporated Church Building Society
NMR   National Monuments Record
OS   Ordnance Survey
RCHM   Royal Commission on the Historical Monuments of England
RS   Rolls Series
SC   Special Collections (Rentals and Surveys)
VCH   Victoria History of the Counties of England
WAM   Wiltshire Archaeological and Natural History Magazine
WRO   Wiltshire Record Office.

BIBLIOGRAPHY

ANON. 1968. *Britford, Wilts., the Parish Church of St Peter* [ed. C.L. Rowe]

ARTS COUNCIL, 1984. *Romanesque Art 1060–1200*, ed. G. Zarnecki *et al.* (Arts Council, Great Britain)

BARROW, E.P. 1889. *Parish Notes* [of Cholderton]

BLAIR, J. 1979. An Early Fourteenth-Century Incised Slab at Odstock, Wilts. *Trans. Monumental Brass Soc.* **XII** (1975–9, published 1981), 370–2

BODINGTON, E.J. 1919. The Church Survey in Wiltshire, 1649–50. *WAM* **40** (1917–19), 253–72, 297–317, 392–416

BOND, F. 1916. *The Chancel of English Churches*

BORENIUS, T. 1932. A Destroyed Cycle of Wall-Paintings in a Church in Wiltshire. *Antiq. J.* **12**, 393–406

BORG, A. 1967. The Development of Chevron Ornament. *J. Brit. Archaeol. Ass. 3 ser.* **30**, 122–40

BOURNE, B.W. 1944. *Coombe Bissett and its Church*

BRAKSPEAR, H. 1934. Ivychurch Priory. *WAM* **46** (1932–4), 433–40

Br. Mag. 1836. *British Magazine* **9**, 258–65

BUCK, A.G.R. 1950–2. Some Wiltshire Fonts. *WAM* **53** (1949–50), 458–70; **54** (1951–2), 19–35, 192–209

Builder 1851. Charlton Church. *The Builder* **9**, 286

— 1880. Obituary of T.H. Wyatt. *The Builder* **39**, 193–4

CHAMBERS, G.E. 1960. The Pre-Conquest Church of St Peter, at Britford. *WAM* **57** (1958–60), 212–21

CHANDLER, J. (ed.) 1979. *The Amesbury Millenium Lectures*

CHINNERY, V. 1979. *Early Oak Furniture: the British Tradition: a History of Early Furniture in the British Isles and New England* (Antique Collectors' Club)

CLAPHAM, A.W. 1964. *English Romanesque Architecture*, 2 vols. I *Before the Conquest* (1930); II *After the Conquest* (1934) (reprinted 1964)

CLEGG, M. 1974. Roof Wanderings in Ipswich. *Suffolk Rev.* **4**, no. 3, 136–8

— 1979. The Wandering Roof and the Cloth Hall in Ipswich. *Suffolk Rev.* **4**, no. 6, 298–307

COCKE, T.H. 1985. The William Butterfield Font from Amesbury Church. *WAM* **79** (1984–5), 248–50

COLT HOARE, R. *et al.* 1824–44. *The Modern History of South Wiltshire*

Vol. 1, pt ii, *The Hundred of Heytesbury* (1824)

Vol. 2, pt i, *The Hundred of Branch and Dole* (1825)

Vol. 2, pt ii, *The Hundreds of Everley, Ambresbury and Underditch* (1826)

Vol. 3, pt ii, *Hundred of South Damerham, Hundred of Downton, Hundred of Cawden* (1835)

Vol. 5, pt i, *Hundred of Alderbury* (1837)

Vol. 5, pt ii, *Hundred of Frustfield* (1844)

COLVIN, H.M. (ed.) 1963. *History of the King's Works. The Middle Ages*, 2 vols.

— 1978. *A Biographical Dictionary of British Architects 1600–1840*

COOK, G.H. 1954. *The English Medieval Parish Church*

DAWSON, R.S. (ed.) 1958. *Silver Treasures of the Diocese of Salisbury*

DORLING, E. 1908. The Heraldry of Wilton Church. *WAM* **35** (1907–8), 453–9

DRURY, W.E. 1978. *A Guide to Wilton Parish Church and the Old Church of St Mary*, 9th edn

DUKE, E. 1837. *Prolusiones Historicae*

EAMES, E.S. 1976. The Tiles. *In* The Medieval Kilns on Nash Hill, Lacock, Wiltshire, M.R. McCarthy *et al. WAM* **69** (1974), 131–45

— 1980. *Catalogue of Medieval Lead-Glazed Earthenware Tiles in the . . . British Museum*, 2 vols.

ELLIOTT, B. 1971. *Bramshaw People, Parsons and Criminals*, 2nd edn

FAWCETT, E. 1939. The Royal Heraldic Achievements in the Churches of Wiltshire. *WAM* **48** (1937–9), 92–117

FERREY, B. 1978. *Recollections of A.W.N. Pugin and his father Augustus Pugin* (reprinted with an introduction by C. and J. Wainwright, 1978)

GARDNER, J. 1970. The Capocci Tabernacle in S. Maria Maggiore. *Pap. Brit. Sch. Rome* **38**, 220–30

GIBBON, R.G. 1978. Cholderton Church and its Builder. *WAM* **70–71** (1975–6), 104–8

GILYARD-BEER, R. 1977. Ipswich Blackfriars. *Proc. Suffolk Inst. Archaeol. Hist.* **XXXIV**, 15–23

GLYNNE, S. 1924. Notes on Wiltshire Churches. *WAM* **42** (1922–4), 167–214, 277–306

GODDARD, E.H. (ed.) 1919a. The Buckler Collection of Wiltshire Drawings. *WAM* **40** (1917–19), 148–90

— 1919b. Drawings of Wiltshire Churches by O.B. Carter 1847–1850. *WAM* **40** (1917–19), 190–1

— 1932. The Kemm Drawings of Wiltshire Churches. *WAM* **45** (1930–32), 254–67

— 1934. Chitterne All Saints – Churchwardens' Accounts, Extracts from 1732 onwards. *WAM* **46** (1932–4), 393–5

— 1944. A List of Wiltshire Churches Containing Old Glass. *WAM* **50** (1942–4), 205–13

GORDON, A.H. 1906. *Sidney Herbert, a Memoir*

GORHAM, G.C. 1820. *The History and Antiquities of Eynesbury and St Neots*, 307–8

GRODECKI, L. 1976. *Les Vitreaux de Saint-Denis: Étude sur le Vitrail au XIIe Siècle*, 2 vols.

GUNNIS, R. 1971. *Dictionary of British Sculptors 1660–1851*

HASLAM, J. 1984. *Anglo-Saxon Towns in Southern England*

HENRY, F. and ZARNECKI, G. 1958. Romanesque Arches Decorated with Human and Animal Heads. *J. Brit. Archaeol. Ass. 3 ser.* **XX–XXI** (1957–8), 1–34

HILL, A.D. 1888. Downton Church. *Archaeol. J.* **45**, 81–4

JACKSON, J.E. 1862. *Wiltshire. The Topographical Collections of John Aubrey FRS, AD 1659–70*, revised edn

1867a. Ambresbury Monastery. *WAM* **10** (1865–7), 61–84

1867b. Ancient Chapels, &c, in Co. Wilts. *WAM* **10** (1865–7), 253–322

1875. Names of Wiltshire Churches. *WAM* **15** (1874–5), 98–110

n.d. Wiltshire Collections, vol. 8 (unpublished scrapbooks), Libr. Soc. Antiq., London

JESSIMAN, I. McD. 1958. The Piscina in the English Medieval Church. *J. Brit. Archaeol. Ass. 3 ser.* **XX–XXI** (1957–8), 53–71

JONES, W.H. 1879. *Fasti Ecclesiae Sarisburiensis*

KENWORTHY BROWN, E.K. 1944. *Notes on St Andrew's Church, Durnford*

KEYSER, C.E. 1883. *List of Buildings in Gt Britain and Ireland having Mural and other Painted Decorations . . . prior to the Latter Part of the 16th Century*, 3 edn

KITE, E. 1860. *The Monumental Brasses of Wiltshire*

1901. Notes on Amesbury Monastery, with an Account of Some Discoveries on the Site in 1860. *Wilts. Notes Queries* **3** (1899–1901), 115–19, 145–54, 221–7, 258–67, 289–305, 354–66, 433–48

1904. Amesbury Monastery. *Wilts. Notes Queries* **4** (1902–4), 74–80, 124–39

MASTER, G.S. 1885. Collections for a History of West Dean. *WAM* **22** (1884–5), 239–317

MILES, P. *c.* 1908. *Memoirs of Odstock* (reprinted 1976)

MONTGOMERIE, D.H. 1944. A Window in St Andrew's Church, Nunton. *WAM* **50** (1942–4), 194

MORGAN, F.W. 1939. Domesday Geography of Wiltshire. *WAM* **48** (1937–9), 68–81

MORRES, A.P. 1888. Britford Church. *Archaeol J.* **45**, 77–80

MOZLEY, T. 1841. Open Roofs [T. Mozley]. *Br. Crit. & Q. Theol. Rev.* **XXIX**, 441–89

1882. *Remains, Chiefly of Oriel College and the Oxford Movement*, 2 vols.

1885. *Remains, Chiefly of Towns, Villages and Schools*, 2 vols.

NIGHTINGALE, J.E. 1891a. *The Church Plate of the County of Wilts.*

1891b. The Priory of Ivychurch and its Wall-Paintings. *Proc. Soc. Antiq.* **XIII**, 352–5

OLIVIER, D. 1881. *A Plain Description of Wilton Church*

OS (ed.) 1973. *Britain Before the Norman Conquest*

PENNY, N. 1977. *Church Monuments in Romantic England.*

PEVSNER, N. 1967. *The Buildings of England: Hampshire* (N. Pevsner and D. Lloyd)

1972. *The Buildings of England: Dorset* (N. Pevsner and J. Newman)

1975. *The Buildings of England: Wiltshire*, 2nd edn (revised by B. Cherry)

PONTING, C.E. 1904. Durrington and Durnford Churches, *WAM* **33** (1903–4), 277–88

1908. Notes on the Church of St Mary, Stapleford. *WAM* **35** (1907–8), 376–80

1910. Notes on the Churches of Boscombe, Idmiston, Winterbourne Gunner, Winterslow, Farley, Pitton, West Grimstead and Ivychurch Priory. *WAM* **36** (1909–10), 13–26

QUINEY, A. 1979. *John Loughborough Pearson*

RALEGH RADFORD, C.A. 1973. Pre-Conquest Minster Churches. *Archaeol. J.* **130**, 120–40

ROBINSON, J.M. 1981. *The Wyatts, an Architectural Dynasty*

RCHM 1952. *An Inventory of the Historical Monuments in Dorset, Vol. I, West*

1980. *Ancient and Historical Monuments in the City of Salisbury, Vol. I*

RS 33. *Historia et Cartularium Sancti Petri Gloacestriae*, ed. W.H. Hart. Rolls Series [33], 3 vols. (1863), 1

RS 99. *Red Book of the Exchequer*, ed. H. Hall. Rolls Series [99], 3 vols. (1896), 2

RUDDLE, C.S. 1901. Notes on Amesbury Church. *WAM* **31** (1900–1), 29–32

RUSSEL, F. and HAGREEN, W. 1845. *Picturesque Antiquities of Ipswich. A Selection from the Remains of Ancient Edifices existing in that Town. The Antiquarian and Architectural Descriptions by John Wodderspoon*

SALMON, J. 1939. Mural Paintings at Gt Durnford Church. *WAM* **48** (1937–9), 144–6

SHORTT, H. 1964. Two Wiltshire Fonts in South Australia. *WAM* **59** (1964), 168–9

SIMMONS, J. 1959. Brooke Church, Rutland, with Notes on Elizabethan Church Building. *Trans. Leicestershire Archaeol. Hist. Soc.* **35**, 36–44

SOUL, J. 1926. *Amesbury Historic and Prehistoric*

STALLEY, R.A. 1971. A 12th-century Patron of Architecture. *J. Brit. Archaeol. Ass. 3 ser.* **34**, 62–83

STEVENS, F. 1937. The Inlaid Paving Tiles of Wiltshire. *WAM* **47** (1935–7), 358–78

STEWART, P. (ed.) 1973. *Diocese of Salisbury: Guide to the Records of the Bishop . . . and other . . Jurisdictions*

SYMONDS, W. 1910. Winterslow Church Reckonings, 1542–1661. *WAM* **36** (1909–10), 27–49

TALBOT, C.H. 1878. Downton and Britford Churches. *WAM* **17** (1876–8), 238–53

1901. Amesbury Church. Reasons for thinking that it was not the Church of the Priory. *WAM* **31** (1900–1), 8–20

1901–4. Amesbury Monastery. *Wilts. Notes Queries* **3** (1899–1901), 549–56; **4** (1902–4), 11–20

TAYLOR, C.C. 1967. Whiteparish: a Study of the Development of a Forest-Edge Parish. *WAM* **62**, 79–102

1968. Three Deserted Medieval Settlements in Whiteparish. *WAM* **63**, 39–45

THOMPSON, H.V. 1896. *History of Tilshead Church*

THOMPSON, P. 1971. *William Butterfield.*

VCH 1955. *A History of Wiltshire* II

1956. *A History of Wiltshire* III

1962. *A History of Wiltshire* VI

1980. *A History of Wiltshire* IX

WALTERS, H.B. 1929. *The Church Bells of Wiltshire, their Inscriptions and History*

WEBB, M.I. 1956. Roubiliac Busts at Wilton. *Country Life* **119**, 804–5

1958. Roubiliac, Architect and Sculptor. *Archit. Rev.* **123**, 329

WHINNEY, M. 1964. *Sculpture in Britain 1530–1830*

WINDLEY, E.J. 1917. *Amesbury Church*

WINSTON, C. 1865. *Memoirs Illustrative of the Art of Glass-Painting.*

1867. *An Inquiry into the Difference of Style . . . in Ancient Glass-Painting . . .* 2 vols., 2nd edn

WORDSWORTH, C. 1910. Marlborough Chantries and the Supply of Clergy in Olden Days. Part I: Wiltshire Chantries. *WAM* **36** (1909–10), 525–50

INDEX